Chasing Normal

A Memoir

Beck Thompson

Note to the Reader

Please be aware that this book contains reference to incest and sexual abuse. It may be disturbing for many readers. If you have been sexually abused, this book may trigger extreme emotions and re-traumatise you. Please be aware of this before you read this book. And of course, please seek help and support if you need it.

To my husband, for holding my hand.

Foreword

Every time I read Rebekah's story – I tear up! I am not one for doing this, as I have grown very resilient over the many years I have worked in this field of trauma-aware education. I have heard so many stories of harm done to people, young and older, and have met and known many of these people. What keeps me working so hard in this field, are people like Rebekah!

Rebekah is the epitome of someone who I refer to in my work as becoming more and more "resolved" from the trauma she endured, as time goes by. This has not happened easily or without an extreme amount of endurance and hard work, but people like Rebekah are the evidence that – what we do and how we support our children and young people who have lived through complex trauma – particularly in education settings – is so very important!

I teared up again when I read Rebekah 's manuscript for this book. I believe this is because I know the (mostly) resolved and adult Rebekah, a beautiful young woman who exhibits such strength and passion for caring for others. It sincerely hurts me to read about the vulnerable and victimised child Rebekah and the long-suffering younger adult, Rebekah.

However, Rebekah has chosen to openly share with you, both the child and the younger adult Rebekah, in the hope that this will encourage others who have lived through complex childhood trauma, to fight for their healing and for all the goodies in life that they need and deserve – health, love, family, career, calm, happiness.

Rebekah is a courageous survivor of complex trauma- who is determined to prevent any intergenerational transmission of this harm by being a great (informed and responsive) mother. She is also someone who is determined to heal herself, and to be her best self, so that she can then support the healing of others.

Her memoir is an admirable project – to do just that – to support healing in others. This project would not have come easily, as it is no small thing to recall the details of suffering and to analyse one's self and one's experiences to the degree that Rebekah has done. I feel so privileged to write this introduction to Rebekah's heartfelt story and I look forward to hearing of many more great chapters in Rebekah's life!

Associate Professor, Dr Judith Howard

Queensland University of Technology, Brisbane Australia.

What educators are saying about Chasing Normal

Beck's memoir of chasing "normal" is heart-wrenching, awe-inspiring and hopeful. While she bravely walks us through her years of abuse, neglect, struggle, identity crises, and multiple attempts at healing, the underlying determination to be free of her torment and address the damage of her childhood shines through. This is must-read for any educator who wishes to deepen their understanding of the effects of childhood trauma. Beck's story provides a compelling motive for "why" we need trauma-informed education for all those young people who need someone to walk beside them, offering safety, warmth, and a chance to be seen.

Dr Lyra L'Estrange, Trauma-Aware Education, Queensland University of Technology

I could not put this book down from the moment I started. As an Early Childhood Educator, Leader, and Consultant this book reaffirmed the importance of relationships in Early Education and beyond for all children but in particular children dealing with trauma. This book demonstrates the valuable role educators and teachers play in children's lives. I commend Beck for her courage to share her story in such a vulnerable and articulate way.

Tracey Yeomans, Early Childhood Specialist and Consultant

Beck's survival in the face of significant abuse and parental neglect is overwhelming and heartbreaking, but you cannot help but be inspired and in awe of Beck's courage and resilience. Beck's story is the finest illustration of human strength, spirt and determination. We are so privileged that Beck has been so open and willing to generously share her past struggles of childhood trauma, so that others can learn and perhaps feel less alone from reading her story.Chasing Normal is an essential book for anyone who works with children and wants to understand the true power of relationships, kindness and compassion when caring for children. Chasing Normal is an especially important book for teachers to appreciate the critical impact they can have on students exposed to abuse, neglect and trauma. Beck's survival in the face of significant abuse and parental neglect is overwhelming and heartbreaking, but you cannot help but be inspired and in awe of Beck's courage and resilience. Beck's story is the finest illustration of human strength, spirt and determination. We are so privileged that Beck has been so open and willing to generously share her past struggles of childhood trauma, so that others can learn and perhaps feel less alone from reading her story. Chasing Normal is an essential book for anyone who works with children and wants to understand the true power of relationships, kindness and compassion when caring for children. Chasing Normal is an especially important book for teachers to appreciate the critical impact they can have on students exposed to abuse, neglect and trauma.

Dr Emily Berger, Senior Lecturer and Psychologist, Monash University

Beck's moving memoir 'Chasing Normal' is a very honest and sometimes confronting account of her experience of childhood trauma, but more than that, of her dogged determination to keep moving forward, trying to make sense of her inner and outer worlds, striving to be the person she innately knew she could be. Beck writes in a very raw and intimate way about how trauma has impacted, and continues to impact, on her life. 'Chasing Normal' provides those dealing with childhood trauma with an accessible, hopeful and insightful portrayal of one woman's incredible trek to reclaim her life, from fragmented to healing.

Sue Harding, Counsellor

Beck's honest and heart wrenching memoir shows us the strength of the human spirit. Her story is truly inspirational, as she struggles to face the truth of her past in order to heal. This memoir is invaluable to anyone either on their own healing journey, as well as anyone working with children. I highly recommend this book to other educators interested in trauma informed practice. Through education, we will slowly heal the world.

Tanya Cassidy, B. Soc Sci (Crim/Psych), Master of Teaching (Primary),
Former NSW Police Officer, Current Teacher, Sydney NSW

For many, our family are our 'safe people' and our home is our 'safe place'. Sadly, far too many children do not feel safe and are not safe at home. In Chasing Normal Beck Thompson bravely and selflessly shares her experience of child abuse. Beck's memoir provides valuable insight to help us better understand the dynamics of child abuse and the vital role safe and trusted adults can play in a child's life. Protecting children from harm is a shared responsibility and we can all play a role in the care, safety and protection of children.

Kayelene Kerr, Dip(PublicSaf), AdvDip(PublicSaf), BA(Just)
Child Safety Advocate and Founder of eSafeKids

'Chasing Normal' is a story of courage written by the deeply insightful and articulate Beck Thompson, where she outlines with unflinching honesty and rawness, the ongoing impact of her childhood trauma. Beck had to deal with more childhood adversity than most of us would encounter in a life time, all without supportive adults (apart from some great teachers), and as an adult had to deal with the crushing weight of self-doubt, loneliness, anxiety and later on, Post-Natal Depression. Ultimately her life story is one triumph and transformation over real adversity, and choosing through sheer force of will (and support from wonderful people in her life), to get off the trauma roller coaster. Your journey will be an inspiration to many who are seeking to find their own 'normal'.

Tony Jamieson, PhD Candidate, Griffith University

Chasing Normal is heartbreaking and so incredibly inspiring. Thank you for sharing your story so I can be reminded that some of the little people I teach have the weight of the world on their shoulders when they come into my classroom.

Mandy Rock, Primary Teacher

Chapter 1

Our small shabby, white weatherboard house looked like it had been plonked dead centre of the good-sized block in our narrow Melbourne suburban street. It left ample space out the back for an overgrown veggie patch—that successfully grew weeds and not much more—and had a rusty, decrepit tin garage off to the side. Puffs of blackened smoke regularly billowed from our backyard incinerator, where we tossed domestic rubbish to burn for hours on end.

Most houses in my street were single storey weatherboards, with just a few double-story status symbols towering over little houses like mine. One imposing brown brick double-story a couple of houses down appeared so tall it almost blocked the sky view from my tiny bedroom window. Sometimes I wondered what it was like to live in such a big house. Did those kids have their own rooms, or did they have to sleep in bunks like I did? How many rooms did they have that they needed another entire floor? There must have been lots of space for play and maybe even to do cartwheels without knocking into anything.

Mum was just twenty-two years old and already busy with my brother and sister—born fourteen months apart—when I came along in June 1977, exactly two-and-a-half years to the day after my eldest brother. Three-and-a-half years later, Mum and Dad would have another son and round our family unit out to six people crammed into that shabby shoebox weatherboard.

Mum's only ambition was to be a mother. She happily stayed at home to look after her four children and tend to the wifely duties, while Dad went to work, as it was 'supposed' to be.

With little room to play inside, Mum and Dad scooted us outside as soon as we'd chowed down our breakfast. Not that it was a bad thing. We got to play unencumbered all day with friends in the street, or my sister and I would host delightful tea parties under the shady tree out the front of our house whenever there was no school. Sometimes my siblings and I took turns riding the billy cart Dad hand-built up and down our street until we grew tired of pushing each other. One time I accidentally let my foot get caught in the front wheel and my brother had to carry me back to Mum to fix me up. My blood left little drips on the footpath that stayed there until the next rain.

Play was running through the sprinkler on a hot summer day or peddling my half-rusted metal trike around the front yard with my favourite stuffed blue chook toy wedged under my arm. Most of the time, my siblings and I could roam as far as we wanted as long as we stayed in the street, only leaving if we let Mum or Dad know, and we stuck together. Our days were fun and adventurous. Our imaginations ran wild and long until the sun met the horizon and then we'd trundle home for dinner, showers, and bed. It was the ultimate freedom for a kid with next to no worries.

While us kids got along for the most part, my parents were polar opposites in almost every way imaginable. Not exactly a match made in Heaven. They met at a police ball, and after only three short months, they married on the suggestion and approval of their parents. Perhaps that explained why I never saw them relate in a loving way; they barely knew each other. There was no shared laughter over sweet dating memories. No cuddles or affectionate touches as they passed each other by. Nothing flirtatious, and never any compliments or adoring looks from across the room that us kids could get squeamish over.

Almost like a betrothed couple who barely tolerated one another, they existed in the roles society expected of them and carried on, but there was no genuine happiness between them.

Mum was the nurturer epitomised: subservient to her motherly duties, taking care of her children, prepping school lunches, keeping her brood dressed and fed, and for the most part, keeping us out of Dad's hair. So softly spoken, rarely—if ever—did I hear Mum yell or lose her temper. Her voice lingered like a warm embrace. She was the one I went to for hugs on a sleepless night, comfort when I was sick, or to rest in the nook of her arm in front of the TV when the bogeyman who sometimes lurked under my bed terrified me in the dark.

With Mum, I felt safe, secure, and loved.

Dad, on the other hand, was a stern and serious man. Not much for piggyback rides or goofy play or shenanigans. More of a do-as-you're-told, toe-the-line kind of a Dad. Even his dress sense matched his strict, controlled persona: ironed short-sleeved shirt, knee-length shorts, sandals, and knee-high socks. He was always clean-shaven, with his short dark hair neatly combed to one side. Nothing about Dad was sloppy or unkempt. Not ever.

He had high expectations of his wife and his young children's behaviour that killed any hope of laughter and joy when he was around. There seemed to be a rule for just about every step we took. Mum knew, either by way of a menacing glare or a stern talking to, there were rules to follow, standards to be met, and ways you did not question. The house was her 'job' to keep clean and tidy before Dad, 'the boss', came home from work. Any trace of child's play scattered on the floor or dishes stacked in the sink was a sure-fire way to unleash Dad's scornful tongue.

Even in the absence of his coarsely unsympathetic tone, Dad's presence could frost the warm air the moment he entered a room. He was not one to tolerate nonsense, disrespect, or unruliness. He was quick to anger when our innocent attempts to appease him failed, and along with disobedience or insubordination, simple errors were matched with strict discipline that sometimes meant a belting with his thick leather belt. If we argued or fought with each other—as kids often did—he'd bang our heads together, leaving us to cry quietly and sometimes wonder what had happened. Rarely were we afforded the grace of a mistake, a learning curve, or a gentle guiding hand as we navigated our childhood.

There was never a moment to relax in a house dictated by order and obedience. Time spared was time wasted, so evenings were not for sitting lazily in front of the TV—'the idiot box', as Dad called it—but for learning. He bought a set of special children's illustrated encyclopaedias to study things our young minds 'should' know. Often these 'sessions' ran like a Q&A trivia type night. We were expected to keep up and follow Dad as he read and lectured us on a topic I barely understood, and it was our job to answer questions he'd throw out at a moment's notice. Often, I'd tune out, dreaming, gazing around the room, wishing I was asleep or at least reading a more interesting book. If Dad caught me staring into space, he'd shout out, 'Hey, dream boat, come back to us, pay attention!'

Saturdays were for cleaning and tidying around our already tidy house. Sundays were for rare days out to an annual show or watching his favourite footy team on the telly. Only very occasionally did my father break from rigid, uptight Dad. If he did, it was brief and oddly out of the blue: laughing at something random on TV, blaring Beatles or Moody Blues music on his record player, or after a couple of beers, bellowing out "Carn the Blues," while watching his favourite Aussie football team score a rare goal before pulling one of his kids in for a bear hug. If we were quick enough, we could latch on and enjoy a rare fun-Dad moment, before he switched back to serious old Dad mode. I'm certain my body even straightened up automatically as he did.

Though I never saw Dad physically abuse Mum, at times Mum's droopy eyes and down-turned mouth told me she'd incurred Dad's wrath for disobeying him. Sometimes she'd emerge despondently from the kitchen or the bedroom with red, watery eyes. She would never argue back. She took whatever came silently, like penance. Sometimes an argument would erupt into a screaming match, and as if my older brother knew where it was headed, he'd quickly usher us outside to play farther down the street. The yelling grew louder and louder, with what sounded like shards of ice being thrown across the room. Their voices would muffle and go quiet, but we knew not to return until the noise died completely or until my father slammed the front door and drove off in his car.

In the aftermath of these arguments, Mum never took it out on her children, even if the fight was over something we had or hadn't done. Her eyes wore her sadness but also her love for us. If nothing else, we knew we were her joy, her life, and we were worth the pain behind the tears she shed.

As I grew, I noticed Mum's whole demeanour would switch instantly from relaxed while Dad was out, to cowering like a child the minute he walked through the door. She would wait silently for his nod of approval that her home duties had satisfied his high standards and then there was relief that she'd avoided being yelled at. She wouldn't have to endure his cold shoulder or angry glares for the evening.

While she stayed between the lines almost exclusively, she broke free from the person she held herself to when Christmas, Easter, or birthdays came around. I don't know if it was an unspoken defiance, or a joy no male authority could contain, but she revelled in these celebrations. She became childlike, happy, excited; a far cry from the obedience of every other day.

At Christmas she'd eagerly put up the plastic tree, meticulously hanging each ornament with a wide smile as each piece completed a perfect picture for her. She played carols and openly sang along. Sometimes when my father was absent at night, she'd let me stay up and watch Christmas movies, while during the day she'd leave the television on to play continuous Christmas cartoons.

She seemed a different person—a happier, more relaxed person. She delighted in sharing with her children a simple joy in an otherwise structured and disciplined life. It was a time to feel alive, regardless of the watchful and critical eye of my father. She loved the element of surprise that placing presents under the tree brought, too. Even on a low income, she made sure to budget, so we never missed out. I remember an unbridled happiness on her face as she watched us open them one-by-one. I don't recall much more of my younger years. My mother often paints a very sweet picture of the little girl I was. If I asked, she'd say I was a quiet, timid child who rarely misbehaved.

I know I loved going to school, following in the footsteps of my older brother and sister, walking under their guardianship every morning. I was four-and-a-half when I started. With four children under seven, Mum was pretty keen for me to start as soon as possible, relieving her of a child to look after during the day.

At school, I was the shy, well-behaved student, always eager to help my teachers set up the next activity. Sometimes I'd even beg to stay inside at break times just so I could help out. School opened up my world and sparked my lifelong love of learning and reading. Mum was an avid reader herself, a trait I believe I inherited. There was something about writing stories I loved, imagining worlds and characters, where time and space disappeared.

My teachers even made special mention of my writing ability that 'surpassed my years'. If I wasn't eagerly writing my next story, I was sitting wide-eyed up front on the classroom floor, soaking up the story read enticingly by my teacher, or I'd be the first in line to visit the school library for story time and the chance to read and borrow from the endless shelves of colourful picture books. With a book in my hand, I could daydream and imagine myself within the story, escaping to beautiful places. Escaping to anywhere.

Once, after story time in the library, we were asked to imagine and then draw a picture of what animal we would be if we could be anything. I dreamed I was a bird so I could fly. Completely free to go anywhere, anytime, without anyone holding me back. I often dreamed of escaping, wondering what it must feel like for a bird to be uninhibited.

Tuckshop Monitor was the prized task of the list of classroom jobs to get. Two children from each grade were chosen to deliver the red handled wire basket filled with lunch orders from the tuckshop that smelled of delicious oven baked pies and sweet pastry treats. If I was lucky enough, I had a lunch order too. My choice was always the same—a meat pie and a mini can of soft drink. It was a treat and a break from the same old sandwich and fruit Mum packed. Especially when she went through a phase of making her own bread that tasted like a hard, dried up crust of yeast. On those days, I'd deliberately ask for cheese and vegemite, just so I had something to eat, while I threw the bread out.

Once a week, I watched my older sister get dressed in her Brownies uniform: a brown pinafore, brown beret and yellow skivvy. She'd joined a year ago, and I was keen as mustard to become a Brownie Girl, just like her, as soon as I turned seven in a few months.

When Mum and I walked to pick up my sister, I'd leap up the steps and squish my face against the window to watch all the Brownies chanting and sign off to their leader. I couldn't wait to be a part of it. One day, as Mum and I waited outside the hall, I asked her when I could join. A question I'd asked her a hundred times before.

She turned to me slowly, with a pained look of disappointment. "Unfortunately, you won't be joining Brownies, Rebekah," she said apologetically.

"Why, Mum?" I whined back.

"Because we're moving to live with your grandfather in another part of Melbourne."

"But why, Mum?" I urged. She wasn't talking about *her* father, Pop. Trips to see him were really long, driving past bare paddocks, and trees as tall as the sky lined the roads for hours and hours.

Mum didn't say anything else. She just looked ahead, purposely avoiding my long-drawn face and my own disappointed expression. As the news sank into my young mind, I peered through the glass doors. I saw all the Brownies happily chanting their goodbye song, realising I would never get to be a Brownie, ever. It wasn't fair. I wanted to cry.

Over the next few weeks, Mum and Dad packed up the house, emptying it of everything familiar and mine. All of the furniture was thrown away. All of my special things, my plush chook, my blue metal trike, my ABC book, and my most favourite bed and bath toy, all tossed into a skip bin. Why could I not take my things with me to the new house? Was it even smaller than our house now?

I never went back to my school. No chance to say goodbye to my teachers, my friends. There was no closure, no time to look back on everything I knew. Now suddenly, I was moving to a new place with a grandfather I hardly knew.

I was leaving everything behind and starting a new life, and I didn't even know why.

Chapter 2

True to my mother's bombshell that afternoon at Brownies, a few weeks later, our car pulled into a long driveway, past the large, white wrought-iron gates affixed to two white pillars, each with a concrete lion head mounted on it.

At first glance, 'The House'—as I would come to refer to it—looked so grand. My eyes widened as I took in the large-scale, two-storey Victorian-style home. This house was like nothing I'd ever seen before—a complete contrast to the small, shabby weatherboard we'd just left. This might actually be an adventure after all.

As I reviewed the pale exterior, the double-storey balcony with its intricate wrought-iron lattice between the second-floor balcony posts, the asymmetrical bay windows, one above each other, excitement bubbled in my stomach knowing this would be my new home. It looked so fancy, like something out of a fairy tale, with its strategically placed trees and manicured shrubs planted around the large, lush green garden. Along the front of the House were half a dozen tall green conifers, like they were deliberately planted to create a private screen.

I imagined all the games we'd play in the spacious garden and all the tea parties I'd have sprawled out on a blanket amongst the large shrubs. The long concrete driveway would be ideal for riding a bike and skipping with ropes, or even the wooden billy cart Dad made. *Was it packed?* I wondered briefly.

My father pulled up to the double garage doors around the back of the house, well hidden behind the grand façade so as not to spoil the initial impressions.

Promptly I was ushered out of the car with my siblings, where four women and nine children of various ages—all standing in a perfectly straight line, in military-like fashion—waited to greet us. *Who were they all?* I wondered. Confused, I looked up to Mum for an explanation, but she remained silent, keeping what appeared to be a forced smile across her face. With so much uncertainty, I desperately wanted to cling to something familiar, like my favourite chook toy, but I didn't have it with me. So I clutched the side of my dress in a tight grip and quietly hoped my mum would explain everything to me soon.

Shortly after arriving, an austere but strikingly tall woman called Agnes walked us into the House and showed us our new bedrooms. Agnes was my grandfather's second wife. She was very slim, with mousy brown hair that sat just above her shoulders. Dressed in long black pants, a long-sleeved top, and a pinafore that draped to her knees, her clothes made her look like a boy. One dark brown mole sat obtrusively above the crook of her mouth and moved every time she spoke.

On the way to my new bedroom, I walked through the biggest laundry I had ever seen. A gigantic commercial-sized washing machine sat right next to the laundry door and on my left was a dryer so big it nearly reached the ceiling. A large rectangular table centred the next room, surrounded by floor-to-ceiling built-in cupboards. A grey double bowl trough sat under the only window in the room. The concrete floor chilled the room, giving it a cold, industrial feel.

"Here is where you'll be sleeping, Rebekah." Agnes pointed to the top bunk bed. Yes! Finally. I'd always been on the bottom bunk back at my old house.

My new room was small, given I'd be sharing it with two other girls, with just enough space for a wardrobe, a single bed under the window, and a bright red bunk on the opposite side. Everything in this room, like the laundry, was perfectly in its place. It was hard to believe a child could keep it so clean.

Where were all the kids' things? Even at my old house there'd be full toy boxes tucked into the corners. *Why are there no books?* The perfectly made beds had plain woollen blankets; no pretty designs or 'Holly Hobbie' on the doona cover, like I used to have.

Where are all the toys, the shoes? Where are all the storybooks, the pencils, the dolls, and the teddies? Maybe they're kept in the wardrobe? Perhaps this is how they lived? Perhaps they aren't allowed to have their toys or books out? Even my dad let me have some things out some of the time. *Maybe they cleaned up before we got here?*

So far, I'd been shown *my* room, the large boys' room next to mine, the large laundry, and the bathroom and the toilet all the girls had to share. The boys' bathroom was just outside another door in the laundry room. There had to be so much more to be seen in this huge house. Where was the lounge room with the TV? Perhaps, I wondered, we'd be shown soon.

We walked outside the lower floor of the house and up a flight of stairs that ran just above the laundry door below and shuffled in through another white door that was much fancier than the laundry door with two pretty Victorian patterned glass panels. *Maybe this was the beautiful part of the house I'd first seen?*

The moment I walked inside, an eye-blinding burst of light shone from the distant window ahead, illuminating the white floor tiles and crisp white walls around me, uncovering not a single trace of dirt or dust in sight. No stains, kids' hand marks, nothing. Everything was so pristine white it reflected the sunlight. How could it be that so many kids lived here and yet everything was so spotless? Much more spotless than my old home, and Mum did such a good job there.

The hallway led to an upstairs kitchen. *Another kitchen?* I'd already spotted a kitchen on the ground floor when I'd first arrived. How could it be that there were two kitchens in one house? The upstairs kitchen, I learned, was the main eating area for all the children and a few women to supervise us all. It looked too small for the number of children eating here, especially with a large rectangular table taking up most of the space and a breakfast bench with four stools crammed into the corner.

Agnes's tone suddenly became serious, warning us never to use the door next to the kitchen or use the internal staircase leading down to the bottom kitchen unless we were given permission to do so.

Directly at the bottom of the internal stairs was a beautiful formal dining room so fancy it looked like a museum of antiques. Its plush white carpet oozed a cosy feel, a stark contrast to the cold, hard laundry and my bedroom floor. A long antique mahogany dining table centred the room with intricately carved chairs and cushioned white seats. A grand mahogany buffet took up an entire length of wall. So shiny and fancy was the polished furniture it reflected the light here too and bounced off each piece throughout the room creating little sparkles. Grand as it was, I'd finally spotted the only thing I was looking for: a TV. *Surely this was not where all the children would watch TV? There wasn't even a couch!*

As I wondered how thirteen children would squeeze into one ill-fitting room to watch TV, Agnes moved us into the large ground floor kitchen where the smell of freshly baked bread wafted through the air. This kitchen was huge. One big, long bench stretched across the room, with multiple ovens and cupboards that ran from one side of the wall to the other. A large fridge with clear doors showed everything inside, and around the corner a little nook housed a large stainless-steel meat slicer.

Permission was a word Agnes repeated a lot as she walked us through different parts of The House. Where we could go, where we couldn't. What we were allowed to touch and what parts of The House were off limits. Maybe this house would not be such an adventure after all. None of the kids were following behind us, giggling, or running around us as we toured. Everything seemed bleak, silent, and ordered. How could it be that a house full of children was so quiet?

No one had yet mentioned play, where the toys were kept, or where we could run around. There was no invitation to grab a piece of fruit or snack when I was hungry. *Can I just help myself to fruit? Can I go and open the fridge?* Still no mention of when we could watch TV.

I had so many questions about my new life, my new home, but no answers. Maybe Mum would answer them soon enough. I stayed quiet.

Later that evening, everyone ate their dinner in silence. The children didn't chat amongst themselves, nor ask me any questions. No one asked what we might get up to tomorrow or sniggered at something funny. It was all so serious. As soon as dinner was finished, like well-trained soldiers, the children began collecting dishes and tidying up, while I was led to my bedroom to get ready for bed. When the other children came down, there was no whinging, no night-time chaos, no running around to delay bedtime, no reading stories, no jumping on each other's beds, laughing and giggling. They were all so well behaved. It was frightening.

As I tucked myself into bed, I peered over the bunk rail, looking for my mum. She was nowhere to be seen. Would she be coming down to tuck me in and kiss me goodnight as she always did?

I had not seen my father since he left us that morning, and I didn't know when or if he was coming back. He didn't say. He'd only told us to behave and then drove away in our car. I was trying so hard to be good. To be quiet and obedient.

In the silence, I laid still, waiting for my mum. Listening intently for her footsteps to draw closer. The final night-light switched off moments before the sound of the sliding door closed. Pitch dark and silent, I felt my bottom lip pout, realising Mum was not coming. I desperately wanted my mum to tuck me in and tell me everything was going to be okay here. Just to feel assured she was still with me in this big House. To feel her warm breath on my forehead as she kissed me goodnight, as she always did. I pulled my blanket up to my face and hugged it tightly. Would Mum ever come down and tuck me in, or was this how it was going to be from now on?

Whatever peace and order I noticed the day before swiftly changed as I woke the next morning to women bellowing orders from outside my bedroom.

Agnes stormed in and ripped my bed blankets from me. Was there an emergency? I rubbed my eyes, still half asleep, as the two other girls in my room moved swiftly to make their beds.

"Hurry, Rebekah. Get up and make your bed," Agnes yelled.

What has happened?

Sarah, I learned, was Agnes's eldest daughter and was sixteen. She slept below me on the bottom bunk. She smiled reassuringly as I looked to her for answers, a reason for this mad rush, shouting, and noise.

"Rebekah," she spoke softly, "Come down and get dressed. Here." She pointed to two drawers at the base of our bunk. "These are your clothes. We need to get ready for our chores."

Our chores? I looked to the window where the blind had already been lifted. The sun had barely risen. *What time is it? And why do I need to do chores? When do I get to have breakfast? Do we get to watch TV this morning?*

I opened my new clothes drawer, and nothing looked familiar. Where were *my* clothes? Where were my jumpers, my t-shirts, my dresses? Had they not been packed? I walked over to the wardrobe, opened the sliding door, and saw nothing of mine in there either.

I popped my head outside my bedroom, hoping Mum was there somewhere. Instead, Agnes stood glaring at me.

"Where are my clothes? Has my mum got them?"

She stomped towards me. "Rebekah, your clothes are in here." She pointed to the drawers Sarah had shown me. "This is what you are wearing. Now hurry up and get dressed!"

"But, but," I said, stumbling on my words. "Where are *my* clothes? Where is my mum?"

Agnes turned swiftly, her eyes piercing me like daggers, and shouted, "Rebekah, hurry up and get dressed. Don't you dare ask me again. Now hurry up!"

Fighting back tears, I hurriedly dressed in the foreign clothes. I was so confused. Why was she yelling at me? What did I do wrong? Nothing made sense, and yet, I'd be in more trouble if they saw me cry. I just knew it.

After dressing, I scurried to the laundry, where the other children were already lined up. Agnes, who looked to be in the same clothes as yesterday, addressed us like young army cadets in training: harsh, loud, and cold. While I stood, frozen, trying to take in her instructions, every so often my eyes wandered around the room, looking, wondering why Mum still wasn't here. Why hadn't she come down to wake me or at least say good morning? I wanted to see her familiar face as I'd done every morning and hug her. Where was she now? I missed her.

"Rebekah," Agnes yelled again, interrupting my chaotic thoughts. "You have two jobs every morning before school. These must be done quickly and properly before you come up for breakfast. If you are late or do not do your job properly, you will miss out on breakfast and go to school hungry. You have enough time to get up and get your chores done, just like everybody else."

Chores? Like a penny dropping, now it all made sense. The spotless house, the manicured gardens, the kids obediently collecting dishes, the order, and the quiet children. No mention of play. Now I knew why. There would be no playtime. This house was super clean because the children worked around the clock like prisoners to keep it looking spic and span.

Every child had chores here. They varied depending on our age and level of trust. Chores included wiping the skirting around the hallway, making the women's beds in the front section of the House, sweeping the driveway, raking leaves, watering the garden, cleaning the bathrooms, sweeping floors, washing dishes, and prepping food with the ladies in the kitchen. Enough jobs were handed out to keep every part of The House consistently spotless.

I must have drawn the shortest straw with my chores. One was to clean the narrow space behind the dryer and the other was to sweep the small path between the laundry door and the garage door.

As quickly as the meeting was over, everyone quickly disappeared to start their tasks. Agnes stood over me, pointing her finger towards the dryer where I was to begin my first job.

I scrubbed as quickly as I could, matching the furious pace of the children working around me. Breakfast was at seven am, giving me twenty-five minutes to get both my jobs done, checked, and ticked off. I'd not eaten since six the night before, and I was starving.

When I thought I'd finished, I asked Agnes to check my first job. I'd done my best, but I wasn't sure how well I needed to work. I'd helped Mum and Dad out at home before, but my jobs were never henpecked like this. This was all so new to me.

Seeing the children still working hard, sweeping floors, tidying things up, and scrubbing, I worried I'd finished too soon. Had I done this too quickly? How much time do you really need to scrub behind a machine with only four inches of space? Surely it wasn't supposed to take long. Besides, what was the point of cleaning somewhere no one ever saw? Surely *this* was not a big deal.

Agnes inspected my work carefully. She nit-picked at some dust I'd missed, and sternly warned to improve next time or I'd go without my breakfast. I nodded, waiting earnestly for my signal to hurry on to the next job.

Breakfast was the first time I'd seen my mother since we were given the tour the day before. While she stood at the kitchen sink washing a mountain of dishes, she glanced over at me and winced a half-smile before quickly turning back to her own chores. She made no attempt to come over and hug or even speak to me. I could only sit and watch her as I ate my disgusting semolina porridge—it tasted like sloppy, grainy, sand mush—wondering why she was not speaking to me. What was happening here?

Just like the chores meeting earlier, the children were given another dressing down of the rules for walking to school. School? Where was I going? Who would be my new grade two teacher? Would Mum walk me to my new school and into my classroom to meet my new teacher?

Again, no questions were answered because there was no opportunity to ask. All children had to walk to school in pairs. Even beyond The House gates, even without an adult watching, we were expected to walk in straight lines so we didn't look like 'brown cows in a paddock', whatever that meant. The same rule applied at home time, though we also had a curfew. We were to be home no later than a quarter to four. This, we were warned, was plenty of time if we followed the same route to school and we didn't dawdle back. Of course, there'd be consequences if we were just one minute late. I wasn't privy to what those consequences would be, but I got the feeling it wouldn't be good.

I didn't know if what I had woken to—the order, urgency, the jobs, the yelling—was a daily thing or whether this morning routine was a necessity given the number of children to be organised before school. Maybe things would be different after school? Perhaps we would play until dinnertime? Maybe I'd get a chance to see Mum and share my first day at school, even watch some TV together? My toys I missed were still nowhere to be seen, but I quietly hoped I'd be reunited with them soon.

My hopes were cruelly dashed when I came home after school to yet another meeting of more chores to be done until dinnertime and then bedtime shortly after eating.

Great! I grumbled as I tuned out Agnes's constant yelling. *Was she ever nice?* I wondered. I looked around at the other children. I waited for someone to at least whinge and moan how unfair it was! Why couldn't we play? When do we get to go outside and run around, play chase, have tea parties under one of the many trees in the yard or watch TV? But the children remained silent, like they were in some sort of weird trance, following every order like mindless robots.

No more games, no more play, no more TV, and as it seemed so far, no more mother. Now I understood why I never saw any toys of any kind, because there were none. Not a single book, bike, or anything indicating a child existed in this House. Every single part of my life in The House instantly revolved around order, structure, routine, and definitely no fun. Without any warning, without any explanation, my old life was gone. The House was like prison for kids, and the adults were our wardens.

So much of my life with Mum in our old home became memories too soon before their time. Seeing her first thing in the morning and the last person to tuck me into bed before sleep. Sitting on the kitchen bench, watching her bake, watching her eyes light up when we'd walk in from school. Making me a warm drink on a cold wintery day or running a warm bath when I'd come home soaking wet from a rainy day at school, were all still fresh in my mind and I tried to hold onto them because now, I couldn't even touch her. Forbidden from nestling in arms, to talk about my day, to sit on the kitchen bench as she prepared food while I shared a breakdown of my new school, my friends, and teacher. I couldn't go to her for anything anymore.

Mum was all I knew and now she was nothing to me. And it seemed I became nothing to her. Most of the time, we passed each other by, like perfect strangers, leaving me to stare into her distant eyes and wonder why she wasn't my mum anymore.

Did I do something wrong?

Despite being surrounded by so many children and adults, I'd never felt so alone with no one to cry to, no one to run to, and no one telling me why I was living in this new world.

Everything I was to learn in The House, I'd need to figure out on my own, never knowing where the boundaries were until I overstepped them and did something wrong. I now existed in a new world I knew nothing about, with no safety net—like my mum—no protection to fall back on.

Structure and order flourished like a well-oiled machine, thanks to an explicit hierarchy of power directed by my grandfather at the top, whom I was now ordered to call Dad, like all the other children, for reasons no one ever explained. He had complete control and the final word over all matters. Most of the decisions and actions concerning the children were authorised by Agnes, but often carried out by the lower ranking women.

Order of rank started to become clearer. I knew reasonably quickly who to take direct orders from, what their responsibilities were, who had authority, and who had none.

Out of the six women in The House, three of them were the higher-ranking women who were more like sister-wives and also mothers to eight of my grandfather's children. They did administrative things rather than menial tasks and household jobs. They were allowed to leave The House and drive the car. Almost exclusively, they spent their time in the front, more luxurious, part of The House. We didn't see much of these women, except for Agnes, who dealt with serious mistakes and misbehaviours, or when my grandfather sent her to deliver an urgent message that us kids needed to hear immediately.

The other three women at the bottom of the rank—like my mother—did not have sister-wife status. They got lumped with the most labouring crappy tasks: cleaning, scrubbing floors and preparing food for the entire household of twenty people, as well preparing special meals that my grandfather and Agnes requested. With virtually no authority or voice, they were expected to simply obey whatever orders were thrown at them.

An older lady with streaks of white and grey hair and a heavily wrinkled face sat a rank above my mother. Her name was Mildred. Her fearfully loud voice outdid her scrawny old frame, and aside from the laborious tasks, it was also Mildred's job to beat the children with a thin leather strap either when ordered directly or when Agnes couldn't do it herself. Seeing

Mildred storm into a room with the belt in her hands was never a good sign.

Mum was tacked on to the bottom of this hierarchy ladder. She had no rank, authority, or input into the running of The House whatsoever. Not even when it came to her own children. She had no say in how we were treated at all, nor did she dare challenge our punishment.

Mildred constantly barked orders at Mum. She bellowed so often, I think she enjoyed treating Mum like a nuisance child. She gave Mum all the horrible jobs none of the other women wanted. Sometimes I'd see Mum hanging from the top floor, cleaning the outside windows with a petrified look on her face. Other times she'd be wiping the metal venetian blinds, one silvery white length at a time, or on her hands and knees scrubbing every single tile on the large floors until they sparkled and the grout was back to white. Her every move was monitored, timed, and scrutinised by Mildred, who demanded nothing less than perfection, diligence, and obedience.

Mum tried so hard to keep everyone happy. Trying to obey everyone's instructions at once, she'd often get caught out trying to appease everyone. If she was found doing something she wasn't initially told to do, she'd be berated like a child and forced to kneel on the floor with her head down while Mildred stood over her and screamed. Mildred would withhold Mum's rationed morning tea, or she'd have her meals restricted or taken away completely. Mum was constantly pulled in so many directions and controlled in every way imaginable. My heart ached seeing my own mother treated so badly. Despite yearning for my mum to rescue me, sometimes I wished I could have saved her, knowing she too was reduced to being treated like a wicked child.

There was also rank amongst the thirteen children in The House, though it was based on age, from eldest to youngest, and not so much who was favoured and who wasn't. But this rank was only ever enforced when we stood in a straight line for inspections or walked from one part of The House to another. Or sometimes, when it wasn't enough to have everything we did monitored or listened to, they'd assign our leaders—the child above us in age—to watch us like hawks and report back on all our wrongdoings to Agnes or Mildred at the end of each day.

Each night I would fall into my bed exhausted and defeated. This is not how other children had to live, so why did I? I wanted to ask my mother to take us away from The House, but how could I when I wasn't even supposed to talk to her and she acted like I was a stranger?

"Rebekah, Rebekah, come on, wake up. You have to get up."

Strong, cold hands gripped my shoulders as I was shaken awake, a quiet voice urging me to get up quickly. As I blinked my sleepy eyelids, Agnes's face stared at me as she whispered, "Come on, Rebekah, up you get."

It was very early Saturday morning so I wasn't sure why I was being ushered out of bed. Both girls in my room were still asleep. *Why am I being woken ahead of everyone else?*

Agnes pulled the blankets back and ushered me to quietly climb down from the bunk. "Quickly," she whispered. "Here, put on your robe and follow me."

A chilly silence filled the air. No one, not a single child, was up. No washing machines ran, no food being prepared. No gentle slam of doors or thump of feet on concrete floors.

Agnes remained silent as we came to the door adjacent to the top kitchen. The very door I remembered was off limits. She knocked softly and then paused before gesturing me to walk in when it opened.

Stepping into the dimly lit room, I immediately felt the softness of the carpet as my feet sunk into the lush pile, a complete contrast to the cold, hard, concrete floor I'd become accustomed to. The far end of the room revealed the only source of light, coming from a bathroom, allowing me to see two single beds in front of me, both adorned with floral bedspreads. Nothing quite like the plain, old, weathered blankets I had but nothing special either.

Agnes directed me to the bathroom with what looked like two toilets, but one had an unusual looking oval porcelain bowl similar in height to the toilet but with taps at one end.

"Remove your clothes, Rebekah," Agnes demanded.

Confused, I turned around and waited for more, for an explanation.

"Hurry up, Rebekah, quick. Take everything off."

As I hurriedly obeyed, I looked for my mum. *Where was she?*

I'd never undressed in front anyone except my mother, and now I was stripping bare in front of women I barely knew.

The tiled floor numbed my feet as I wrapped my arms around my cold, naked body.

Mary filled up the porcelain bowl, occasionally checking the temperature with her fingers. I'd seen Mary a few times. She was mother to six of the children in The House and the only one I ever saw hug her children and speak warm and lovingly to them. Being higher ranked, a sister-wife, she was one of the few women allowed to leave the house. She dressed in pretty blouses, pencil skirts, and high heels when she was going out. Her thick, black, wavy hair bounced around her shoulders. Her trademark bright red lipstick coloured an otherwise gloomy room.

"Rebekah, come and sit. Just put your bum here." Mary positioned me at the end of the bowl to allow my legs to hang over the edge.

What is happening? I wondered again.

Agnes vigorously began washing my private parts with a bar of soap, nudging me farther forward to wash my bottom before I was abruptly lifted off the bowl and onto my feet before both Mary and Agnes worked quickly to dry my body. My eyes now darted around the room for Mum and my confusion began to turn to fear.

"Put your dressing gown back on and follow me, Rebekah," Agnes instructed.

She led me to a new door. Once opened, there were two identical sets of four stairs, one on the right and on the left. We moved to the stairs leading right, to another door, where Agnes knocked and waited again.

Agnes walked in after a short time, leaving the door ajar while she spoke quietly to someone inside. Moments later, she opened the door. "Rebekah, come in."

Nervously, I tiptoed in. Immediately to my right, I noticed a dark, wood-stained, shiny dressing table with a large mirror making the room look double in size. Thick twisted timber edged the mirror.

As I turned to my left, my grandfather lay bare chested in bed alongside another woman, Linda. Both wore what appeared to be warm and welcoming smiles, like they were expecting me. I wondered if I had done something wrong and was about to be admonished before all the women of The House. It must have been bad. I must have been bad.

Linda was second in rank to Agnes and the older sister to Mary. Her seniority kept her from household duties and my section of The House, so I barely saw her, but I knew who she was.

Of the three people in the room, I still waited expectantly for my mum to come in, hoping she would explain why I was in my grandfather's room, wearing nothing but a dressing gown.

"Rebekah," Agnes said. "Let's take off your robe and I want you to go and jump into bed."

I was too terrified to ask why. Why would I get into bed with my grandfather, naked?

As soon as Agnes took my dressing gown off, I instinctively jumped beneath the covers, immediately feeling warmth emanating from him. To protect myself and shield my body, I turned away from him and curled up in the foetal position, bringing my knees to my chest, and wrapping my arms around my legs. I was so uncomfortable. I wanted to get up and run away, to find my mum.

Where was she?

Slowly his hand reached over and touched my cold, shivering body, stroking my shoulder down to my bare bottom. He grabbed me gently and pulled me closer against his warm stomach, rolling me until I was in the middle of the bed. It was then I realised, my grandfather was naked too.

I looked around, wondering what was happening. *Why is he doing this? Why is he naked? Why is his penis so hard and wet?*

Where is my mum?

Please help me, Mum, I cried on the inside. On the outside, I remained quiet. This is what they had taught me since my arrival. Don't ask. Don't talk back. Don't talk.

"Rebekah. Did you know you have the smoothest bottom? Just like a baby's bottom," my grandfather whispered as he continued to stroke me with his large, warm hands.

Was I meant to say thank you? I didn't know. I was so frightened. I continued to lie frozen, too scared to move. His hands moved around from my bottom to my private parts, and ever so gently, he began stroking.

My eyes darted furiously around, wondering when it was going to stop. Was anyone going to stop this? How long would this go on for? Linda, the only remaining adult in the room, lay still on the other side of me, agreeable and silent the whole time.

I needed to escape, to focus on something else to take me away from what was happening. I fixated my eyes on the curved detailing on the dresser I'd noticed when I first walked in.

How does the wood curve around like that? Look how shiny it is? How do they get the wood to look so shiny? I wondered intensely on what lay in the drawers with the gold handles. The clothes in there must be beautiful, special. I counted the number of drawers. *Wow! Six big drawers! They're so big. I don't think I'll ever have enough clothes to fill six big drawers. So* entranced I was by this piece of furniture, I blocked out everything that was happening to me, the pain and then embarrassment.

"Rebekah, Rebekah."

"It's time to get up now. Here's your dressing gown. Put it back on and I'll take you back downstairs," said Agnes. I hadn't even noticed her in the room.

Abruptly, I was taken back to the bathroom and re-showered. I put my pyjamas back on before being led to my bedroom. I had no idea how much time has passed, but everyone was still fast asleep. Still quiet, I climbed underneath the covers and pulled the blanket up to my face. What happened I didn't quite understand. Shame and violation cloaked my entire body like I'd never felt before. I brought my knees up to my chest as an uneasiness I couldn't resolve hovered around me knowing the little girl who'd entered The House was forever gone.

That I was certain of.

Chapter 3

Another force, God, an omnipotent power, outranked everyone in The House. Except my grandfather apparently, who often proclaimed himself as God's Messiah. This God, an invisible being to which the women and children blindly answered, scrutinised and judged my naughty behaviours, my attitude, and my very existence; although I didn't know how he saw all those things. Even my thoughts came under His watchful eye. There was no escaping this God who demanded perfection and righteousness, and only my grandfather was ordained with the task of unleashing God's wrath upon us errant children.

Before moving into The House, my family didn't go to church on Sundays or say grace at mealtimes. Prayers weren't recited before bed, nor was our home decorated with Jesus statues or any other religious symbols. God was not someone to be afraid of and never lurked behind doors or hid in wall cracks, watching me with judgemental eyes. We used to celebrate Christmas; believing Santa delivered presents to good children, and families gathered for delicious Christmas feasts. The Easter Bunny came once a year to hide delicious chocolate eggs around my house and at Nana's place for me and my siblings or cousins to find.

School taught a little bit about God and Jesus as invisible people in the sky who loved us. A couple of times a year, religious education teachers showed pictures of Jesus as a very special baby cradled in a hay-filled manger who was a Christmas gift to a sinful world. Later at Easter, he would be brutally nailed to a cross and our sins would die with him. Then we could live in a happy, sinless world and it was all thanks to Jesus's sacrifice. Seemed like such a brave thing to do for a man I'd never met. And all I had to do was be grateful and say thank you.

But in the House, my young life's purpose was to serve an almighty, conditional God who only accepted perfection. No mistakes—that never used to be mistakes in my old home—were allowed here. Reminders of my imperfections were frequently barked at me, and no matter how hard I tried, this God always seemed angry.

God was central to everything. Serving Him through my daily chores, my attitude, and willingness to work happily and obediently. Constantly reminded: don't be glutton or complain of hunger because God doesn't like greedy people. Don't begrudge doing that job because God doesn't like laziness. Always have a happy attitude because you're doing God's work. Always keep The House clean because you know cleanliness is next to godliness. You can't play because you need to serve God. You can't watch TV because it reveals what the devil inspires. You can't eat sugar because it's the devil's food. Showing your skin to another person was immoral, except for the times I was naked with my grandfather. Apparently, that was acceptable in the eyes of God. The way I walked and talked, even expressions on my face, how I performed sexually despite my tender age, nothing was left unevaluated.

Sundays at The House were usually devoted to Him. Learning about God. Trying to please God. Seeking God's forgiveness. It was the only day of the week we didn't do chores. But I'd rather do chores than sit through a day where God lashed my sinful soul, and all my supposed sins were laid bare.

Immediately after breakfast, we dressed in our God-pleasing outfits, exclusively set aside for Sundays. The girls were draped in long paisley-patterned dresses, and the boys wore perfectly creased pants, long-sleeved shirts, and knitted jumpers. Just like our school walks, we marched the path in pairs to a purpose-built 'Church Room' attached to the side of the House.

This room was given the Midas touch. Built to either please the God we worshipped or serve as a reminder of my grandfather's wealth; a wealth kept hidden from the cold and gloomy section of the House I lived in. Rows of chairs were lined up against the far-left side of the room, leaving a large rectangular space on the right. At first glance, the layout didn't make sense. But I'd soon learn the space was for sinners to lie down and bury their faces in shame, whilst openly repenting their sins of the week. The sinner's cry began loudly— "I'm sorry, I have sinned."—and the charade would continue until all transgressions were aired. A remorseful apology followed, before waiting for forgiveness, which was usually slow to come and reluctantly given. It was a humiliating spectacle and another show of our worth reduced to nothing.

Sunday routines became so predictable that I quickly learned to mentally prepare for the most boring two hours of sermons, testimonies, and relentless badgering of all the ungodly ways we'd stuffed up during the week. My grandfather glared from behind the lectern, preaching and chastising us for all the ways we'd disappointed Him and him, and how we could only strive to improve ourselves in the forthcoming week. It was futile. Perfection in The House was like a mirage in the desert. Often as he pointed his finger down upon us, I wondered whether he was talking to us about God, or whether he believed he was God. *What made him so special that only he could hear God's voice?* I often wondered.

Most of the time, I really had to listen to every word, being careful not to space out, just in case we were quizzed in the follow-up meeting. It wasn't long before I'd daydream of my old life outside the House. Anything, even cleaning the long skirting boards with a toothbrush, was better than sitting through Sunday sermons. Every so often, a hymn, a cough, or an angry voice brought me back to my dreary reality. With every long pause, I prayed it was the end.

There was rarely anything to look forward to in The House except for Sunday lunch. It was *the* treat of my week. A break from a bland diet of salads for school lunch every day; nothing sweet, no cakes or biscuits to eat, and never any lollies. Just fruit, barley salads, and soya bean salads which made you gag. The only reason you ate everything on the plate—besides being forced to—was knowing we couldn't snack between meals, and anything was better than a growling tummy at bedtime.

Usually Sunday lunch alternated between pancakes or a roast. Not that I cared which was served, but the pancakes were the largest, fluffiest pancakes I'd ever tasted. We even got to choose which topping we had: lemon juice or maple syrup. I savoured every mouthful of my sweet pancakes. It was often the only time I got to fill my empty stomach with something I actually liked to eat. Sunday lunches made sitting through the long monotonous speeches and ear bashing sermons almost worth it. But one of the things I learned living here, was no sooner had you become used to something, or if we let on we liked something, the more likely they were to change or remove it without warning.

One Sunday, I'd quickly tuned out, thinking ahead to the day's lunch choice, when my grandfather suddenly changed the routine. Apparently, he'd received 'word' the children's behaviour wasn't pleasing Him and the only way to redeem ourselves was to voluntarily give up our Sunday lunch.

Agnes, my grandfather's faithful messenger, gathered the children into the laundry room where she asked, "If you would like to please God today by giving up your lunch, put your hand up. Otherwise, you may eat."

What? We have a choice? Choices here were as rare as hen's teeth. I scanned the room to see what the other children would do. *Surely they wouldn't give us a choice, if there wasn't one?* No way would I foolishly choose to go without my favourite meal of the week. And I was certain the others wouldn't 'choose' to either.

Standing firm, I clasped my hands together, not willing for a second to raise my hand. But as I held my grip tight and steady, all the children's hands rose around me. Should it have been my cue to join them? Perhaps, but they gave me a choice, and I was choosing NO. I served this God every day. *How was me starving going to please Him? Nothing I did pleased Him, anyway.*

I stood, waiting for Agnes to start shouting, labelling me greedy and selfish.

But it didn't come.

"Rebekah, why don't you come with me for a chat?" Agnes spoke calmly.

A chat? No one ever chatted in The House. Surely this was a trick.

As I was taken to a bedroom upstairs, I began to regret my decision and wished I could change my mind and run back to the others. Her calmness scared me more than the fear of being thrown into my room or beaten, something I was used to whenever I misbehaved.

Agnes began lecturing on my duty to please God.

"Rebekah," she started. "How do you think it looks when you choose to sit and eat lunch while the other children go without? What do you think God will think if you eat and the others fast? Don't you want God to be pleased with you? Don't you want to show God how much you love Him by giving up a meal? Do you really want to let Him down?"

Agnes left me alone in the room to 'rethink' my choice.

Hopelessly, I stared out the window. What was the point? If I didn't eat, then I'd have to wait until breakfast the next morning, and I was already starving. I wanted to jump up and down and bury my head into the pillow and cry. I just wanted to eat! My stance was futile. They'd tricked me, and I'd fallen for it. Until that moment, I'd not understood why the children raised their hands so willingly. They knew it was a trick. There was never a choice at all.

Agnes walked back in soon after and asked calmly, "So, Rebekah, what have you decided to do?"

"I'm choosing to fast," I grumbled, not caring how insincere I sounded.

It hurt to give in. It was yet another blow of defeat in The House. It showed the extreme lengths they would go to take everything away, to increase their stronghold on an already suffocating grip. I could feel my misery begin to fester.

Sometimes at night, I'd lie in bed, looking up, scanning the ceiling for the invisible God I was warned was constantly watching and listening. Why didn't he speak to me and explain why I was so bad? What had I done wrong to make him hate me so much? Could I do anything right? Pleasing God was like pushing water uphill with a rake.

Never did I understand why we were badgered to idolise a supreme being who wanted all the joy sucked out of life. Didn't anyone want to be happy here?

There was never any reason to look forward to another day because all the mistakes I'd made were carried over and then more were added to the list. Even though every Sunday they teased we could 'wipe the slate clean' with penance. It wasn't true. Nothing was ever forgiven, forgotten, or erased.

After Sunday lunchtime whether the children ate or not, there would be more meetings to discuss the morning sermon, just to make sure we really understood our sins and how much effort we could put in to make up for being awful, naughty children.

Sometimes all the children would be forced to have an afternoon nap rather than give us an ounce of time off to just play. If we were judged as deserving, we were taken for a walk around our local neighbourhood.

Beyond school, the orchestrated Sunday walks were a rare outing into the outside world, the only glimpse of what was happening beyond the imprisonment of The House. It was time away from chores, abuse, solitude, church, and lectures. It was colour to my grey and dreary world.

What could have been an adventure, though, was another opportunity lost to control. No freedom to run or chase each other wildly along the path, to explore, to stop to admire or touch anything. But despite walking like prisoners in shackles, I took careful notice of everything, including the flowers I'd pass by, even the bottlebrushes' red spiky blossoms. If I was really quick, I could pluck a flower and suck the sweet nectar and discard it before anyone noticed.

From the path, I'd peer in through the shopfront windows, gazing at all new items on display. Kid's toys, books, dolls, and bikes. Sometimes even dresses. I missed wearing pretty dresses. Other kids, wearing clothes I could only dream of wearing again, ran ahead of their parents while laughing and holding ice-creams that melted down their wrists. Families walked their dogs, while stray cats purred up high on wooden fences. If we were lucky enough to take the route near the beach, I'd wish time would slow down long enough to view the vast ocean before me and wonder where the water led beyond the horizon. I would imagine how it would feel to float on the surface, feeling as light as a cloud, as the rise and fall of the waves smacked against each other.

The Sunday walks were a bittersweet reminder of a world I used to live in. When I played tea parties under the tree with my sister. Riding my trike with friends up and down our street. The children passing me were smiling and giggling, sharing what sounded like funny stories. I wondered what their homes were like. Did they have to do chores all the time? Were they beaten with a leather strap when they were naughty? Did they have their own toys? Or were they taken away from them too? They looked so happy. I missed feeling happy.

In these moments, I wondered why my life had changed so much.

All the things I once enjoyed were no longer allowed. Things I never considered were bad at all. My grandfather constantly painted the world as the devil's playground. People "out there" were doomed to live in hell for their immorality, their evil wicked ways, the way they dressed, what they watched on TV. He said the world was full of bad people and he was protecting us from them. Everything he took away from me was for my own good, apparently.

I dreaded walking the final stretch home. Each step towards The House was a step back into a world I despised. Like a prisoner let out into the yard before being sent back to the cells, I felt trapped. My freedom was out there. My old life was out there. The childhood I wanted back so desperately was out there, and I couldn't grab it.

I couldn't have it anymore.

Chapter 4

Memories of my old life slowly eroded until it seemed they were nothing more than a fantasy I'd dreamed up. The House was my cold reality now. Complete absence of warmth, love, or nurturing was my new normal. Not even a hug or a smile. Arguing or attempts to resist, reject, or defy my new existence were futile.

Eventually, I even stopped wondering about my mum every day. As much as I missed her cuddles and the sound of her voice, I would soon come to accept I no longer had a mother or mother figure in The House. I hadn't seen or heard from my dad since he dropped us off the day we moved in. Like the rest of the children—my grandfather's children—I slotted in, took my orders, tried to stay within the rules, and just learned to get along without anyone to go to for anything.

The days of being a child were well and truly over.

The rules became tighter every day, week, month and the punishments more severe and given out for the most trivial of mistakes. Using too much conditioner in my hair had me banished from the dinner table and left to sit alone in the cold laundry, with nothing more than a slice of dry, stale bread and a cup of water.

Most of the time, I had no idea I was heading towards another misstep. No gentle discussions to explain where I'd gone wrong, so at least I'd understand for next time. I was just expected to know, like I should have a sixth sense of what to avoid. Fear and anxiety dogged my every action, not knowing what I'd do to bring about another consequence.

While doing my chores one day, I stopped to go to the toilet. When I came out of the bathroom, Agnes was waiting with her arms folded and her lips curled with disgust.

"Rebekah, did you ask if you could go to the toilet?" she yelled.

My body trembled as she towered over me. "No," I answered, confused.

"Right, go stand and face the wall and stay there until I say you can move again!"

I shuffled over to the wall next to the industrial dryer. My body shook so much I needed to use the toilet again. I shifted into a comfortable position, bending one knee and putting weight onto the other leg that wasn't wobbling as much.

"Stand up properly, hands by your side!" she shouted from behind me.

Too overwhelmed to move, I stood frozen with terror. Braced for a belting.

Out of the corner of my eye, a small clock hung on the wall. I could scarcely see much of it except for the second-hand as it ticked by on the last twenty seconds of each minute.

Time might pass quicker if I counted the second hand as it ticked by, I thought. Every so often the sound of feet shuffled behind me, but no one said a word and I didn't dare move.

Have they forgotten me?

My body was still for so long that my legs began to ache as blood pooled in my feet. I desperately needed to move to stop the throbbing. *Why isn't anyone helping me?*

Tears burned my eyes as I thought about my mum, wishing she would help me.

Forty-five minutes later, a stern voice broke the silence. "Rebekah, you can leave the corner now."

Slowly, as my legs released, I turned around, terrified this wouldn't be the end of it. A beating would sometimes follow.

"You are not to go to the toilet whenever you please. Next time you'll get the strap, do you understand me?" Agnes warned.

"Yes," I sulked.

"Now, go back to your jobs!"

Sometimes the rules changed while we were at school, catching us off guard when we arrived home. Agnes, with her arms crossed and her usual angry face, stood waiting at the gates as we marched home one day. She started yelling, ordering us to hurry and form a line in the laundry in our ranked positions.

What had we done? I worried. *We were on time.*

Once inside and in line, Agnes began shouting. "I am sick and tired of seeing you all come home with dirty marks on your clothes. We're not washing your clothes every single day. You have two uniforms, and they must last the entire week, clean and tidy. There is no early changeover. You wear the same uniform for the first half of the week and the next uniform for the second half. Too many of you are coming home with filthy dirt marks, and we've had enough! I will not have you children embarrassing our family name by showing up at school in dirty uniforms! From now on, you'll come home, immediately stand in line, and we will look over you. If we see any dirty marks, you will get the strap. Starting now, I am going to look at your uniforms one by one, and if I tell you to, go and wait by your bedroom!"

Now? Dirty marks? My knees trembled and threatened to give way as I hurriedly scanned my uniform for any dirty marks that might seal my fate. In the cooler months I had two track pants and two zippered jackets to wear to school—a dark maroon colour, which easily concealed most marks, and a pale-blue one that only served to highlight the faintest of dirty marks. Today, as luck would have it, I was wearing my pale-blue uniform. A sickening wave of panic rippled over me as I gazed down at the green, muddy stains on both knees from tripping over on the school oval.

Anticipating my fate, I began inconspicuously rubbing my forearms and hands to numb the sting, knowing from experience the strap very rarely landed on my hands. Jumpers had to be removed, ensuring the full impact of the strap was felt no matter where it hit.

I was the fourth youngest child, ninth in order of rank. In these situations, being at the end of the line gave me more time to prepare, mentally and physically. Besides, I secretly hoped Agnes might ease up by the time she got to me.

When my turn came—as it always did—my stomach churned as I anxiously prepared for what I knew was coming.

"Rebekah, look at your knees!" Agnes yelled. "This is an absolute disgrace. Go and wait over by your bedroom."

I wanted to cry and scream out loud, *"This isn't fair!"* To stomp my feet in protest. Running away was futile. Screaming in defiance would only get me more lashings, so I dragged my feet to wait by my bedroom door. I couldn't flee to into Mum's arms to shield me from the punishment of doing what kids do. I didn't even know where she was. She was no longer my protector, my safety, my security. I was on my own.

After a time, I was beckoned. "Rebekah, come here."

My lips quivered and tears blurred my vision.

"Put your hands out," Agnes demanded.

The strap began lashing my forearms. The burning, stinging sensation intensified after each strike until my arms started to numb. Sometimes the numbness worked in my favour to protect my pain senses and allow me to focus on keeping up with the speed of her belting. If I hesitated and kept my hands back, it only infuriated Agnes, spurring her on to belt me longer and harder.

Keep going, Rebekah, don't lose rhythm. Don't let her miss a hand, because you know what that means. Strap. Strap. Strap. *Keep going.*

"Right," she yelled when she finally stopped. "Now make sure you keep your uniform clean. Do you understand, Rebekah?"

"Yes," I whimpered.

The after-burn was a terrible feeling. As the numbness faded, it gave way to a long raw, burning heat. Leaving the room to start my long list of before-dinner chores, I bowed my head and allowed the tears to quietly stream down my face.

There was never anyone to run to after a belting. Not that we were ever given time to even soothe or comfort ourselves. Once the beatings were over, we were rushed on to the next chore. Though I longed to be hugged. To feel attached to something, to someone, especially Mum. Wishing I could run into the safety of her arms and gently assure me I wasn't naughty. Promising me she'd never leave or allow anyone to hurt me. But she was never there for me in my times of need. Never.

Maybe I'm just a bad little girl? Maybe I deserve this? Maybe I'm not good enough...

I spent every day scared witless. Sometimes my body shook automatically, never knowing if I'd be on the end of a swift blow as I passed an adult. It wasn't unusual to get to bedtime, completely zonk out, wet the bed through the night, and not even realise until I woke up to the strong stench of urine and a wet patch the next morning. The only question that rattled me was whether to admit to it or not. Usually, it depended on the week I'd had. Could I take another beating? Or risk covering it and hope I'd get away with it?

Here I was again. I'd woken to another saturated mattress, but not wanting another belting, I chose to hide it, hoping it would dry while I was at school. While the children slept, I pulled the blanket over the wet patch and quietly stepped down the ladder. I went into the bathroom to wash myself clean, before shoving my urine-soaked pjs behind my drawer.

Feeling triumphant, I walked to school a little lighter, relieved to have escaped without punishment. I knew the risk, but some days I just yearned for a break. A moment without someone barking orders at me, beating me, casting me to a big empty room to sit on my own for hours. Risky as it was, I needed it.

I'd forgotten about my bed by the time I got home from school, but as I showered that evening, I remembered how I'd left it. Now a shower seemed pointless, knowing I'd be sleeping in urine.

Drying myself, Agnes suddenly roared from outside the bathroom.

"Rebekah! Get out here now!"

Oh no... Scrambling to get my pyjamas on, I ran towards my room.

"Come in here." Agnes pointed to my bedroom. The stench hit me instantly and fear made my body ache.

"Did you wet the bed last night?" she demanded.

My whole body trembled. "Yes," I murmured.

"And you just left it? You disgusting little girl! That is the filthiest thing, you dirty, dirty girl!"

I wanted to cry out, *"I'm sorry. I'm sorry, I didn't want to get in trouble!"* There was no use. She wouldn't listen and the more words I said, the worse my punishment would be.

"You're going to strip your bed and leave the mattress on its side to air out. You will sleep on the floor and think about what you did. I am completely disgusted with you!" She stormed off, heading straight to the intercom, and yelled out to my mother. "June, come down immediately and make Rebekah's bed!"

All the lights had been switched off by the time my mother came toward where I cowered in the corner of the room. For a moment, I hoped she might sneak in a rare cuddle in the dark where no one would see and assure me it was all going to be all right. But instead, without a word, she began to lay the sheets of newspaper she held in her hands on the bare concrete floor. I knew better than to throw myself at her like I'd tried a few times before. She would unwrap my arms from her waist and push me away. Again.

Tears poured down my cheeks, soaking my pyjama top. "Mum, Mum, please, please don't do this! Don't make me sleep on the floor, Mum. Please don't do this! I'm sorry I wet the bed. I won't do it again," I begged and pleaded.

Mum never uttered a word. She kept her head down as she continued laying each sheet of paper, not daring to look at me once. Once finished, she turned and walked away. I ran as far as the laundry table, screaming for her to come back. "Mum, Mum, come back, please!" Not caring that my screams may incur another beating.

Like a robot, she just walked ahead and never looked back. For once, I wished Mum was brave enough to break rank and rescue me, even if it meant taking a beating for me. Wasn't I worth that much?

It seemed there was nothing my own mother would do to save her little girl, not even from the clutches of my grandfather's wandering hands on my naked body, being beaten until bruised and numb, or tossed aside like garbage.

I meant nothing.

Alone and broken in the darkness, I dragged myself back to my newspaper bed on the freezing concrete floor and sank down in the foetal position. Hugging my body tight, I cried myself to sleep.

I was eight years old and all alone.

Chapter 5

The morning after I was made to sleep on newspapers on the floor like a dog, I woke freezing cold, stiff, and sore from holding my body so tight, trying to keep myself warm against the icy concrete. Relief and pain flowed simultaneously as I slowly stretched out my shivering limbs, allowing blood to course through my fingers and toes.

Scanning the room, I paused briefly and stared at my bed, hoping tonight I'd be allowed to sleep on my cushioned mattress with warm blankets.

As I got up, it dawned on me that no one came to check on me during the night.

No one came to place a warm blanket over me.

No one came to usher me back into my bed.

I was discarded like a stray animal on the bitterly cold floor.

This was the final straw. A punishment so callous, I could scarcely contain my hatred for The House any longer. I was so sick to death of this place and I ached to scream, "I hate this house!" everywhere I went, to release every single rebellious thought I held back. I didn't deserve any of this. This time they'd gone too far. They had beaten me, abused me, isolated me, cut me down to nothing, and for what? What had I ever done to deserve this? There was not a shred of joy under this roof—no fun, no laughter, no happy stories.

Nothing about this horrid house was good, and I was done with it all!

Using my mum to punish me yet again was the lowest blow, the most hurtful thing they'd done, and they'd done it twice now. The first time Agnes had ordered Mum to repeatedly lash me with the strap while I cowered and begged and screamed for her to stop.

Now I don't care anymore.

Beat me all you like.

Put me in a corner. Starve me, lecture me, do whatever you like, because I don't care!

After that day, I wore my hatred for this place like an oversized coat. Stomping around the House, begrudging the endless cycle of chores. Gritting my teeth, holding back the very thoughts I wanted to scream out loud as I passed the crabby, mean old women. No more confessions for stupid trivial mistakes, another belting for folding towels the wrong way—for goodness' sake—or breaking the string on venetian blinds. I was done owning up and being punished for stupid stuff.

On a wild, windy day, I was ordered to rake the leaves on the nature strip. Outside, a sudden gust of wind swept up the leaves and carried them swiftly through the air. What a pointless exercise. *How stupid*, I vented inside my head.

I snatched the rake and black garbage bag, stomped my feet, while snarling angrily to myself, "This isn't fair, this isn't fair! Why should I have to do this?" Tears streamed down my face.

I threw the rake down, stabbing the leaves, and collecting as many as I could while holding the garbage bag down with one foot to try to keep the wind from blowing it away. I manoeuvred my hands and feet to open the bag and shove the leaves in as fast as I could before another gust of wind whooshed past.

Suddenly, I was grabbed from behind and thrown to the ground.

I looked up and saw Agnes glaring at me. "Get up! Get up now, Rebekah!"

"What?" I shouted. "What have I done?"

"Get inside, you naughty girl!"

"What have I done? I'm trying to rake the leaves! What have I done?" I screamed back, finally standing up to Agnes.

Agnes dug her claws into my arm and dragged me inside. "Get inside. You're going to get a belting!"

I had no idea what I'd done, but this time I wasn't going down without a fight. Not anymore! I'd had enough.

Once inside, I swung my arm violently from her tight grip, and bolted to the top kitchen. Agnes flew into a rage, screaming like I'd never heard before. "You stop right now, Rebekah. Remove all of your clothes! You're going to get a beating!"

"No," I screamed defiantly. "No. No. No. No more. I hate you! I hate this house!"

Running around the kitchen table, Agnes furiously tried to catch me, but I had unknowingly cornered myself as I tried to sprint past her and out the kitchen door.

She grabbed me and forcibly began tearing my clothes from my body as I wriggled and struggled, beating me with her hands, over and over and over, pounding into me wherever they landed. The more I wriggled to escape her clutches, the more tired I grew. As I weakened, she snatched the strap from her back pocket and continued lashing me.

Curled up on the ground, I cried out, whimpering between each plea. "Please stop, please stop. Leave me alone, please!"

Her yelling was muffled, like she was talking under water, as I held my half-naked body on the floor, numb and sobbing.

That afternoon I was sent to bed without dinner. A double blow. My body ached; my stomach was empty. Through puffy, blurry eyes, I gazed out the window and saw the day drawing to a close. I wondered about my life in The House. *Is this it? Will I stay in here forever?* I fixated on the green trees that towered above the coloured roof tops of neighbouring houses, and the pink clouds stretching across the sky. Simple things I barely got the chance to stop and notice living here.

I missed regular, normal, and everyday things. I missed Christmas—singing carols, decorating the tree, presents, and the excitement of counting down the days with Mum and my siblings. For three years in The House, my birthday wasn't ever acknowledged. The first year, Mum managed to mouth Happy Birthday as she walked by with a handful of towels. Dad didn't even visit. There were no presents, no cake, no chanting. Just another meaningless day.

I missed having fun. Riding a bike, eating ice-cream on the footpath in my street, racing to finish it before the sun melted it. I wanted to watch TV, my favourite cartoons. To listen to Mum read a bedtime story. I missed reading. Playing with my brothers and sister. Lazily waking up in my pyjamas on a Saturday, with time on my side, leisurely eating breakfast without any thought to what I might do for the rest of the day. I missed everything my life once was.

School was my only solace, an escape from control, punishment, and abuse. My only chance to play and be a kid. I sidled up to my teachers for any ounce of nurturing, warmth, encouragement, and attention The House starved me of. Most days, I showed up in survival mode, spaced out to the noise around me. Sometimes I'd unconsciously say something witty, causing spontaneous laughter from the teacher and kids. These were rare moments where life sprinkled colour before I'd revert back to the frightened, withdrawn child I'd become to survive.

Memories like these triggered an idea to somehow escape The House forever. *Perhaps I could escape during the night.* I knew where they kept the key to the laundry door. I could tiptoe out and run straight to the side gate to freedom. *But where would I go? It would be dark, and I don't know my way around; other than the same route to school, I'd taken hundreds of times now. Perhaps I could run to the neighbours and beg them to send me away somewhere, anywhere?*

My stomach rumbled and broke my train of thought. I huddled myself further underneath the blankets to muffle the sound of hunger. I'd have to wait until morning to eat again.

Perhaps I could find a way to my paternal Nana's house? She lived on her own in Melbourne for years ever since my grandfather walked out on her when my dad and his brothers were young. She didn't drive. *But maybe if I rang her and told her I wanted to visit, she might help me get to her house.* So far, it was the only plausible plan I could come up with. She was the only other person I knew on the outside besides my father. But I never saw him anymore.

Nana was such a sweet lady. Every time we used to visit, she'd prepare a plentiful feast of delicious biscuits and crackers with cheese, laid out on her special China platters, just for these occasions. She'd wouldn't sit down and chat much, too busy fussing over everyone and making sure we were all looked after. Just as our visits ended, she'd grab a glass jar full of white peppermints, insisting my siblings and I take one.

Maybe Nana *was* my only way out. I missed her.

As I lay in bed, I hatched out a bold plan to escape. I'd need to ask Mum for Nana's phone number, being careful to pick a moment that wouldn't arouse suspicion as to why I was talking to Mum or why I wanted the number if someone did hear us.

Sometimes, like a game of cat and mouse, I had to plot and plan to outsmart the women who stalked and waited to pounce on us kids. Like the time I was being punished for something and told to sit in the laundry room, while the kids and adults watched some scary movie with a moral message designed to keep us from being tempted in the 'devil's world'. I was not allowed to join them all until eight o'clock. No one was watching me, so I dragged my stool up to the wall clock and manually moved the hands until it showed eight o'clock precisely. I went to Agnes to report the time, and she never bothered to check. A small but satisfying win.

As it happened, the next day, Mum was standing in the laundry, folding a large pile of clothes. Instead of pacing quickly past her, I slowed right down and whispered, "Mum, do you know Nana's phone number?"

"Yes, I do," she replied. Mum had this uncanny knack for remembering phone numbers and long distant family member's birthdates.

"Can you write it down for me, please?" I pushed the scrap bit of paper in front of her, urging her to write it down quickly before we got caught.

I snatched the paper and quickly hid it inside a sock in my bedroom drawer.

First step accomplished!

It was too risky and virtually impossible with a thousand eyes watching me all day to use The House phone, but I remembered seeing a pay phone at the side entrance of the main building my classroom was in, right next to a popular area of the school yard for playing ball games. How I'd get there without being seen was my next challenge.

Every day, as soon as the home bell rang, all House children had to meet under a large tree at the school's front gates. We weren't allowed to leave until all children were there and still be home by 3:45pm, otherwise we'd all be in trouble.

Two things would foil my plan; one of the House children seeing me run in the opposite direction of the meeting tree or being seen at the phone box.

Perhaps, I could zip out of the classroom as soon as the bell rung, quickly grab my bag and run straight towards the phone. There'd be no way of knowing if I could do this unless I did a dry run first.

The next day, as soon as the home bell rang, I jumped from my desk, grabbed my bag, and darted from the room, running down the stairs, making sure I looked every which way for anyone to spot me. Before I knew it, I'd made it to the side door and none of the House children were anywhere to be seen.

My dry run was a success. *I can do this,* I thought! *This is how I'll escape.*

Brimming with pride, I joined the pack, trying to curtail the spring in my step and disguise my wide smile, knowing the end to my nightmare was in sight. *Is this the last time I'll walk this path? Will this be the very last night I spend in this awful House?*

That night, I eagerly prepared for bed. For once, the women barking orders didn't bother me one bit. I tucked myself in, thinking only of impending freedom.

The next morning, I sprang out of bed, got dressed, remembering to retrieve Nan's number and stuff it inside my sock. For once, I completed my chores with a smile on my face. *Today is the day. My last day in here forever*. Nerves of joy bubbled through my body. A part of me was terrified to follow my plan through. But I reminded myself that freedom was more important than fear!

The school day dragged on. With every minute that ticked by, all I could think about was getting to that phone booth. When the home bell rang, my heart raced as adrenalin flooded my body. I immediately sprinted out of the classroom, bolted down the stairs, and without any obstacles, headed straight towards the side exit.

This is it! I made it here so quickly and so easily without anyone stopping me or noticing where I was going. Freedom was a mere five feet away. All I had to do was open the school gate, step outside the school grounds, and pick up the phone.

But I froze. I couldn't move. My legs fixed to the ground like concrete pillars. I looked down at my feet, willing them to take the steps, but I couldn't do it. *Come on, Rebekah, just go! Go to the phone box. Call Nana, and she can take you away. We don't have much time! Come on, Rebekah!*

But no matter how much will was there, my legs wouldn't budge. I glanced over in the direction of the meeting tree, where everyone would be waiting for me. A deadline to be home loomed.

The futility of my plan dawned on me. *What would really happen if I called Nana? She couldn't come and get me. She didn't have a license. She'd probably call my dad and he would call my grandfather. I'd get into so much trouble once they found out I was trying to flee. They'd watch me even closer, that's for sure.* I could only think of questions and repercussions, questions I'd never considered until now. What about the consequences for the other children who would be late because of me?

"It just isn't fair! I can't escape!" I mumbled to myself through tears. *There's nowhere to go. I'm trapped in The House I hate!* I couldn't walk the last five measly feet towards freedom because it didn't really exist. No one would believe me or what I was living through. The adults, the children, they'd all deny it. No one would take me away. I was stuck here forever.

Resigned to my fate, I remembered the time, flashed one last glance at the phone box—a symbol of my vain attempt at freedom—and swiftly turned around, speeding through the school building and over to the tree to meet the other children.

I never made any more attempts to escape, nor did I entertain any wild plans. As much as I hated The House, as miserable as I was, I buried my wish for a normal life because it seemed impossible.

Memories of what life used to be like were now locked away, somewhere safe and sound. Needed only for my dreams while I slept or daydreamed at school. No one could take them away from me. No one could steal my dreams where life was rich and as colourful as a rainbow. They were mine to hold on to. They were mine to hope for. And maybe that's what dreaming was for.

Chapter 6

It was Wednesday, 26 November 1986, a day just like every other day before it. Mum laboured through the mounds of washing in the laundry room, while Mildred bellowed orders at her like she'd done so many times before. Mum, instead of her usual obedience, responded with unusual defiance, catching Mildred completely by surprise.

In an attempt to quash her tiny attempt at rebellion, Mildred snarled back and withdrew Mum's morning tea, a sure-fire tactic that usually worked. Mum loved her food. But Mum, who no longer seemed to give a damn, threw back an insolent, "Fine!"

Mum's defiance was new territory for Mildred. Mum always obeyed her orders, knowing the harsh discipline she'd receive if she didn't. But something different was happening that day. Mum was fighting back. Mildred kept upping the ante, threatening to take away all her meals; but no matter what she threatened, nothing Mildred did was pushing Mum back into submission.

Mildred, with nothing left up her sleeve, demanded Mum go and pray to release the demons driving her roguish behaviour.

By this time, Mum shuffled down towards the front gates where she sat looking despondently down at the ground. Brent, the eldest child, followed shortly after and sat next to her.

Less than ten minutes later, Mum stood up and walked out the gate. It was the first time she'd left The House in three years. She wasn't a wife or high-ranking woman, nor did she ever have permission to leave.

Where was she going? I wondered, standing at the top of the outside stairs, feeling as though a part of me left with her.

She'd never step back into The House again. She'd left us behind.

As days and nights passed, I agonised over Mum's absence, not knowing what the future held for me here without her. Would she come back to get her children, or leave us behind for good? Though my relationship to Mum was severed in The House, her presence at least connected me to my old world, my old life.

Two weeks went by. My grandfather and Agnes gathered my siblings and me into the formal dining room to try to brainwash us into choosing to stay with them instead of leaving with Mum. Apparently, Mum had phoned to tell them she was coming to collect us. No good would come of it if we were to leave, they warned us. We belonged in The House. So convinced that we would never leave, they asked us to choose a new mother in her place. Which seemed rather odd, given they'd already taken my mum away and never replaced her in the three years I'd lived there.

The next day at school, without warning, I was called out of my classroom and led into the school staff room. Mum was standing there, frightened and visibly upset, between two policemen, who towered over her noticeably smaller frame. She'd lost a lot of weight, too. It was the slimmest I'd ever seen her.

She watched on nervously as I was ushered to join my siblings about ten feet away from her. The police presence told me *this* was a big deal. Something was about to change. No other adult from The House was present, just us four kids and Mum—the original family, minus Dad.

Time stood still as an eerie silence filled the room. I could barely breathe as I anxiously waited for someone to tell me what was going on.

As the policeman spoke, I looked at Mum. Her mouth moved along with the words he spoke. Perhaps she couldn't speak; too afraid she'd collapse. The very presence of police told me she could not do this on her own.

"Your mum has come here today to collect you and move away to live with your other grandparents." A long pause followed as he looked at each of my siblings and me. "Would you all like to leave today and live with your mum?" I waited for my siblings to speak, already knowing my decision as soon as I laid eyes on Mum. I wanted to run into in her protective arms and sob for the loss of three years of my life to that House. It had been so long since I'd been in her arms. So long since I'd been comforted.

My whole body shivered like I'd been thrown into an icebox, trying to hold back an avalanche of emotions that had been shackled for too long. This was a moment I'd waited so long for. To be free of The House, the control, the abuse, and the misery. The life I despised with every fibre of my being.

My voice broke as I fought back tears. "I want to go home with you, Mum; but they don't want me to go with you."

I stood, weeping, holding myself back, trying to mask the overwhelming desperation to just run. Was leaving a real possibility, or was this a test? Mum had always caved to the women's demands in The House. For a moment, I wondered if there was a chance we might well be taken back there. If we leave now, do we leave forever?

Tears welled in Mum's eyes. Our eyes locked, and we both knew we belonged to each other. She was my mother, and I was still her little girl.

My siblings and I unanimously decided to leave with Mum. Since my father didn't live with us anymore and my grandfather didn't have legal custody, Mum was free to take us and leave The House forever and never ever return.

The policemen escorted us out the school gate, where we were met by my mum's father, my Pop. A familiar face I hadn't seen in three long years. My siblings and I squashed into the back of the cream-coloured wagon where we sat awkward and dead silent. No tears, no joyous raptures, or screams of relief.

Mum strapped her seatbelt on as she turned to us and smiled, obviously happy to have her children back. Relieved we were finally together again as a family and our horror was now over.

As we drove away, I stared at the school and surrounding streets as the landscape faded into the distance. A wave of emotion came over me. I was so happy to leave The House. Happy to never have to wake to chores again. Happy to never have to go into my grandfather's bedroom again. Happy to never be beaten or punished again.

But I would miss my school, my teacher who I looked forward to seeing every day. I wondered if my teacher knew where I was going and if he would miss me. Would he wonder why I abruptly left the school without saying goodbye? I hoped he understood I couldn't stay. I'd hoped my teacher knew how much he meant to me.

I would miss the friends I made too. My closest friend Aashvi. She was my only true friend in the school. I wished I got to say goodbye and explain why I had to leave. She would notice my absence. Who would look after her as we looked out for each other? We were all we had. I hoped she would find a new friend who cared for her as much as I did.

I would miss the other children in The House—my aunts and uncles, technically, since they were all born to my grandfather. I wished I could take them all with me, knowing what their lives would continue to be like. Knowing they were trapped there. Maybe one day we would see each other again. *If there is a God,* I thought, as I glanced out the window. *I will pray for the children. I will pray for them to one day be free like me.* I hoped God would hear my prayers and look after them.

As we drove farther away from the suburb of my old existence and into a new life, I was quietly optimistic everything would be better from then on. That happiness and the chance to be a child once more was on the horizon.

Chapter 7

We moved into my maternal grandparents' home that day, more than two hours away from The House. It was a temporary solution until we found a place of our own. Nana and Pop lived on a rural property just outside of a little town and some thirty kilometres from the nearest regional city. It was a completely different landscape from the suburban life we'd just fled.

Properties out here in the bush stretched for miles. Houses scattered in paddocks, some close by the road, others down long, rocky driveways. The landscape was dry, arid, and dusty. Hot summer days killed any desire for flowers to blossom. Only trees that thrived on neglect survived out here. Without access to town water, water was scarce. Whatever rain fell was a welcome relief to the dry, barren ground. Water tanks were deliberately positioned by every house to catch each drop of rain. If it was a good winter of rainfall, you'd be rewarded with a daily shower. Prolonged absence of rain rationed showers to every couple of days just to get clean and then get out.

Each room in my grandparent's timber log house was packed full of a lifetime of memories, experiences, and souvenirs collected from their travels abroad. Treasured items stood proudly on display and collected dust—family photos, awards, spoon collections. A complete contrast to the cold, sterile, lifeless House I'd just come from. This home exuded a warm, cosy feel.

Nana's small study directly adjacent to the kitchen/dining room became my temporary bedroom. A bunk bed was set up along the wall for my sister and me. Nana's knitting bags, balls of wool, and sewing machine filled whatever space was left. A stack of excess books that couldn't fit on her library wall were piled in the corner, teetering and threatening to fall. I worried I'd knock them over and be punished. There was no room for drawers or cupboards. Not that there was any need, since we left Melbourne with only the clothes on our backs.

The next morning, I woke and scanned the room, trying to piece together the last twenty-four hours. The events of yesterday exhausted me completely, and I barely remembered falling asleep.

I tiptoed down from the top bunk and stood in the doorway, immediately covering my eyes from the morning sun beaming through the dining-room window.

The warm sunlight felt glorious and yet surreal at the same time. I'd forgotten just how bright the sun shone. In the House, the sun never coloured the grey walls and dreary light in my room. On a good day, a single ray of sun would sneak through the corner of the laundry window. If I was lucky enough and no one was around, I'd pause momentarily, taking in its beauty, seeing the long, pink clouds stretched across the early morning sky. A reminder that, if for nothing else, it was going to be a beautiful, warm day.

Standing frozen to the spot, I wasn't sure what I was allowed to do. Where was I to go? Did I have jobs or chores? I knew what I normally had to do, but here, I was unsure. Nana's eyes lit up as soon as she saw me. She walked over to the dining table, pulled out a chair and called out, "Rebekah, darling, come sit down and I'll get you some breakfast. What would you like?"

I looked at her with a blank stare. I mumbled nervously, scared to ask her to repeat herself. Missing a question the first time would be met with anger and hostility in The House. Miss the point a second time and it was a beating.

"Um, what would I like?" I asked.

"Yes, Rebekah, what would you like for breakfast? We have toast or cereal. Or you can have both if you're very hungry," she replied. Her voice sounded warm and her smile was so very friendly.

"Um, can I have some cereal, please?" I asked, still nervous. Wasn't there a chore to do first to earn my breakfast?

Everything about this moment felt strange. There was no yelling, no commands, no urgency. Just an odd calm, like everything around me was being played out in slow motion.

As I sat and waited for breakfast, music played from a radio sitting on the bench nearby. Radio music I hadn't heard in three years. Not biblical hymns or classical pieces, just regular music. It was Paul Simon's song, *Call Me Al*.

I'd woken to a completely different world. A world I vaguely remembered from years ago but now felt foreign, almost frightening. What were the rules here? What if I did something wrong? Would the punishment be as severe as The House? Would it be worse?

This time, the nine-and-a-half-year-old me wanted to know immediately before I messed up big time and found out the hard way.

For three years, I'd been controlled in every single way. Conditioned to only to speak when spoken to, only move when instructed, only eat when food was placed before me. Forced to do things I didn't want to do. Now I had no idea what I could do and where I could go. Even still, I couldn't help but fear this 'freedom' wouldn't last and we'd return to The House of horrors.

For all the times I imagined going back to 'normality', to what I once knew and yearned to experience again, now it was right in front of me and yet it unsettled me. The uncertainty felt even scarier. I needed rules and control, so I knew what was right and what was wrong, what the consequences would be if I stuffed up.

Simple things like sitting and talking to my nana, my mother, my brothers, my sister, were just too surreal. I could eat, enjoying every spoonful of cereal at my leisure? I could choose my own clothes? There was no daily uniform? I could watch TV or go outside and play? I could do my most favourite thing and read a book? I can grow my hair long again and not have it cut off to look like a boy, like they insisted on doing at The House. Every time the boys at The House needed a cut, my sister and I were ordered to line up too and get the same: short back and sides. Soon after, I'd whimper as I looked in the mirror, grabbing at my short tufts of hair.

Now I was free to roam around the property, pat and play with the dogs and cats and chooks, and even wander across the paddocks to visit the horses. I could be a child again.

These simple 'normal' things now felt strange.

Such a colossal flip of my life made adjusting to a 'new normal' difficult to embrace, but worse yet, difficult to trust. I'd been previously stripped of my free will, my ability to make choices, and conditioned to be obedient in all things. So accustomed had I become to tread with caution and fear of punishment, I still tiptoed around, terrified to slip up and step out of line. I was always wondering, was I being good? Good enough? Was God still watching me here, too? I moved around the house, nervously fidgeting my fingers, while my legs often shook, expecting I'd get into trouble soon. After all, punishment was never too far away.

Some nights I lay in bed wishing I was back in The House. I hated it there, but at least I knew what to expect. Control became normal to me. I wanted to know where I belonged. And I simply didn't know if this new place was where I was meant to be.

Even the smallest, most trivial mistakes sparked instant fear and trembling. Accidentally pouring too much milk on my cereal, or worse, spilling it. I'd quickly try to soak it up with my jumper to avoid a punishment that was certain to be dished out. I'd make my bed as soon as I woke, just in case anyone came to inspect it. Not knowing what to do every moment, I constantly analysed my every move. Questions consumed me. It was tortuous and exhausting.

No one helped me adapt to my new environment, and it only served to heighten my anxiety. Mum never attempted to explain or correct the past three years, and neither did my grandparents. Mum didn't try to reconnect with me either, to bridge the massive gap that severed our attachment. There were no extra cuddles, no opportunities to discuss my confusion, or my guarded approach to my new life. She never spoke to me about the years of living in hell. She never checked in on me emotionally.

Just like The House at the very beginning, I was once again forced to adapt without any explanation. I buried my thoughts and my feelings, remaining quieter than any nine-year-old should be. My fearful, nervous state was passed off as shy to anyone who commented. I was scared and scarred, and I simply didn't understand how to navigate my way through these huge shifts.

I don't believe Mum's silence was intentional. Maybe she just didn't know how to repair what was damaged or to apologise for what was done. So much time had passed since we'd been together as mother and daughter, and I longed for her to sit and spend time with me. To wrap me in her arms and assure me everything would be okay. I longed to hear her reassuring words, to do the little things that would help build our trust again and help restore our broken bond, to help me feel safe in the world again. I needed to know she was here for me now. I had so many questions, so much confusion, so much anxiety and fear.

Her silence left me wondering why I still felt abandoned when no one was holding her back from reaching out to me.

The week after our move, Mum enrolled my siblings and me into the only public school in town where I could finish the last two weeks of grade four.

Our new school was tiny in comparison to the suburban school of three hundred students I'd just left. It had a total of fifty kids from prep to grade six, split into three classes that were divided across two portable buildings for the lower grades and a stand-alone red brick building with a high church-like steepled roof about ten metres away for the combined four/five/six grades. A large cast iron bell, which was rung by a specially chosen child to alert the whole school of break times, hung in the corner outside.

Resources were scarce at this school, with one small Apple computer in the corner of my classroom, compared to an entire room of computers in my old school. The headmaster wore many hats, including teacher and receptionist. Answering the phone was often delegated to the grade six students if he was busy. We only borrowed books when the mobile library truck travelled through our town, and lunch orders were filled by the local general store.

There was a relaxed, country vibe to this school that was so different from my previous suburban school. Everybody knew everybody, which made it harder to blend in and be overlooked, like I wanted to be. I was obviously the new girl, self-conscious, awkward, and shy. I tried my best to adjust, since school was a place I could attempt to be myself, where no one from The House had control. But try as I might, I held myself back until I could find where, if anywhere, I might fit in.

Amy, who was also in grade four, was one of the first girls I met. She lived just a few kilometres down the road from my grandparents' house on a big farm property with scores of sheep and cattle. We caught the same bus to our small school, where she held the prized Bus Leader job. The Bus Leader got to sit right up the front on a single seat of their own, straight across from the bus driver, while the rest of us squished on double seats. It was the Bus Leader's job to make sure everyone on the bus behaved.

She must be so cool and popular! I thought.

Maybe it was the fact that it was such a small school that made Amy stand out as the 'it' girl. The one everyone seemed to want to be around. To me, she seemed to have it all. Her long toned legs towered over shorter girls like me, and her long golden blonde hair sat perfectly in place compared to my untamed wild wavy hair.

It was so easy to be around her. She kept a smile on her face like it was tattooed in place. She was warm and friendly to everyone, no matter what grade. Other kids seemed to gloat over her, following her around the school with giddy smiles and happily obeying her every instruction on the bus just to please her. Compared to my shy and fearful nature, I wondered how it must have felt to be so comfortable around people like she was. She never looked scared or afraid of anything like I was. Her appearance and popularity epitomised everything I could only wish to be.

Around Amy, it was easy to forget about the trauma of my old life and finally be a part of a world that was normal and fun, like regular kids my age. The more we saw each other at school, the closer friends we became. I got hang out with her after school and sometimes even have sleepovers on the weekend, something I'd not been able to do before. We became so in sync with each other, we often spent the bus ride home planning our matching hairstyles for the next day at school. Two ponytails or one plait, or two. We sat next to each other at school and playfully competed against each other to see who'd done more work.

Despite being close and often chatting endlessly for hours, Amy never really asked where I'd come from, a topic I was more than happy to avoid. Questions like, where's your dad or where did you live in Melbourne, were quickly shut down with brief and vague answers before I'd quickly change the subject. I was scared if she knew too much about my old life, she might not like me, and I needed her friendship to feel a part of something normal.

My teacher/headmaster—Sir, as we were to address him—was an older man, tall and lanky with tanned, wrinkled skin. He was a warm and friendly teacher, greeting everybody with a 'hooroo' in the morning and a 'cheerio' in the afternoon as we bolted out of the classroom at home time.

Every day, he wore the same outfit: white short-sleeved shirt, a tie, shorts with twin creases down the middle of each leg, and long white socks pulled up to his knees. Whenever he stopped to explain something, he'd take his glasses off and hold the tip of the temple in his mouth, revealing his one gold tooth that sparkled in the light when he spoke.

He expected good behaviour, good values, and good manners but not in a scary way, balancing his expectations with a funny side, often breaking from class lessons to tell us a yarn or two from the *good ol' days*. I enjoyed his stories. At least they weren't bible stories where you had to listen for the hidden message.

Like my old schoolteacher, his good-natured style made school a safe place to be. It was only on occasions when I'd wave him over for help that unnerved me. He'd sit next to me, resting his arm on my shoulder and sometimes brushing his fingers up and down as he listened to my question. My whole body would stiffen, alarmed by his unwarranted touch, triggering flashbacks and more fear.

I wondered if all old men were like that. Were they just allowed to touch me? I'd scan the classroom to spot some sort of shocked look from the other students, but no one batted an eyelid. Just like the women and kids in The House, no one questioned nor stopped any type of inappropriate behaviour. It must be normal, I concluded. But whether it was innocent or not, I didn't like how icky it felt.

The schoolyard, though vast, lacked luscious green grass. What tried to resemble an oval was just a brown, rectangular dustbowl. Small patches of grass only grew where the water pooled. A row of small shrubs and colourful flowers lined either side of the school entrance. Large gum trees, native plants, and foliage clustered around the edges of the school grounds. With minimal play equipment, we made the best of what we had, often creating our own fun out of oddly placed structures in the yard and nature itself.

Massive gum trees provided ample opportunities to play, climb, eat, and chat. Four poles, at least six metres high and connected by steel beams at the top forming a metal square, stood surrounded by sand. Sometimes the girls and I, with our sandwiches clenched in our mouths, would climb the poles like monkeys and eat our lunch perched high in the sky.

On the outskirts of the oval, nestled among the smaller trees, was a large concrete pipe. When we'd get bored of sitting in the trees, we'd play on it, since it just sat on top of the ground rather than under it. As soon as the play bell rang, kids would bolt down to the pipe, jump inside it and wait for the other kids to stand on top and roll it backwards and forwards.

On the third day at my new school, the kids were keen for me to have a turn in the pipe. Sitting on the inside edge, I placed my hand on the outside of the pipe to hold on and keep myself from slipping, not realising that as we rolled forward, my hand would go with it. Suddenly, I felt an enormous pressure in my fingers and realised they were being crushed between the ground and the pipe. Blood squirted everywhere as I jumped up, screaming and clutching my hand to my chest. I bolted to the classroom ahead of the other kids who were running and freaking out too.

Miraculously, I hadn't broken any bones, but I'd split open three of my fingers. For six weeks, my right hand was bandaged and in a sling.

My mangled fingers throbbed most at night. Mum gave me Panadol and suggested I sleep with her to keep an eye on me. I squirmed as images of my grandfather's bed flashed across my mind, reminding me of what used to happen when I shared a bed with an adult. Was there more to this? Would someone else sneak in? Would Mum stop them this time?

I huddled towards the edge of the bed, curled up in a ball, a tight fist clenching my bandaged hand close to my chest, isolating myself as much as I could from any possible contact. I didn't sleep much, unable to rest my mind from a possible intrusion throughout the night. I woke regularly, startled by a noise, a door opening, footsteps, anything, double-checking the door was closed, so no one else could get in.

The next time Mum offered for me to sleep next to her, I refused.

Aside from school events and activities, I hadn't celebrated Christmas for three years. At school, kids made long red, green, and white paper chains and hung tinsel around the room. Christmas carols played in the background, while kids spoke excitedly about their holiday plans and the presents they were hoping to get. What a treat it was to finally be able to enjoy the festivities from one environment to another and not have to switch off once I was home.

This year we celebrated Christmas at my Mum's sister's house in Melbourne. As soon as I walked into the house, anxiously keeping close to Mum, I could hear my aunties and uncles chatting and the sounds of children tramping over the wooden floors, laughing loudly and having fun.

My cousin Charlotte, who was five years younger than me, grabbed my hand and pulled me towards her bedroom. Stepping into her room was like entering an enchanted world I'd only read about in fairy tales. There were Barbies, pretty bedspreads, pink things, frilly things, boxes of toys, and shelves full of dolls. Her wardrobe overflowed with lovely dresses and shoes. I, on the other hand, still had barely any clothes, no toys, and definitely no Barbies.

As I moved freely around their home, in the corner of the lounge room stood a tall, sparkly white Christmas tree with red baubles and silver tinsel hung randomly on it. What a sight! Underneath the trees were gifts, perfectly wrapped and stacked haphazardly upon each other. There were so many. *Who were they for? Would I receive any gifts?* I knew Mum probably had no money for gifts. But still I hoped.

As the family gathered around the tree, I smiled, just happy to be here, celebrating, surrounded by my family once again. That in itself was a gift. Everyone was happy, laughing, and giggling. Joy and love filled the room.

A wave of gratitude and longing flowed over me as I remembered how it used to be for us years before.

As the gifts were handed out, I heard my name.

"Rebekah, this one's for you."

I looked up to see Nana's hand extended towards me, holding a small, wrapped box. I nervously thanked her as I reached for it. Staring down at this little box, I couldn't help but pause and bask in the simple pleasure of receiving my own gift, completely and utterly mine, while my cousins tore through theirs like wild animals.

I unwrapped the paper so very slowly, trying to savour the moment and not rip the wrapping. Inside the box were three small, single ornaments. A gnome-looking man in a red suit with a black belt around his rounded waist, leaning against a pale brown stump of wood with a long, white beard and a pointed red hat. On either side of him were two children, also wearing red clothes and a hat, lying forward on their bellies, with their legs kicked up behind them. I didn't understand what they were for, but I didn't care. These ornaments were the first gifts I'd been given in a long time. They belonged to me. I squeezed them tightly in my hands. Suddenly they became the most valuable things I owned in the whole world and little did I realise that even in adulthood, I'd never let them go.

Chapter 8

In 1987, my mum, siblings, and I were still living at my grandparent's house. Starting a fresh new year in grade five and soon to be ten years old, leaving single digits behind. Life was settling down, and I was adjusting better each day as the routine and parameters became more familiar and safe.

Each moment with Nan and Pop, was a chance to bridge the gap and re-connect again. I helped in the kitchen, washing the dishes as Nana cooked breakfast or prepared the weekly Sunday roast. Feeding their cats and dogs, carrying a bucket of veggie scraps to the chook pen and collecting the eggs, were not considered chores as a condition of earning my keep, but jobs I did willingly and enjoyed.

When Pop came home, he'd sit down at the kitchen table and slap his hands down on his knees, prompting me to jump on his lap as he jigged his knee up and down pretending to be a horse.

My guard was slowly coming down, and I was learning to trust a warm smile, a cuddle, a kiss on the cheek, all the while learning what safe and trusting relationships were like again.

Unfortunately, it didn't last long.

It started out innocently enough. He would prompt me to sit on his knee and then tickle the side of my ribs, as I came to expect. Sometimes it annoyed me, but I thought he was showing his affection and I didn't want to make him angry by asking him to stop. But then after a while, he began to move his hands underneath my top so that he was touching my skin. At first his fingers played on my belly, but gradually his hands moved to my breasts and nipples. As he circled his fingers around, his breath hitting the side of my neck felt heavier and warm. The bulkier the jumper I wore, the more insistent he became and the longer he touched me.

When I tried to push his hands away, he'd lock his elbows against mine so I couldn't move and made small talk to keep me on his lap while he molested me. If there was any chance Nana or Mum walked in, he'd quickly withdraw his hands from underneath my jumper and pretend he was just tickling me again.

Another part of my heart shattered, not quite believing this was happening all over again. If I told anyone, is that when the punishments would come? Would I be to blame? Would it even stop, anyway?

But the more comfortable he felt, the riskier Pop's behaviour became. Usually, he touched me in the kitchen in full view of my Nana. Each time he made his way underneath my top, I'd watch Nana move about the kitchen, hoping our eyes made contact, desperately hoping she'd catch him in the act. *"Look what Pop is doing to me,"* I screamed inside; but unless she saw it, I knew she would never believe me. My biggest fear was if I said something, we'd be asked to leave and go back to The House. I could endure this if it meant never going back there.

Pop had a study in the back of the house, away from the common areas, where he read and played games on his computer in solitude. He didn't like anyone going in there without permission, especially us kids. One day, he asked me if I'd like to play on his computer. It was a rare but exciting opportunity, something I could lord over my siblings later, that I had played the computer and they hadn't.

I quickly accepted and followed him to the room where he told me to take a seat in front of the computer. He showed me how to play the game and I felt special. As I sat, he kneeled behind me; I thought he was going to watch me play.

That wasn't his plan. He applied pressure to the insides of my knees, trying to part my legs. I tensed in resistance, but softly he whispered, "It's okay, just keep playing the game."

I eventually relaxed. I knew better than to argue or fight back. I spread my legs while he placed one hand around my waist to restrain me and the other hand inside my pants. As soon as I felt his touch, it immediately triggered flashbacks to the abuse in The House. All I could do, like an automatic reaction, was to completely engross myself into the game on the computer screen to block out what was happening to me.

Nana shouted something from the kitchen, and he wrenched his hands away from me. He stood to leave the room but told me to keep playing the game.

I didn't know how much time had passed, but once he left the room, I immediately closed my legs together. I felt dirty and violated. The thought of him that close to me again repulsed me and sent a shudder down my spine. Right there and then, I vowed never be lured away in secret ever again, doing anything I could to keep my distance. But my attempts to avoid him only encouraged him to become more creative in trying to isolate me.

Pop was a retired policeman. He supplemented his pension as a performing magician, mostly for kid's parties. Sometimes he'd show my siblings and me his favourite tricks when he practised his performance, never revealing the solution, abiding by the cardinal 'code of the magician'. Sometimes we were so desperate to know we'd plead for just a hint.

Now he had another way in.

One afternoon he created a 'seek and find' game, randomly hiding objects around his home—behind the curtains, things blue-tacked under windowsills, and tucked behind the couch. The purpose of the game was to find as many objects as you could, and the winner was the one who found the most. The prize? To be his assistant at his next magic show.

I knew what that meant—a long drive, alone, giving him free rein to do as he pleased, without fear of being caught.

As the game started and my siblings frantically searched for these objects with whoops of joy, he stared at me and nudged his head towards an object he wanted me to find. I pretended to look confused. There was no way I was going to win any game so he could molest me again.

Realising he was never going to leave me alone, pursuing opportunities to repeatedly abuse me, I would never accept any other offers to play computer games or go for a drive, no matter how enticing he tried to make it sound. Sometimes it was hard to come up with creative reasons in front of Mum and Nana. I kept myself busy, wandering in the paddocks all day with the dog, so the opportunities weren't as available. Sometimes Nana insisted I sit on his lap, which I reluctantly did, but only to keep her from suspecting something was wrong.

No longer was he my Pop, a man I could trust. Now he was just another disgusting old man I despised, just like my other grandfather. The double life he led revolted me. Hearing him preach his high morals and righteousness, bragging about his days in the police force, sickened me. He'd chide me for doing something wrong and then preach the riot act. I wondered how he lived with himself. How could he betray my mum like this? How could he betray me, and all the while keep an innocent smile on his face?

When Mum announced she'd found a place for us to live, I looked up to the sky in silent gratitude. Finally, a place of our own. Hopefully, an end to abuse.

Chapter 9

In July 1987, we moved into the old headmaster's schoolhouse about ten kilometres down the road from my grandparents' house. Since our new home was on the main road leading to the nearest major town, Nan and Pop could still stop by and pick Mum up every Thursday to do the weekly grocery shopping together, since Mum didn't drive.

Our town was a small, under-populated country town with one school, an old pub, a general store, a town hall, and a large river that acted as the local swimming hole for kids in summer. The only thing that put our tiny town on the map was the world-class golf course, where tournaments and events brought people in from all over the state to play on its lush fairways and bentgrass greens. Luckily for my siblings and me, living in a small township gave us plenty more to do and farther to roam than the boundary paddocks of my grandparents' property.

Our new home, a tidy single-storey weatherboard house, smelled stale and mouldy. Knee-high grass spread across the backyard, suggesting it had been vacant for some time, but still I considered it our palace. With three small bedrooms, a square lounge room, kitchen, bathroom, and an outside toilet, it wasn't big, but it felt spacious enough for a family of five. The enclosed yard out the back had a gate leading directly to my school and a small rusty tin shed with a pile of rubbish abandoned in the corner from the last tenant.

It was truly a new beginning, moving into our own home. For the first time in three and half years, there was no one else already living in the house. No more surprises. Just Mum, my three siblings, and me.

Without any possessions, we needed to furnish every bare room. As a family, we decided how to set up our home. It was the simplest of things, but it represented a new start. Freedom. Everything was ours, and this time no one could throw our belongings out or take them away.

My drawers were soon filled with clothes that I mostly got to choose, like other girls from my school did. Every time Mum came home from a day in town, she'd have something new to fill our home. Even though virtually everything was second-hand, I loved that everything was ours. Mum even made sure *this* house had a TV we could watch without seeking permission first. A brand new slim tv on wheels, with smooth push-in buttons for changing channels and volume. Very modern for 1987. Not like Nana and Pop's big old box TV that took up a lot of space.

Waking to see Mum first thing, greeting me with her warm smile, reminded me I was her little girl again. I'd missed that so much. With every new day, seeing just her, without anyone keeping us apart, helped to slowly rebuild our trust and reconnect.

Though I was ten years old now, Mum tucking me in at night was a ritual from our earlier days I longed to resume again. Sometimes I'd still toss and turn, crying out, needing her to sit and comfort me. Or I'd sit snug within her arms in the lounge room until I grew sleepy.

One night I woke, drenched in sweat, a dark wave of impending doom threatening to end my life with a flick of a switch. Panic-stricken, I cried out to Mum.

"Mum, I don't want to die," I whimpered against her shoulder.

She stroked my hair and kissed my forehead. "You're not going to die, darling. You're going to live a wonderfully long life."

Her soothing words eased my fears as she continued to stroke my hair until I fell asleep again.

Mum, a single parent, ran the house in complete contrast to Dad's authoritarian style and The House's militant schedule. She was far more relaxed about almost everything. Apart from bedtimes and knowing our whereabouts around town, there were no fixed rules, no forced chores, and no specific routines to follow.

Instead of gathering around the table for meals, we'd eat in the lounge room like campers, resting our plates on our laps while we watched television together, unless we had company. Our diets also changed dramatically since leaving the House. Sugary foods were reintroduced. Rice Bubbles, real cow's milk—not soy—white bread, jams, peanut butter, soft drinks, cordial, chips, ice creams, lollies, were all back on the menu, much to our delight.

Chores weren't forced upon us or used as a condition to be fed. Dishes were often left scattered in the lounge room and kitchen. Beds were left unmade; doonas we wrapped around ourselves to keep warm in front of the television on a Saturday morning were often left in the lounge room for the whole day. Full grocery bags were left unpacked until someone eventually put them away in the cupboard. Mum cleaned sporadically and with more intent if she was expecting visitors.

Sometimes, when she knew my father was coming to visit, she'd obsessively clean for hours before his arrival. Luckily, this didn't happen very often. In the few short years after he'd dumped his kids at The House, he remarried and now had four stepsons to take care of. He only ever tried to visit during school holidays.

The other times the house got really messy, she'd ask us to help; but there was never any force or punishment if we didn't do something quick enough or good enough.

Living within the hub of town, there were so many things to do within walking distance. Mum's brother Harry, who'd recently moved up from Melbourne to the back of my grandparent's property with his wife and three boys, offered to teach me how to play tennis so I could join the local tennis club. Sometimes I'd catch up with friends from school who lived nearby. Sometimes I'd wander onto the school grounds to practise cartwheels and handstands on a long, narrow beam of wood half a foot off the ground. It acted as the perfect apparatus for trying to dismount, pretending I was a graceful gymnast. Or I'd swing around on the uneven bars, looping my arms through my knees and spinning until my eyes blurred.

Sometimes I'd sit under the local bridge, just gazing at the water, listening to the rippling sounds it made as it trickled over and around the rocks. Something about the sound of water felt soothing. I could sit there, mesmerised, for hours. Perhaps it was the novelty of it that excited me? Perhaps it was the gentle quiet? I'd missed out on so much.

With so much freedom, I was discovering more about myself and the world again. What did I love to do now I could do pretty much anything? How did I like to fill my time now that there were no chores? What made me happy? What made me laugh? What made me cry? What did I like to eat? Who was I without someone telling me what I could and couldn't do?

I didn't know the answer to many of these questions yet, but I loved having the space to find out. This was all a period of discovery and I was loving it.

Most of the time I still withdrew and kept to myself, remaining quiet, and shy, especially when I went to friend's houses. My skin crawled with nerves and my body stiffened with fear, worrying I'd make a mistake and get into trouble. I was so afraid to muck up, that any clues as to what I was allowed to do in someone else's house were completely missed.

Seeing friends outside of school was sometimes really hard because I didn't have the same life experiences as the other ten-year-olds. I barely knew anything about the current pop stars, the latest music, actors, or movies. There was Australian slang, lingo, jokes, songs, hidden meanings in conversations I'd never heard of. Mum's naivety regarding what was worldly didn't help. She just didn't know much about all that. She spoke 'proper' and wore old-fashioned pleated skirts and blouses that her own mother's age group wore. Mum didn't even listen to the radio. She just plonked herself in front of the TV to watch reruns of Hogan's Heroes or Mash or movies like *Sound of Music* and *Chitty Chitty Bang Bang*.

When the other kids talked about their weekends and the exciting places they travelled, I wondered what that was like. I could only go as far as my legs would carry me, unless a rare opportunity was granted, and Nana and Pop took us all into town, or Uncle Harry would let us kids pile into the back of his panel van.

Those same kids bragged about new stuff they got, the new car Mum and Dad bought, or seeing the latest movie at the cinema, and wearing new clothes. *They must be so rich*, I often thought.

I'd also wonder how other kids seemed to talk so confidently when they shared stories? How did they find so many things to laugh about? How did I know what was *meant* to be funny? I didn't understand how they switched from one topic to another so seamlessly. I barely had enough time to take in everything before they started chatting about something else. It was enough to make my head spin.

Sometimes I tried so hard to concentrate, to see when my cue might be to say something funny, but I either missed it or my response came off completely weird and I'd only get strange looks. Most of the time it was just easier to copy other kids when they snorted and giggled, just to feel like I fit in.

When I felt completely invisible and I needed a boost of attention, I'd invent games, 'pretending' to be a bitch to my closest friend, Amy, and the other girls at school. Playing the mean-spirited girl came so easily that I'd get so caught up in my role play and sometimes go too far.

Amy would pause, caught off guard by my viciousness, and then yell, "Hey! That's a bit mean!"

I'd quickly apologise, just to get back in her good books, but I never fully understood why I did it or why I always went too far. There was something about playing the feisty girl that felt so satisfying. For once, maybe I could be good at something.

There were so many social rules I didn't understand, and with no one to explain them to me, they went into a figure-it-out-yourself box, along with just about everything else I had to figure out myself. Nana and Pop were often the only ones who corrected me if I ever asked a question or if they noticed something I was doing wrong. And just like in The House, if I did stuff up, they made such a big deal out of it, like I was just magically meant to know. But how could I? It never seemed fair.

No-one in our town had letter boxes. Instead, all mail was delivered to the post office/general store. One day, when Nana and Pop visited, I offered to get their mail while I collected ours. A brown envelope addressed to my older brother looked interesting enough for me to tear it open as I walked back home. When I returned, Pop glanced at the torn envelope as I handed it to my brother and asked me if I'd collected it from the post office like that.

"No, I opened it. I just wanted to see what it was."

"You never open someone else's mail!" he scolded me angrily. "That was not yours to open. That is none of your business!"

"But I just wanted to see what it was," I repeated, genuinely confused.

"Was it addressed to you?" he demanded.

"No, but—"

"Then you do not open it! That's very naughty of you. Don't ever do that again!"

Baffled by his anger, I looked to Mum for answers.

"Your grandfather's right, Rebekah. We don't open other people's mail," Mum confirmed in a gentler tone than Pop had used.

How was I meant to know that? I stomped off to my bedroom, puzzled and upset. It didn't seem fair to be told off for something I didn't even know was wrong. At least it got me away from his wandering hands. Now that he was angry with me, he wouldn't coerce me into sitting on his lap.

His blatant contradiction angered me. *How can opening someone else's mail be worse than touching my private parts? Dirty old man!*

Another Christmas fast approached. Miniature Christmas trees perched on the teachers' desks, tinsel hung along the shop countertops, and wreaths were nailed on the front doors of all the local houses.

This year we celebrated our first Christmas together in our new home, just us. The first time since 1983. Mum was back in her element with a spring in her step, reviving the unbridled joy Christmas once inspired in her. Celebrating Christmas with her children the way *she* wanted, with no restrictions or disapproving looks from my father or anyone. She could hardly wait to assemble our brand-new tree and decorate it with tinsel and baubles as soon as the first day of December arrived. Happily and unreservedly, Mum sang along to the Christmas Eve concert on TV. A tradition she continued for many years after.

Most of my sleepless nights in The House were out of fear and uncertainty, but this time my restlessness was wonderfully different. I couldn't wait to find presents under the tree. I didn't care if I got one or ten; I knew Mum would do her best to get us each something we really wanted.

Early morning light seeping through the edge of the curtain woke me, so I leapt out of bed and ran straight to the lounge room. Christmas morning was here! Four large Santa sacks, each labelled with our names and filled to the brim with presents, stood upright around the Christmas tree. I didn't know if I believed in Santa anymore, since he seemed to have abandoned me for three years at The House, but these bags overflowing with gifts made me wonder if he'd helped Mum with extra presents this year. There seemed far too many for her to possibly afford all of them. A wide grin stretched across my face as Mum shuffled into the room in her slippers and robe. She smiled and then nodded to let us know we could start opening our presents.

One by one, I tore through them all until I came to the very last gift. A tall rectangular box, perfectly wrapped as Mum loved to do. I wondered if it was the very thing I'd asked for: a *Hot Looks* Doll. There were six dolls in the collection. My favourite was Elke. She had long black hair, blue eyes, a stylish mini skirt, and a shiny black jacket. I'd told my mum how much I loved these dolls, but they were a lot of money and there was little chance she'd been able to afford it.

I unwrapped the box carefully, slowly, all the while wondering if it was the right size and depth for the doll I'd hoped for. As I pulled the last strip of paper off, there she was: Elke, my *Hot Looks* Doll.

I gasped, hardly believing it. "Mum, Mum," I cried, running to her. "Look what I got! Look what I got!"

"How wonderful, darling!" Mum responded, smiling as she shared in my delight.

I gazed at Elke, taking in every square inch of my beautiful new doll, still not quite believing she was mine.

Mum had given me the one thing I truly wanted. As I wrapped my arms tightly around my new doll, I beamed at Mum with the biggest smile. "Thank you, Mum," I said. "Thank you."

Quietly, and with a look of sheer delight, she replied, "Merry Christmas, Rebekah."

In moments like this one, it was easy to forget the past years of misery and scarcity and feel like a normal kid again, just like everyone else.

Finally, I had an exciting story to share with my friends about something new and expensive that was all mine.

Chapter 10

Normal was beginning to grow on me until one day I arrived home from school to Mum being unusually domestic, scrubbing the house clean, like she had a sudden case of OCD. The only times she cleaned like this was when my father was due for a visit, which usually prompted the same question. "Mum, who's coming over?"

She hated when any of us kids asked that. "Why does anyone have to be coming for me to clean?" she'd bellow, before slamming a dish into the drying rack. Despite being divorced, Dad's presence still rattled Mum.

Today was different.

While she paced the house, tossing clothes into the laundry and collecting every dish left scattered around, she greeted me with a gleeful smile stretched across her face. "Hello, darling. How was your day?"

"Good," I stuttered. "Is someone coming?" I asked, out of habit.

"Yes," she replied with enthusiasm. "Jack's coming over for dinner."

Mum met Jack through a mutual friend in April 1988, nearly a year after we'd moved into the schoolhouse. Seeing Jack pull up in his rusty ute more often, a cloud of dust and bits of hay billowing into the air, I figured things were developing between them. If there was any formality to their status, I don't recall. But just like The House, I didn't expect there to be any discussions or opportunities to share how I felt about Jack becoming a bigger part of our lives.

Mum sure fussed more over dinner preparations though, meticulously setting the table and tidying the house more when he visited. As Mum served dinner with a giddy schoolgirl grin, Jack stood patiently at the head of the table, removed his wide-brimmed oil-stained hat and waited for Mum to sit first, trying to impress each other like two love-struck teenagers.

On appearance, you couldn't have paired two more mismatched people. Mum dressed in pleated skirts, clean, creased blouses, and hair tied neatly back from her perfectly clean face. Quite formal for someone who didn't work and stayed at home.

And then there was Jack. His missing front teeth stood out beyond his scruffy ginger hair, ginger whiskers, and thick, coke-bottle glasses. The deep lines etched in his weather-beaten face did not speak of a man who hid from the harsh elements in a desk job, but typified a hard, rough life on the land.

His attire matched the rugged landscape he worked. Thick tartan flannelette shirts, torn, oil-stained jeans, and his beloved Akubra hat he took everywhere. His worn, scratched-up boots had seen better days and had travelled far. There wasn't much finesse with Jack. Every time he smoked a rolled cigarette, he'd use the dip of his hat to tap the ash into, or smear it into his jeans, blending in with the oil marks, rather than use an ashtray, as convention would have it. The smell of tobacco, sheep manure, and oil accompanied him, so whenever I smelled that combination, I knew Jack wasn't too far away.

He was a simple man, a bachelor most of his life. He'd travelled extensively around Australia, working on remote stations, droving cattle. He loved the wide, open spaces and peace of the vast land, never caring much for material possessions, only accumulating necessities for his nomadic lifestyle. He preferred all the simple things, like the company of his beloved animals. His horse, Flamingo, travelled from farm to farm, along with his two loyal black sheep dogs, Aggi and Nig, who went everywhere on the back of his rusty ute.

Accustomed to the simplicity of bush life, nothing ever needed to be replaced, just fixed. He'd find odd bits and pieces around the shed, often revealing to us kids his time-honoured bush-hacks for getting a man out of trouble. And if you questioned his ways, he'd simply reply, "It was rough enough for the bush."

Jack was a larrikin and a storyteller. Too many years of travelling and encounters, he always had a yarn to tell of his misfortunes, of being down to his last few dollars, rum-drinking shenanigans with the locals, looking for work in every town, his cattle-droving days, and the many different people he'd met along the way.

He didn't mind setting up the odd prank, being the shit-stirrer he was. Something so comical that would make you look a bit silly always gave Jack a real belly laugh. Sometimes he'd sneak into my room and threaten to pour a bucket of icy water over my head if I didn't get out of bed. I'd learned very quickly calling his bluff would only encourage him to go fetch an icy cold pail of water.

As much as he joked around, Jack enforced discipline when I'd mess up, and sometimes I did in a big way. One day Jack mentioned the possibility of taking us kids to the local show. A real treat. I hadn't been since I was five years old. One Saturday afternoon, he invited his boss over for a cuppa. I hung around, listening to the two men having a yarn before I interrupted their conversation to pester him about the show. He stopped mid-sentence and then blurted out, "I'll take ya if you don't misbehave."

I knew he was kidding, but I decided to throw back a smart-arse response, thinking he and his boss would laugh it off. "You're just showing off in front of your boss," I joked with a cheeky smile.

He slammed his coffee down, grabbed my arm, pulled me into the bedroom, and swiftly kicked my behind.

"Ya don't speak to me like that in front of me boss, kid!" He slammed the door behind him.

While I sulked and sometimes held a short grudge, Jack never went any further, and he didn't hold any of my mistakes over my head. Discipline ended as quick as it began. I'd lie low after, keeping quiet until I got some nod from Jack that we were okay again. Jack never held a grudge and pretty soon we'd pick up from where we left off, like all was forgotten. So completely different to 'discipline' in The House, where it felt like weeks before I had mildly redeemed myself.

Move on and learn the lesson was Jack's way, helping me to trust that he wouldn't forever banish me as the 'bad girl.'

Sometimes, I would bait him on purpose, to see how far I could push him. Cruel and unrelenting punishment was all I knew, and it's how I learned to receive the attention I craved. Sometimes it felt weird that days went by without drama, without someone telling me off. But with Jack, he taught me I didn't need to be rude or misbehave on purpose just to be acknowledged.

Jack was nothing like my father. Apart from birthdays, or the rare opportunity to stay at his house in Melbourne during school holidays, I rarely heard from my dad. Whereas with Jack, there was always an opportunity to talk, throw out a joke, or find humour in the everyday that usually involved me tripping over something. Whether it was over a morning cuppa, where he'd greet me with, "How's it goin', kid?" as he slouched in his chair, rolling a cigarette while his strong black coffee cooled, or taking the piss and laughing at my dishevelled look as I shuffled around slowly, trying to wake in the early mornings, he was always up for a laugh or light-hearted banter.

Sometimes I'd join him on long days in the cattle truck carting livestock from one paddock to another. The stench of animal waste wafting into the truck cabin reeked; but having one-on-one time with him more than made up for it. He never said much on those trips other than the occasional, "How ya goin?" or "You awake?" in his cheeky manner. My nervousness and mistrust just kind of crumbled away on those trips with Jack. For once, I felt special to someone, and I cherished those times.

The thirty-minute drive from our small town to the next regional city was smattered with small talk of the cold crappy Victorian weather he hated, or a crude joke tossed in for a bit of a laugh. Often Jack reminisced about his days living up north, under the dry hot sun he loved. Other times I'd share a problem, to which he'd reply, "You'll be 'right, kid," or, "Don't worry about it, mate" or, "Just tell 'em to bugger off!" in his classic 'occa' Australian accent.

His solutions were simple, the bush way of dealing with issues. "Don't let them get to you." He rarely held grudges unless a fellow bushman really burnt a bridge.

Usually he accepted people and situations as they were.

His ways were uncomplicated, and he lived by an unwritten bushman's motto: You helped people out of a jam, you paid your way, you always did the right thing, and never expected anything in return. It was good-natured, simple bush living.

Jack became a consistently reliable and trusting presence in my life. He helped me to feel safe, more connected, and trusting enough let my guard down now and then, instead of always having it up to block out potential harm.

As I reached my teenage years, I started playing sports and got my first casual job. He didn't hesitate to pick me up, even if it meant multiple trips into town late at night or early in the morning. Without so much as a grumble or any expectation in return—albeit sometimes I'd have to wait an hour or so until he knocked off from work—he just did it. I learnt very quickly not to complain when he was late to get me, as it was the only ride home I was going to get.

With Jack, I didn't have to play a role to be loved. There were no conditions or some far-reaching criteria to meet, just full acceptance of me as I was. I imagined that that was what most other children felt with their own fathers. Having a father figure like Jack reminded me that not all men were dirty, filthy bastards like my grandfathers. Jack showed me what a normal, loving, safe relationship was. Of course, naturally I had reservations at the beginning, not trusting if he'd repeat the patterns of the men before him who'd used, abused, or abandoned me.

As time went on, Jack kept proving he was different. When there were lessons to be learned, he imparted his wisdom from his own life experiences, and I understood. He was never preachy, and I didn't have to try to be a step ahead of him to avoid punishment. It was almost like he spent time with me because he wanted to, not because he had to. We had an actual father-daughter type of relationship and I cherished it.

In May 1989, Mum gathered my siblings and me at Nana and Pop's house to announce she and Jack were having a baby, due in November. I didn't know what this meant at first. Having a new baby around would be exciting, but it also left me with so many questions. Would Jack be my new dad now? Were we an official family? Would all of Jack's love go to his own child now?

I never asked Mum any of my burning questions. I figured, like any other time my life changed, I'd have to work that out for myself. But at least I had some time now to prepare.

In August 1989 we moved about twenty kilometres from the schoolhouse to Jack's farmhouse on a huge 1600-acre property out the middle of nowhere. It was more isolated than I'd ever experienced, with much less to do, and so far away from my friends.

The farmhouse, set two kilometres back from the road, was perched up on two-foot-high stumps, and weirdly positioned right alongside the foul, manure-smelling sheep and cattle yards, and across from the sky-high grain silos. It was only meant to be a temporary solution while a permanent place for the house was arranged, that never eventuated.

The farmhouse gave new meaning to run-down. Missing tiles exposed grubby grout from the grotty kitchen countertops, and ripped lino revealed fist-sized holes through the kitchen floor so you could actually see the dirty ground below. In the bathroom, a pink enamel bath matched the pink bathroom walls. With river water from behind the house as our only water supply, it was a good day if the brown water ran clear in time for a brief, hot shower. Without any insulation, the wind ripped through the house, shaking the walls, while the broken metal blinds crackled. Our only source of warmth was a small electric heater that worked sporadically and never spread far enough to reach our freezing bedrooms. Jack barked at us kids if he caught us huddled by the heater. There was no air-conditioning to cool us down when we were sweating, either. Luckily, on scorching hot days, we could cool off in the river a short distance from the house.

Behind our house were the remains of the old, dilapidated farmhouse Jack lived in before it burned down. The chimney and the old cast-iron stove were the only things that remained amongst the burnt, crumpled tin and piles of ash and bricks.

Being so far out of town, early mornings were the worst thing about living at the Farmhouse. A semi-rural bus service picked up all the farm kids and dropped us off at a central bus station, where we then caught another bus to our respective high schools. The bus stopped at our property gate at 7:20am sharp, and with the two-kilometre walk to get there, I'd need to allow at least 25 minutes whatever the weather. Mum still didn't have a driver's license, so we had to make our own way. The bitterly cold frosty winter mornings were the worst. Sometimes we'd be lucky to catch a lift in the back of the ute with Jack, but it was rare. Sometimes I'd find the cattle barricading the paddock gates to pass from one paddock to another, stopping me from getting through. I could never predict whether one would break away from the pack and charge towards me, so I was forever wary of the beasts. Occasionally, on the home stretch in the afternoon, if we were lucky to see Jack driving down the road, he'd sit me on his knee so I could take control of the steering wheel and drive us home.

My stop was the first on the school bus route, giving me pick of the seats. I wasn't confident or cool enough to sit at the back and I didn't want to sit at the front, so usually I hunched myself down low on the window seat somewhere in the middle. It wasn't long before you knew who the popular kids were, the ones who owned the back seat. The kids who kept to themselves sat up the front.

Most kids on the bus ignored me, assuming I was shy. I guess it looked that way, and even though I didn't go out of my way to start conversations, some kids with easy smiles and friendly greetings would sit with me and we'd chat. That's when I could relax the most and enjoy the easy banter. Most of the kids down the back were boisterous and could be overheard insulting other kids. I didn't care for drama, petty fights, or idle nonsense. I preferred kids who were down to earth, who would talk about stuff rather than people.

There were a few cute boys on the bus, but even if I did kind of like one, I'd never dare let on I did, unless some big, bright neon sign flashed that he liked me first and I didn't think that would ever happen.

After a few months of catching the bus, one particular boy caught my eye. He was every bit the cliché. Tall and lanky, with dark hair and to me, he was so cute. We went to different high schools, he was in year eight, a year ahead of me, and I could tell he was popular by the way he'd bounce up the steps and swagger down the aisle with his hands gliding along the bag shelf above, chanting, "Hello" to everyone in a cool, confident manner that always beckoned the other kids to stop and notice him. I'd secretly wish my seat was vacant by the time we came to his stop, but I'd also quickly look away when he passed.

I don't know how, but word of my crush whispered around the bus, immediately stirring butterflies in my stomach. Now I definitely hoped he wouldn't come near me. Soon after the gossip took hold, he approached, eyeing off the empty seat beside me. His eyes met mine. Blood rushed to my face and burned my cheeks. Like a deer in the headlights, my body froze as he plonked heavily into the seat beside me, bellowing out a cocky, "Hello" without a shred of nervousness.

I could only manage to mumble out a barely audible "Hi". Butterflies were going crazy in my stomach. My head scrambled for something cool to say, but my mind had clamped down and I could only hold my breath, waiting for him to speak, and hope to God I'd respond with something half intelligent that didn't make me seem like a weirdo.

After a long, torturous minute of silence, he blurted out, "So, do you have a boyfriend?"

I searched for a confident response, some clever banter or even something flirtatious, as if I were playing hard to get, because wasn't that what you were supposed to do with boys? I finally muttered, "Um, no?" Would he make fun of me and broadcast my single status to a bus full of students? I held my breath, waiting.

"Would you like to be my girlfriend?" he asked.

"Okay," I replied nervously.

"Okay." He leapt from the seat and joined the cool group at the back of the bus.

Now we wouldn't see each other until we caught the afternoon bus together as boyfriend and girlfriend, apparently.

In the afternoon, I made sure to get on the bus before he did. Same position, hunched down, knees resting on the back of the seat. I glued my eyes to window, waiting for him. My stomach clenched itself into a tight ball. *What am I meant to do? What do girlfriends say?* Even worse, had I imagined this morning's conversation? After all, even I knew the way he asked me out and then bolted was just odd.

From the corner of my eye, he appeared, walking towards the bus. I squirmed under the sudden weight in my chest, making it difficult to breathe. Quickly I turned away, praying he wouldn't see me.

Suddenly, there was a thud beside me. "Hello," he said.

Trying my best to appear relaxed, I sat upright and threw him a closed smile. Without warning, he swung his arm around me, causing me to flinch like a frightened animal.

He pulled away, confused. "Sorry... Can't I hug my girlfriend?"

Why did he have to touch me? People who like each other don't have to touch. Can't we just be girlfriend and boyfriend? Now he'd definitely think I was weird. Around school, kids like me were labelled frigid. Scared to do anything and easy prey to be mocked and ridiculed.

His touch felt suffocating and icky; but what could I say that would make him understand? I barely understood. I muttered something, but it didn't matter now. He didn't say anything else. I slumped back and looked through the window, embarrassed and upset. I'd blown it. As soon as the bus pulled up at his stop, he said goodbye and left. My whole body relaxed into the seat as I let out a sigh of relief. I was safe once more. Until I had to do it all over again tomorrow.

After I'd rejected his touch, I wasn't even sure he'd bother to sit next to me again. I spent the entire night stewing over what had happened and rehearsing possible future scenarios, so I was better prepared. I decided I'd let him place his hand on me if he tried again.

When he got on the bus the next morning, he did sit beside me, but kept his hands to himself. We didn't talk much, except to ask if I wanted to go to the cinemas to see the latest Batman movie. *Is this a date? Or do I bring someone else along?*

Just in case, I dragged a friend from school along, but when we got there, I couldn't find him anywhere. Maybe he'd decided not to come. Just to be sure, I waited outside the cinema after the movie had finished. I looked around, farther past the main door to a dark corner behind the stairs, and there he was, sitting down with both arms wrapped around another girl.

What an utter fool I was. *See, I knew he never liked me.* He hadn't stood me up. He made plans with someone else. Was it my fault? *Did my rejection cause this?*

A lump rose in my throat as tears welled. The fool I was.

He never saw me that night, so I could pretend I was never there. I phoned him the next day and dumped him before quickly hanging up. Relieved as I was, it bothered me. The whole touchy thing freaked me out, and yet seeing his arms around another girl crushed me. I wished it was me he had his arm around, and yet I had flinched away. Why did his touch make me shudder? Why did it seem so easy for her? I wanted it, yet it repulsed me and left me panic-stricken. Confusion set in, and I didn't like how the whole thing made me feel.

From then on, I stayed huddled down in my seat. Safe.

The farmhouse property had enough to keep us entertained and busy if you went looking for it. I made my own fun exploring the paddocks, riding my bike, climbing up and down the silo ladder, or swimming in the river behind the house. There were cats to cuddle and dogs to throw balls and sticks to, as well as wild rabbits and sheep to chase. The property was so vast that most of the fences were boundary fences.

Jack owned nine horses, and with so many to look after, he gave one to each of us to be responsible for. My horse was a chestnut colour named Kitty.

Owning a horse meant we were expected to learn to ride. Jack showed us how to place the bridle on and carefully but swiftly feed the bit into the horse's mouth without getting your fingers chomped on. Jack spent time showing us how to behave around a horse, including where to walk, so you didn't get a swift kick. He taught us what to do if our horse abruptly broke into a trot or canter. He guided us the first few times, but after that, we were expected to know what to do, otherwise he'd get angry. If the horse played up, *we* weren't doing something right. It was never the horse's fault.

Jack said the way to be the best riders was to learn to ride bareback. It stopped us from relying on the saddle and therefore retain more control over the animal. It was hard going, though. You had to dig your thighs into the horse's side tight just to stay on. It wasn't too bad as you got used to it; but after the first few times, my thigh muscles seized, making it unbearable to walk the next day.

I became so adept at bare back that on the rare occasion I rode with a saddle, it felt too stiff and uncomfortable. Most weekends I'd bring Kitty into the sheep yard and practise riding, putting the bridle on and off, being careful not to leave my fingers in Kitty's mouth before she'd chomp on her bit. I rode Kitty until sweat dripped from my thighs, a sign I could stay on without falling. An accomplishment of how much I had learned.

Living on the property often felt isolating. I missed seeing my friends and strolling to the shops. I missed the busyness of town and hearing the traffic pass by. With Mum not having a license, we didn't leave the property very often other than for school or Nana and Pop's house—which I preferred to avoid, even if it did give me somewhere else to be. I'd rather spend hours searching the property to find Kitty than go to their house and try to steer clear of Pop's wandering hands. He didn't visit the Farmhouse much since it was too far out of his way. Those were the only times I was grateful for the distance.

Sometimes I enjoyed the open space the property provided, preferring my own company to the anxiety of sitting on a bus with relative strangers. I never knew how to strike up a conversation to fill the awkward silence when someone plopped themselves down next to me, even though I did go to school with some of them. On the property, I didn't have to pretend to feel comfortable, nor did I have to force a smile when there wasn't much to smile about. I just wandered the paddocks and did my own thing.

Retreating to the river for hours with my deep thoughts and unanswered questions as I watched the current flow by.

I was twelve going on thirteen. My body was changing. Hair was growing in places I hated, and even though I tried to shave it off, it kept coming back. My breasts were growing more. Mum tried to pull me aside a few times to show me a bra, but I'd bolt out the door and as far down the paddock as possible, knowing she'd never run after me. Mum was the last person I wanted to talk to about this stuff, not that I wanted to talk about it at all. Pretty soon I'd get my period. At least that's what the Sex Ed teacher at school said. Mum never mentioned periods, and I knew that would be another awkward conversation that I definitely wouldn't be able to avoid forever. I had no idea how I was going to deal with all that on top of continually finding ways to avoid Pop and his wandering hands.

Sometimes I'd rest under a tree, wondering about life. Perhaps it was existential, I don't know. My thoughts tended to run deep. Probably deeper than most teenagers my age. I'd wonder who I really was. At times I felt so disconnected from my body that when I looked down at what connected my head to this body, it seemed foreign. Like I wasn't even sure my body belonged to me. Was that even normal, I wondered? I'd wonder about all of my experiences that had led me to where I was now. Where would my life take me as I got older?

On those lazy days exploring, I'd wonder if my family was normal? If abuse was just normal. Deep down I knew what Pop was doing wasn't right, because it didn't feel right. It felt disgusting and grubby, and surely if I didn't like it, then it was wrong wasn't it? But I couldn't be sure since no one ever said anything. Just like in the House, with so many adults around, touching granddaughters seemed to be a thing that was just accepted.. Maybe it was normal, and I was supposed to just shut up and let my grandfathers touch me? I couldn't help but wonder if I would ever escape Pop's wandering hands and if it would ever stop

The one thing living on this large property gave me was distance. A place of solace. A haven to protect me and my adolescent body. As long as I was out here—boring and isolating as it was—no one could hurt me. I was safe.

Chapter 11

In March 1990, after only eight months of living at the farmhouse, we moved again, but this time to a commission-area suburb (government subsidised housing) in the regional city close by (I'll call this town Rushton). The farmhouse property became too difficult for Mum without a license to do her weekly shop and pay the bills. At least now she could catch the bus into the town's centre and not have to rely on Jack or her parents.

The houses in our street were very basic but affordable for people on low incomes like us. Though simple, I liked how clean, uncluttered, and intact this house was. A welcome improvement on the farmhouse and its random holes in the floor and the walls.

Living in the suburbs was so much better. Though Rushton was only twenty-five minutes away from the secluded farmhouse, I'd almost forgotten what it was like living a stone's throw from the neighbours like we had at the schoolhouse. Rushton's suburbs were far more populated. Almost identical houses stacked next to each other lined every narrow street.

Living in a regional city with a bus stop nearby meant I could go to the shops or cinemas, instead of being stuck like I was at the farmhouse or beg for Jack to drive me into town, which he rarely did anyway. A few girls from my school lived in the same area, so we could ride our bikes to school or catch a lift when their parents offered to drive us.

Jack moved in too, but without the space of the farmhouse property, Jack's monstrous green, rattly old sheep-carting truck almost barricaded our narrow street when he parked outside our house. The truck's loud clattering when Jack started it up at sunrise was familiar to me, but I couldn't help but giggle, knowing the loud noise must anger the sleepy neighbours.

The street culture here was an eye-opener. Most nights, our street lit up like a festival with boisterous booze-drinking teenagers, foul language, parties, loud cars, blaring music, and fights erupting spontaneously after one too many cans of Bourbon. Frequent yelling and screaming became white noise, while the rare silent night became eerie and made me uneasy.

Our house was at the upper end of the street, which mostly kept us away from the drama. On one side we had a quiet family who kept to themselves, while on the other side of us a loud teenage boy, Rob, lived with his grandmother.

Rob was tall and scrawny, with a pimply face and rotting and missing teeth. He swaggered around the streets in his tight-fitting jeans, a smoke in one hand and a tinnie in another. Every time he took a swig of his beer, he'd throw his head back to brush his greasy brown hair away from his face.

My bedroom window was directly across from Rob's. Any night of the week, I could peer through my window to see him and his mates drinking and smoking outside, or catch an eyeful of naked ladies on his big TV through his sheer curtains while music blared. It wasn't unusual to hear him singing off key to *Great Balls of Fire* or ACDC's *Thunderstruck*.

Mum didn't like us kids being outside after dark, but that didn't stop me from climbing out of my bedroom window when Rob and his mates were laughing and carrying on outside late at night. I didn't join Rob for his looks, just the attention he and his mates piled on me. They would tell me how much older than thirteen I looked, with my 'nice tits, toned legs, and skinny body'. Their comments mostly made me feel special, or at least acknowledged, and with that came some kind of rush.

Sometimes they'd go further than taunting and dare me to give them sexual favours, but they were over eighteen and I was never sure if they were serious or not because of all the laughter that followed the dirty words. I'd just laughed nervously along with them and then distract myself with a swig of Jim Beam and Coke that left a disgusting mothball after-taste in my mouth.

I wasn't quite sure if their sexual conversations were wrong, or if they were really trying to lure me into something that I was maybe too young for. Kids at school and teenagers on the telly flirted and made sex-jokes all the time. And from what I could see, those were the kinds of things that got you more attention and made you more popular. I didn't want to make the same mistake with these guys like I did with the boy on the bus. And I liked these boys. They seemed nice enough and were always mucking around and having fun. I wanted to have fun, too.

Even though I'd been exposed to more sexual stuff than the average thirteen-year-old, I was still quite naïve. Sexual lingo for erections or the liquid that came out when my grandfather was 'happy', still went way over my head. When the boys said they had a 'fat' just thinking about me, I had no idea what that meant, but their tone told me it was a 'good thing' so I laughed along.

Before I moved into the street, I'd never really cared about what my hair looked like or what clothes I wore. Mum never wore makeup or kept up with the latest fashions, so neither did I. But I discovered the boys in the street stared more when I straightened out my curls with Mum's flat iron and wore shorter skirts and more revealing tops. Sometimes I'd purposely stand outside my house when I knew the boys were coming home, or I'd lie in bed waiting to hear them talking outside and quickly look out the window, hoping they'd see me and throw a flattering line my way. If Mum or Jack had plans that took me out of the house and kept me from a street party, I'd lie and tell Mum I had too much homework to go anywhere.

One night, during one of Rob's heavy drinking sessions, he invited me into his bedroom. He sat on his bed and gestured for me to join him. Music blared while his mates laughed and carried on. Rob offered me a swig of Jim Beam and Coke. The mix was so strong it burned my throat and made me cough and splutter. All the boys, including Rob, thought it was hilarious and laughed at me. They did that a lot.

When his mates left the room, Rob switched off the light.

I'd imagined how this moment would go hundreds of times, but now I was filled with fear. Draped in darkness, with only the smallest patch of moonlight seeping through the sheer curtain, I clutched my hands in my lap, barely able to predict, much less see, his next move. For the first time in a long time, I was scared. He slowly and gently gauged my willingness to play, gliding his hands up and down my chest. As I fumbled with my words, he slowly moved his hand up my thigh, under my skirt, and towards my underwear, until his fingers reached inside. Every one of my muscles clenched tight, my tummy, my thighs, my insides, until I was completely frozen to the spot.

I glanced over at my own window, where Mum would assume I was asleep in bed, never imagining I was less than ten feet away, being felt up by a boy five years older than me. Not that she'd do anything anyway, I didn't think.

Rob tugged at my underwear, trying to pull them down past my thighs that were clenched together. "Come on, let's just play a little bit more. I promise it won't hurt," he whispered, as a strong wave of alcohol breath hit my face. My stomach churned and images of my grandfather's wrinkly old fingers flashed across my mind. I tried to escape, but the weight of my own body pinned me down. *What had I got myself into?*

I gasped for air as the walls of my throat narrowed. "No. No, I don't want that!" I whispered loudly. I pushed him away and dashed for the door before sneaking back into my own bedroom. I didn't want this. I didn't want *that*. I wasn't a little kid anymore, and he couldn't make me do anything I didn't want to.

From that night on, I stayed away from the street boys and their sexual antics. I never wanted to be in that same position ever again. Just the thought of anything sexual stirred up too many old memories of abuse from The House and triggered the same feelings of grossness in my tummy, when Pop still tried to touch me.

Towards the end of the year, Mum announced she'd found a permanent home back in our old small home town. The same town with the one main highway connecting us to Pop's house. Living in Rushton, there were more opportunities to avoid him. His house was a forty-five minute drive away from our housing estate, so I barely saw him much at all. Moving back meant he'd be stopping in every Thursday to take Mum shopping, then he'd hang around for a cuppa, just like he use to. *Damn it!*

Just the thought of living closer to Pop again burdened my mind. I was done making excuses to avoid visiting his house or making myself scarce when he visited mine. Now that I was too old to be sitting on his knee where he could feel me up, his newest tactic was to try to kiss me directly on the lips. The last time I went to his house, I quickly turned my head so his lips would land on my cheek, but he gripped my face firm and kissed my lips. I quickly pulled away and wiped my lips. *Filthy old bastard!*

Anxiety and fear kept a constant knot in my stomach. Every time Mum mentioned the new house, my chest tightened. I wanted the abuse to stop, once and for all.

After school one day, the move still dominating my every thought, I scuffed my feet on the pavement towards my friend Cathy, who was sitting on the ground scratching the dirt with a stick in between the cracks in the concrete path.

Two sisters, similar in age to me, Cathy and Jenny, lived at the opposite end of our street. You'd be mistaken for thinking they were twins with their similar height, apple-shaped figures, and identical bobbed haircuts. One had blonde hair, the other brown. They were different from the other girls in the street. They avoided all the drama, the boozy late nights, and the sleazy boys. We naturally clicked when we met, spending our free time sitting in the street chatting and laughing for hours.

When I sat down next to her, I pressed my lips together, fearing I'd burst into tears if I spoke. Cathy noticed and asked if I was okay.

I buried my head between my knees, trying to hide my face, but deep down inside I knew I couldn't hold the truth in any longer. It was like I had a rubber band holding me together and it just snapped. I was falling apart, spilling all my secrets with it.

"We're moving," I said, but then I paused. I tried to stop the truth involuntarily pouring out of me, but now it felt too powerful to stop. "We're moving closer to my grandfather... and... he... molests me." Teachers in Sex Ed had touched on sexual abuse in class. Even though I knew it was wrong, the teacher's words finally helped to confirm what I already knew. Now it had a name.

Cindy fell back in shock, like she'd been knocked by a gust of wind.

Finally, I'd released what I'd hung on to for years. As I exhaled, this crushing weight I felt I'd carried for years released from my chest. But just as quickly, my truth now exposed me. Now someone else knew. Cindy, sensing my fear, assured me she'd keep our conversation private and not tell anyone.

But the next day, Cathy ran up and grabbed me by the arm just before I walked into my house. "I told my mum what you told me. She wants to talk to your mum," she rushed to say in a loud whisper.

"What!" I gasped. Instant panic for my future engulfed my entire body. I knew Mum wouldn't believe me or do anything. She must have known what was happening at The House and didn't try to stop it then. Why would she try to stop it now? What would happen to me?

Cathy talked me into telling Mum first. She thought it would be better hearing it from me, thinking it would help to have a big chat as mother and daughter first.

It was hard to imagine Mum would protect me. She depended on her parents and was still "Daddy's little girl". There'd be slim chance she'd believe or acknowledge what her father was doing to me. Somewhere inside me, though, I held a glimmer of hope she'd be there for me, her own little girl. Wouldn't she?

Cathy stayed close beside me as I slowly walked towards the front door. My legs felt so weak, I feared I'd collapse. I knocked two or three times, waiting to hear Mum's footsteps approach, while my heart pounded.

"Why are you knocking? You know where the back door is," Mum said, confused as she opened the door. I must have looked as white as a ghost. She kept staring at me, waiting.

My voice trembled, and I squeezed Cathy's hand tight. "Um... Mum, I need to tell you something." I paused, trying to swallow past the hard lump in my throat. "Pop is molesting me." I gazed into her eyes, hoping and waiting for that impulsive bear hug, the kind where she'd scoop me up and promise everything would be okay.

"You've got to be joking," she scoffed, snorting at the ridiculousness of it.

In an instant, my worst fears were confirmed.

Her words echoed through me and shattered any hope she would leap to rescue her little girl. What I'd feared almost as much as the abuse was now a reality. She was not going to rescue me. She was not going to hold me tight, cradle me, and weep for my loss of innocence.

The consequences of speaking out sunk to my core. My world was about to change, and I had no idea how or what this would mean for me. How could I even look at Mum after this? Would she tell Nan or bring it up with Pop? Would I be in for it? Beaten and then banished from the family? To where?

Whatever happened beyond this moment, this was a fight I was leading on my own, at just thirteen years of age.

Cathy chased after me as I fled to my backyard and collapsed onto the trampoline, sobbing, wishing I'd just kept my mouth shut. I started screaming at her. "What do I do now? What do I do now?" Pleading for a solution.

Mum didn't even bother chasing after me. Cathy stayed with me until the sky darkened. I quietly retreated to my bedroom without dinner. Mum still made no effort to see me, triggering the same abandonment as The House. It was an all too familiar pattern. Except this time, Mum wasn't being held back by anyone. This time, she chose not to do anything.

Mum had truly deserted me.

We moved back to our small town and into our permanent home in late January 1991. No more moving, Mum said. After three moves in three years, all within a twenty-five-kilometre radius, I was more than happy to finally have a place to call home. This house wasn't new, but it was the biggest we'd lived in so far. Big enough for us to all have our own bedrooms. Finally, my own private space to hide when Pop visited, and I didn't want to be near him. Even if Mum expected me to come out when he did visit, the front door was right next to my room, so I could still escape and run down the road and far away from him.

Cathy worried about me, knowing Mum refused to address the abuse, even after Cathy's mum had spoken to her about it directly. Even knowing I would be seeing him a lot more now, Mum hadn't uttered a word to me about the abuse since the day I told her. I figured it was forgotten about. I assured Cathy I'd do everything and anything to keep away from the disgusting pervert.

Three weeks after moving in, a loud knock came from the front door. As soon as I swung the door open, a female police officer appeared on the other side of the security screen. My stomach dropped to the floor. I was going to be sick. The girls had dobbed to the police! *Oh no, I'm in trouble.*

"Hello. My name is Constable..." Her voice faded before I caught her name; my mind busy, scrambling for a way out.

"Is your mum home?" she asked.

"Yes," I muttered.

Puzzled, Mum led the policewoman to the lounge room, while I snuck into my room knowing I would be summoned to face my mum soon enough. How could I tell her this wasn't my doing? That I hadn't told the police anything?

Moments later, Mum called me straight back out to sit with both her and the policewoman. The officer removed her hat revealing her shiny, brunette hair, neatly pulled back in a bun. Her dark brown eyes matched her hair perfectly. She looked to be in her mid-thirties, slender with smooth skin and a naturally pretty face.

"Rebekah," the policewoman addressed me in a quiet assured voice, suggesting this was not the first time she'd done this. With her hands clasped together on her knees, she leaned forward to speak. "We received a phone call from a friend of yours telling us you are being abused by your grandfather. Is this true?" she asked. She spoke in such a way that invited me to trust that I was safe to be honest with her.

With Mum sitting on one side, the officer on the other, time slowed right down.

Ultimately, whatever I said would affect everything from here on in. Do I remain silent to avoid the shit storm that would erupt like a volcano within my family, or do I abandon the safety of lies and risk everything to stand up and protect myself? So far Mum proved she wouldn't jump to my defence at all. Maybe it was up to me to defend and rescue myself, knowing I had no parent to fall back on for support. Yet I held some glimmer of hope the officer's presence might make Mum take me seriously. Would she believe me now?

Avoiding Mum's glare, I took a slow, deep breath. "Yes, it's true," I said, my voice quivering. Now there was someone who was willing to hear me, I revealed the abuse of my paternal grandfather as well. I wanted everything out in the open so Mum could understand what had been happening for the past seven years. How messed up my life was.

After everything was said, Mum sat, switching her expression between a stone-faced glare and reserved defiance. Depending on the questions being asked, Mum answered vaguely and appeared to be completely—falsely—unaware, except when the officer broached questions about her own father, to which Mum's voice raised to arrogant objection, emphatically denying her father—a retired police officer himself—would ever do such a thing. Her lips pursed, offended by the complete absurdity of such an insinuation of her perfect Daddy.

I could only shake my head. My mother was essentially accusing me of lying, of making it all up.

The police officer expressed her concerns for my welfare, knowing Mum would do nothing to protect me and still welcome her father into our home. She offered to drive me into town to give an official statement at the police station.

I'm not sure Mum thought I'd accept the offer, but this was my choice and my own act of defiance. I had to show her how far I would go to convince her I was telling the truth. Mum couldn't stop me. Heck! No one could. I was glad Jack was still at work. I'm not sure what he would have done or said with all this going on, but I was glad he wasn't there at that moment. I might have been too scared to accept the offer if he were there, but he'd find out soon enough. The rest of the family would too. I was going to feel the ripple effects from this, and though a part of me was shit scared to know how that would go down, right now I had to think about myself because no one else was.

The policewoman drove me into town alone, without Mum. Mum refused to come in with me, continuing to emphatically deny any truth to my account. When I arrived at the station, I was led into a small room with a typewriter to give two statements, one for each grandfather.

Hours later, in the darkness, the policewoman drove me home. I tiptoed inside, head down, retreating straight to my bedroom and collapsed, too exhausted to worry about what the future held for me now. Mum hadn't waited up.

A couple of days later, I was told Pop had been brought into the police station to answer the allegations I'd made against him. I was invited to listen to his responses that they'd recorded. Of course, he denied everything. I felt so angry listening to him lying through his teeth, claiming I'd misinterpreted his hugs and kisses.

Even though he insisted my accusations were false, the police still advised that I could press charges. They assured me they had enough to go on to take it further. Mum said that if everything that happened was true, then I should take it all the way to court. Almost like she was daring me to fight her and her father now they'd teamed up against me.

As much as I wanted to, in the end I just couldn't. Mum wouldn't believe me whatever I did or said. In her eyes, I was a liar whether I pressed charges or not. There was no point dragging this out any longer. There'd be more meetings, more hisses and cusses from Pop and the family once they got wind of it, even from my own mother. All I wanted was for the abuse to stop. I needed a home, and I needed my siblings. If I testified against Pop, would I lose everything that I had left?

On the silent drive back to our home, one thought echoed louder than the rest. My mother had just proved, without a doubt, that her loyalty was to her father and not with me.

Chapter 12

The very next morning, I woke to a house with a new vibe. Revelations and truths were exposed and could no longer be ignored. The tension was so thick, you could slash the air with a knife. Mum dragged herself around muttering good morning as she attempted to mask the uncomfortable truth she couldn't or wouldn't face. We could no longer go back to pretending, even though she tried. The abuse exposed and shattered her utopian world of her perfect father. Nothing was spoken that morning. My siblings and I kept busy to avoid the elephant in the room everyone pretended wasn't there.

It was 1991, and I was to start grade nine at a different high school. I'd convinced Mum the year before to change schools to be with Cathy and Jenny. Before yesterday's events, I'd looked forward to hanging out with them. But not now.

When the girls spotted me at school for the first since I'd moved, they hurried over to apologise and explain how everything had unfolded. They wanted to warn me of their mother's intentions to call the police but didn't have my new phone number. Their pleas for understanding fell on deaf ears as I stood, body tense, my blood boiling, biting my lip to hold back the words I wanted to scream at them. They'd destroyed my life. Their tattletales enraged me, clouding the bright side they insisted was there. It was okay for them, though. They had 'saved' me. They could go back to their safe, supportive, loving mum. But I was left to deal with the aftermath alone. My mum was cold to me, and her mum was cold to her. It was like a dark storm cloud had dropped over everyone involved in my truth telling.

From then on, I distanced myself from both sisters, avoiding their constant offers to help and support me. I never spoke to them again. Deep down, I knew they'd done the right thing. The abuse had stopped for now. But I didn't want all the other shitty consequences that had followed. I wanted my mum to stand at my side and scream at her father. At my dad's father. At the men in my life who had failed to protect me.

With no one to turn to, I withdrew and disregarded my feelings, just as my family had. Clouds of uncertainty numbed me from engaging with anyone around me at school. Questions filled with burden hovered over me like a perpetual storm cloud. How would I get through each day? Would life ever return to normal?

My whole family on my mum's side lived in and around our small town. Though I was scared to run into them, I wondered how they'd treat me when I saw them. Would they speak to me? Would my cousins attack me for destroying the family's peace? Most of the time, it was easier just to retreat, to stay out of the way, and numb myself to the world and just exist.

This shell of an existence I had to create in order to survive.

My family's cocktail of silence, avoidance, and denial made it easier. There were no discussions on fixing the situation, no apologies or even placating lies. There were no 'checks ins' from my mother or anyone else in the family to see how or if I was coping. There were no outward threats of retribution either, which I guessed was good. There was not a lot of backlash at all, except for them to say it was all lies. My family only wondered how I'd lost my mind to think up such a thing. Gradually, everyone just went on as if nothing was ever mentioned, but as though I had done something wrong instead of the other way around.

Everything changed once the abuse was out in the open. Some changes were blatantly obvious. Pop refused to step foot in our house. Not out of shame, but disgust at the lies I'd told. Apparently, I should bear the shame of what I'd done to the family. I didn't.

Instead of coming inside and having a cuppa after dropping Mum off, like they used to, now they parked in our driveway, remained in the car, and then quickly drove off after.

Home was finally a safe place he had no chance of intruding. And for that, I was grateful.

Some changes were less obvious, but I figured these out too. Throughout all Pop's verbal public lashings toward me, casting me as *the little liar*, Nana didn't utter a single word nor defend me. Just like everyone else, she made no attempt to investigate my side. Sometimes, I'd purposely poke my head outside and stare at her sitting in the car, hoping to lock eyes with her, for some acknowledgement. Something that said I still meant something to her. But Nana just stared into the distance, like she didn't even know me. No more birthday cards, no phone calls, no acknowledgement that I existed. Like worthless trash, I was discarded while Pop soaked up sympathy. Nana abandoned our relationship, stripping her home of my photos and erasing me from her life.

There were no tears cried for Pop, but I did feel Nana's loss. When I was a little girl living in Melbourne, I looked forward to staying at her house. She'd welcomed me with open arms as she smacked her whiskery lips against my cheek. We spent long days wearing matching aprons as she baked in the kitchen while I kneeled on a stool, washing the dirty dishes. Other times, I'd sit on her lap in her study while she shared stories of her childhood, and then she'd listen to mine. She'd gasp with so much drama, excited by the tales I spun. Her interest in those silly stories confirmed her love and joy in spending time with me. Her theatrical reactions encouraged me to share more, just to hear her gasps of excitement again. Sometimes I'd wander into her study lined with books, to find her hunched over knitting, or reading under a desk lamp. I'd cuddle in next to her as she wrapped one arm around me while the other hand held her book open or she'd knit over the tops of my shoulders.

Even after we left The House and moved in with her, I looked forward to recreating all those old memories again. Mum always spoke so affectionately about how much Nana loved spending time with me.

Now all the memories we shared amounted to nothing.

Her silence confirmed her unwavering support for Pop, but there were times I missed her so much that in my darkest hours I considered tearing up my statements to the police and telling them all I got it wrong just so we could go back to the way things were and reattach what was severed. But I knew I couldn't. I had to speak my truth. I couldn't lie just so my family could be at peace again. So they could return to their comfort zones that were more like circles of ignorance.

Of course, there were times when Mum purposely threw in more stories of the fallout of our family and the consequences she'd suffered because of my scandalous accusations. Tales she hoped would provoke me to feel ashamed or guilty for destroying the family. Her voice dropped to a guilty tone when she mentioned her parents. Sometimes I think she expected me to renege on the abuse just so she could run to her parents and invite them back into our home. But I purposely ignored it and ignored her. That was never going to happen.

School became another lonely place on my list of lonely places. Without the sisters, there was no one to confide in. Apparently, the school was notified of the abuse, but I was never offered any help or support or opportunities just to have a break from class when learning was the furthest thing from my mind. At best, I sought the comfort of the teacher's encouraging words about my work, or a friendly hello they'd offer in passing in the hallways. I'd cling to their smiles, knowing it was the closest to nurturing I'd get from an adult. Some days it was all I needed just to know someone noticed me. An acknowledgement I existed.

Despite everything, my love of learning never waned. Schoolwork distracted me from my crappy home life, but it could only hold my attention for so long before my anxiety surfaced. As each day drew closer to home time, it reminded me what I'd be going home to.

I chose Textiles as an elective in grade nine. Like my previous school, I picked subjects based on my preferences rather than picking classes just to be with friends. Being alone didn't bother me. I could go a whole session barely speaking or even looking up from my work. As the new girl—the weird and quiet girl—I did nothing to win friends or initiate myself into any groups. My timid and compliant appearance was labelled uncool and weak, and made me an easy target for bullies.

Unbeknownst to me, two girls with reputations for being mean were in my textiles class. Every lesson, they'd chat amongst themselves, carrying on like idiots. I'd tune out, too absorbed in my own task to pay attention to their stupid antics. But during the last class of one particular day, they singled me out.

A loud voice bellowed from across the room, breaking my concentration. I propped up to see two girls staring at me. "So, who are your friends at this school?" Ange asked. It wasn't a friendly tone. The question felt baited somehow.

Kelly, her sidekick, who I knew caught the same country bus home as me, snidely interjected before I could answer. "No one. She's got no friends," she taunted in a childish voice.

I could see where this was going, but I remained silent.

Ange fired another question, and again, Kelly answered.

Fear and rage warred inside me. Fury that this perfect stranger, who knew nothing about me, had never even spoken to me, and had no idea what I was going through, had the audacity to be so mean. I didn't deserve it, and I wasn't going to take her shit for another second. The anger exploded out of me, before I could consciously stop the words, "Why don't you just shut the fuck up?" I screamed across the room.

Ange's eyebrows raised, and her jaw dropped. "Are you talking to me?"

"No!" I yelled and pointed to Kelly. "I'm talking to that fucking bitch. I have done nothing to you, and I don't deserve to take your shit. So just fucking leave me alone!"

Kelly's eyes widened, her mouth gaped open, and she turned to Ange in disbelief.

As quickly as my rage subsided, I was thrust back into reality, fully aware of what just happened. My legs trembled. My heart pounded in my ears, and my mouth went so dry.

Holy crap. I've just gone berserk at the tough girl, and now I've got to catch the bus with her. I'm dead!

This wasn't me. I'd never had an altercation at school before, much less the guts to ever fire back at anyone. Their unprovoked taunts were the final straw. After all, everything I longed to express to my mum was buried under shame and sadness, and something in me just kind of snapped.

I desperately hoped the teacher, who'd witnessed it all, would defend me, but she kept quiet. Silence descended on the room. I sidled up to the teacher, project in hand, half pretending to ask a question and half using her as a shield. I stood there, waiting for retaliation or some sort of threat, anything. But nothing happened.

The girls whispered amongst themselves, and I was certain they were plotting against me. I imagined the pay back in my head. They'd gather their friends, hunt me down, drag me by the hair around the back of the school, and pound me to a pulp. This was new territory, and I had no idea what I was in for.

I took my time packing up, hoping everyone would leave before me. Keeping my head down, I peered around every so often, waiting to spot the shadows of figures behind me while I scurried towards the bus shelter.

The next day, I went back to school after a sleepless night worrying what payback the girls had thought up. I could have said I was sick and stayed home, but school was still the better option to sitting alone in my bedroom, avoiding Mum's depressive moods. I hadn't told Mum what happened in class. Why would she care? Just like everything else, my problems were mine to deal with.

After yesterday's spat, I wondered how long I'd have to watch my back. Kelly was in my home group, so I knew I'd see her first thing. The class tables formed a circle, not allowing me to hide, so I picked the seat farthest from her and buried my head in a book.

Soon after the bell rang, two feet appeared in my view. My jaw clenched shut as my heart raced and my fingers tightened on the pages. She couldn't do much right here in class, could she? There were too many witnesses. If she did attack, how would I react? Could I fight her? Should I? My rage from yesterday disappeared. I'd reverted back to the shy, scared girl.

I slowly lifted my head until our eyes met.

"What are you doing at recess? Who are you hanging out with?" Kelly casually asked.

"Um, I don't know," I replied, heavy with suspicion. Was she baiting me? I waited for the teasing to come, the name-calling or hair-pulling.

"Do you want to come and hang out with us?"

Was this a ploy to isolate me so she and her friends could beat me up?

"Ok," I said, too scared to say no. Besides, the suspense of being punched in the face was killing me and I'd rather it be over and done with.

At recess, Kelly gestured for me to join her group. *Great, witnesses.* I imagined the gossip spreading around the school. *New girl gets tricked and walks right into a catfight.*

But instead, she introduced me to everyone. While they laughed and chatted, I stood awkwardly still, anxiously waiting for someone to tell me what to do or say next. How do I casually join the conversation as though nothing happened yesterday?

With my now unlimited access to what I thought of as the 'cool group', the target was removed from my back, guaranteeing my protection. Now there was someone to sit with in class and hang out with in the schoolyard. I was no longer the *lonely girl* to the other kids. But I still felt displaced. Joining a crowd was just surface stuff to mask my loneliness and pretend I was a part of something. As long as I smiled and laughed when everyone else did, everyone thought I was okay.

I wasn't.

Without any real friends, I drifted between the 'cool kids' and the 'dud group', trying to find a place to belong. At times I wanted fun and distraction, but I also yearned for intelligent conversation and acceptance on a deeper level.

I found more comfort in the studious group. Their conversations were more light-hearted, but at least they were about something instead of nothing. Sex wasn't even on their radar, and they didn't gossip or make fun of others, like the other group. Their funny stories were welcomed distractions from my own turmoil, but still too foreign to my world. How were they so relaxed and happy? With so much upheaval in my home life, I had no light-hearted stories to add. Their conversations eventually became nonsensical to me, too juvenile, too stupid and immature compared to my issues. They probably weren't, but I just couldn't relate and found myself on the outer once again.

The cool girls constantly talked about sex, their crushes, their flirtatious schemes to snag this guy or that. They played with the school's uniform policy, wearing their skirts much shorter than allowed. They experimented with hairstyles, makeup, and jewellery, trying to outdo each other. No topic was off limits, even bragging about sex under the bridge or on the oval on weekends.

They'd ask me if I was interested in anyone. Pfft! I couldn't have cared less. Having sex was the furthest thing from my mind. Besides, the boys were way too immature. They were boisterous, edgy risk-takers, skimming along the edges of the rules and challenging authority. Anarchists in the making.

Sometimes going to school was optional. Not that it was new to me, given the many days I wagged in grade eight. So when some of the girls didn't want to go, most of the time I agreed just so I could escape the chaos in my mind. Most of the time, that's all I wanted from my day.

These skipped days weren't fun. Not in the true sense of the word. I was still quiet. I knew I was little more than someone to rebound jokes off and test out gentler taunts. But I wasn't great company. I just followed the girls like a sheep. We were still in our uniforms, so we couldn't hang around town just in case we got sprung and dobbed on. Usually, we hung out at someone's house while their parents were out for the day, just gossiping and whining about everyone we hated. They'd single out teachers from school and other nerdy kids they hated. While everyone chimed into the ever growing 'hate-club', throwing in more baited opinions and juicy gossip to rouse the group, I mostly remained silent. Even if agreeing gained approval, gossip and ridiculing others didn't interest me.

I never shared any of my home troubles with the girls in this group. It wasn't that kind of friendship. My problems ran too deep for these rebellious teenagers and I knew it would fall on deaf ears, be used against me, or passed around like Chinese whispers for the amusement of others.

My true friendships were outside of school.

In my small town, the kids banded together. No division, exclusion, or class. Teenagers there were friendly, easy going, and welcoming. Completely different from the streets in Rushton where people segregated into their own groups, drinking and doing everything bad. In my hometown, you were welcomed in and accepted without having to pass any tests or scream insults just to prove you weren't a pushover.

I'd met Anna shortly after we moved to the schoolhouse in 1987. She lived about five minutes down the road. We were both ten and in grade five. She went to a Catholic private school in Rushton. On the weekends, we'd hang out, practicing cartwheels or walking aimlessly for hours around town. Sometimes we'd swim in the river. When I moved to the farmhouse, I lost contact with her, but we reconnected when I moved back to town and started catching the same bus to high school.

So much had happened since we last saw each other. We were teenagers now. My home life was in shambles, my self-esteem non-existent. The world was a different place, especially for me. It was like all the weight that had lifted when I'd told my truth to Mum had twisted in the air, gained more weight—like a magnet sucking in all the bad until it stuck—and then it came crashing back down to settle on my shoulders once again. I probably even slouched more because of it. Life had become a lot more complicated since those days of jumping on the trampoline in the sunshine.

When we moved back to town from Rushton, Anna came over to see if I wanted to hang out. I couldn't have been happier to reconnect, not only for company, but another excuse to get away from my mother and our sad home.

Raised in an orthodox Catholic family, Anna was the third of five girls and she was the total opposite of me. Sometimes I wondered in what universe we were ever friends. She was fun and energetic, never taking life too seriously. Not like rigid, uptight me. She was spontaneous and adventurous, taking chances, toying with boundaries, and laughing as much as she could along the way, encouraging me to chill out and relax.

I'd hang out with Anna any chance I could. The more I did, the more I got a peek into how other families lived. Her parents had rules and curfews. Sometimes I thought it seemed strict, but other times I thought it must be nice to have parents who watched out for her and cared when she came home. Her family gathered around the table for meals with the TV turned off and held hands to say Grace. Theirs felt more like a loving and connected family, a bond of unity and care for one another. A part of me felt jealous I didn't have that with my family.

My home didn't have a routine, boundaries, or curfews. I could pretty much do what I wanted. Mum didn't like me being out too late, but that didn't stop me. Family time at the table wasn't a thing in our house. If Mum made dinner, which she didn't do a lot, my siblings and I retreated to our own rooms right after. Luckily, I had a phone line in my room, so I could ring my friends and at least have someone to talk to. Even if I did join Mum and Jack in the lounge room, we just carried on as if the abuse was never mentioned. Laughing at the comedy on the TV and pretended everything was fine. That's how I existed. If there were tears, I saved them for the sanctuary and privacy of my bedroom.

My friends envied my freedom, but they didn't know it came with being ignored, ostracised, and having to look after myself.

Anna was the only one who knew about my home life, the reason I hated being at home, and why I confined myself to my bedroom. Soon after moving in, she invited me to go hang out around town. Once we'd walked far enough away from home to the park nearby, we started chatting and catching up on the last few years we'd been apart. All the surface chat was easy, but it was hard to hide the circumstances in which my life had changed so dramatically since the last time we spoke. To try and talk cheerfully about Mum and my family, when there was nothing good to chat about, was difficult.

Since my close friendship with Cathy and Jenny was over, I'd literally had no one to talk to about the abuse and the fallout with Mum and the rest of the family. My siblings and I hadn't discussed anything, not even away from Mum's ears. There was an unspoken sense among us that talking about it would make the fracture in our family too real.

Everything I felt was still bottled up inside, and while my bedroom walls heard my tears, no words had been uttered to anyone since my statement to the police.

After a brief pause, I bit my lip and tried to hide my discomfort. It was the same familiar feeling when I last exposed the abuse to Cathy, but this time, the only risk was being avoided as the troubled girl. After everything so far, I'd become used to being discarded, so I really had nothing left to lose.

After revealing everything to Anna, I kept my head buried, mainly to hide the tears slowly falling, but also, I was scared she'd just leave.

"I'm so sorry, Beck. That's awful." She leaned forward and wrapped her arms around me, hugging me tight. "I'm here if you ever need to chat."

I sobbed in her arms, embracing her comfort. This is all I wanted from my mum, but I readily accepted it from Anna.

Anna became the one person I relied on. I depended on her more than she realised to keep me afloat when life got tough. So terrified of losing her friendship, sometimes I'd misjudge her other friendships, feeling jealous and left out, believing I was no longer important. I played childish games, stonewalling her when I thought I was being neglected, ignoring her when the attention wasn't on me. I didn't know how to express my feelings or identify or even label what was going on.

Mum had modelled avoidance so skilfully that even when I wanted to talk about what was in my head, I didn't know how. My emotions were so intensely scrambled, so overwhelming, that it was easier to act out, blame, hurt, and avoid her. Playing games to mask my emotional instability became my survival tool. After all, that's what my family did.

Anna stuck by me despite how I behaved, even when she had every reason to run. Knowing my story, the foolish manipulative games I'd play, my reliance on her to be there for me, she never quit on me even when everyone else did. She could have, so easily. She was the only one assuring me I was okay, even when I didn't feel it. She was the one who wanted my shitty company when I didn't deserve it. She cared for me when no one else did.

At a time when I needed to know I meant something to someone, Anna became one of the most important people in my life.

My mother was always physically there, in the background, to the envy of Anna and other friends in town who sometimes remarked how lucky I was that I had a mum who was always home. Sure, she was always home, but she wasn't there for me. Not in any of the ways I needed her to be.

She could have easily been a long-lost relative I didn't know sitting at home all day. It didn't mean there was a relationship. She'd never throw me out of the house, but she would not nurture or support me with dealing with the effects years of abuse had on me or try to make things right. I knew that by now. After everything I'd already been through, nothing was ever discussed. Mum just expected me to invalidate everything, just like she did. That's what we did with problems, it seemed.

Try as she did to push through each day, to put on a brave face, to convince herself and her children she was fine, it was clear Mum just wasn't coping. Sometimes, her cheeks would be red and blotchy from tears she'd shed privately. She walked around with a sad, forlorn look on her face and was distant most of the time. She switched between meticulously cleaning and dusting, to letting the house go to ruins around her. Most days, when I got home from school, she'd be sitting quietly, eyes fixed to the TV, switched off from the reality she wanted no part of.

As I watched her struggle, I wondered why she wouldn't talk to me. Maybe we could help each other through this. It was the perfect opportunity to talk with me, not to stay away from me completely. I just didn't understand what her tears were for, since she was making no effort to connect with me.

A few months had passed since I'd given my official statement to the police for both grandfathers' abuse, when Mum approached me, nervous as hell, stuttering as she spoke. "Beck, do you think you've confused what happened at The House with Pop's attention?"

The short-lived hope in my heart that we'd have a real conversation dropped to the floor like a latch door had swung open beneath me, while simultaneously a burning rage leapt in my veins at her insinuation that I could confuse the two. But it was the first time she'd openly acknowledged she *knew* what happened at The House.

Why was she desperately trying to find a way to make it all better for herself? I wondered. Maybe to be certain I hadn't mixed the grandfathers up, and therefore it would let her off the hook for being the mother of the *treacherous, lying daughter* and get back into Daddy's good books again. She spoke of the abuse like it was a story from a book, not real life. There was no outpouring of grief that my innocence was stolen from me. No moments to compose herself because the revelations tore at her heart.

Nothing.

That's when I realised what was going on.

Her despair, her long wimpy face, the way she dragged herself around the house lying low, had absolutely nothing to do with me. It was the air of disapproval and disgust her father, the man she idolised, held towards *her* for what I had accused him of. That damaged her far more than the idea I'd been abused. She wasn't crying for me. She cried because her daddy was upset with her.

When my own father was notified of the abuse, he promptly drove from Melbourne to confront Mum about the accusations against his dad. His father, like Mum's father, had vehemently denied it as well, threatening to fight the allegations against him with the most powerful lawyers money could buy. Mum and Dad ended up arguing outside like school kids, blaming the abuse on each other's father.

"My father wouldn't do that, it was your father," Mum screamed, pointing her finger in his face, while Dad fired back, "No, your father would do this, not mine!"

Up until Mum's ridiculous question, it hadn't occurred to me that she was just trying to find a way out, so she was no longer the bad little girl her father saw. Mum never had the strength or the courage to confront her parents and investigate whether there was a skerrick of truth to my accusations. She'd never dare. She'd never been a person in her own right around her parents. She was an extension of them: their daughter.

Many times, I observed her cower in their presence, awaiting approval or permission before doing anything that might have raised an eyebrow. She was so easily led by them, by my father. Even at The House, Mum was completely submissive to every order thrown at her, even if it was to the demise of her children. She always did what she was told.

Now she spent her days moping around like a helpless child, waiting, imploring each day to pass, hoping that eventually my abuse could be forgotten so her Daddy could reassure her she was loved and accepted once more.

Mum was a child who'd never grown up, and it now explained why even her own children had to fight for survival in the playground of life.

Watching Mum hurt like that distressed me so much that I wanted to make it better for her. *I* started comforting and reassuring *her*. I already knew I was stronger than her. I'd already notched up a few hits in my young life and managed to bounce right back again. But Mum wasn't like that. She'd never been strong. All of my memories and our history proved that. I'd never seen Mum stand up to anyone, unless it was some political guy on the TV she despised, where she'd rant and rave at the screen, or that one time at The House with Mildred.

When she retold stories of her childhood, there was always a strong thread of dependence and helplessness woven through. She'd recall how her parents barred her from going out on her own in case she had a seizure, since she'd been diagnosed as an epileptic when she was a baby. All the times at school she'd been bullied for being epileptic. Her parents never inspired any hope in her that she could achieve anything because they saw her epilepsy as a disability and coddled her accordingly.

She was the 'poor June' that someone needed to take in and care for. My dad bossed her around, just like his own father and all the women in The House. She took instruction and direction with blind loyalty from people around her and seemingly never made any decisions on her own, always running it by her parents first or allowing others to make decisions for her, even when it came to her children.

Now that the parents she'd depended on so heavily disapproved of her daughter's accusations and had withdrawn from her somewhat, she seemed lost. Mum had reverted to a lost and lonely child.

I don't know if it was witnessing her crumble and abandon her parental role that made me decide to step up and take charge, or whether I needed it on some level, needed to be control of something in my own life, but somehow, I became the mother figure and my mother the dependent child.

I handed out advice and encouraged Mum to stand on her own feet without depending on her parents. "Your parents do not have the final say on your life," were words I echoed repeatedly, hoping this would help her find the courage and confidence I was sure she'd buried somewhere within.

This became our new way of relating. I was the mother who had the answers to help her, and she became the daughter who was learning she could rely on me. Was it sacrificial of me to give up my need to be parented? To be loved and supported by my own mother? I don't know. Maybe I just needed to feel important? That I had something of value to give? A purpose, even if it meant ignoring my own needs.

Maybe I hoped that if she could learn to be strong and decisive, that she might eventually stand up for me and be the kind of mum I needed her to be.

Chapter 13

Whispers of the *little liar* and tensions that previously thickened the air—mostly from the angry remarks Mum drip-fed me—eventually stopped. That 'story' of abuse was swept under the carpet and completely forgotten, like it never happened at all. Avoidance and denial became our new normal. Any mention of Pop's name now only hinted at someone I used to know and was no longer part of my life.

My relationship with Mum changed significantly. Any hope she would be there for me or my needs anymore, was well and truly buried. Time and experience now proved that beyond any doubt. I become accustomed to helping her with everything, constantly making sure *she* was doing okay. I helped manage her diet to keep her weight down, helped budget her limited income, kept her house in order, as well as helping her make decisions for her future, preparing her for the time when her children would inevitably move out.

She'd never pull me into line or remind me I was not the mother and these were not my concerns. She fully accepted the role reversal and became dependent on me.

Now that I was heading into senior high, I was *supposed* to be thinking about my future. Towards the end of grade ten, we had to pick subjects in line with our interests and strengths. How would I know what those were? I saw school as my refuge, not a place for learning and preparing for a future I couldn't even imagine. I was merely passing time.

In the footsteps of my mother, I'd perfected my brave face to the world in such a way that it no longer acted as a shield I wore to protect myself. It shaped me into the person I was becoming. A numb version of a human being who was getting by day-by-day, but not much more.

Every part of my predictable routine would change moving to senior school the following year. My subjects, my 'friends', and my favourite familiar teachers. It was a change I dreaded. The only public senior school in Rushton had an enrolment of around twelve hundred students. New teachers, new people, new classes, and greater expectations. I never liked change. Once I got used to something, I resented having to adjust. I just needed school to keep my mind off my crappy life and keep me away from home for six hours a day. Even though I could see the end of school looming, I couldn't give much thought to that now.

In grade eleven, I enrolled in a grade twelve catering subject as a part of my plan for a certificate in Hotel and Business Management. It was the most obvious career path given all my part-time jobs had been in hospitality. Expectations for grade twelve students, both with cooking assessments and written essays, were higher, as this was the students' last year and everything hinged on getting good enough grades to be accepted into university.

Assignments wouldn't bother me. I loved sinking my teeth into writing essays. Cooking assessments, however, would be my biggest challenge.

I struggled in this class right from the beginning. Cooking time frames and pressure to cook and produce something worth eating panicked me. I preferred the solitude of studying and showing my abilities on paper, not in person. Performing struck me mentally and physically. My mind would go blank, and I'd not have a clue how to proceed with a recipe. I worried that my food wouldn't look as well presented as the rest of the students. Struck with overwhelming anxiety, I'd stand and wait for my next instruction, fearing I'd be ridiculed if I made an error.

When we were required to make a sponge cake, I approached this task with quiet confidence, as I'd made a few before. Mum even proclaimed she could never make a sponge like I could. Not that I thought it was much of a compliment, sponges were so easy to make.

When I gathered the ingredients, I'd misread the bin labels and accidentally scooped from the self-raising flour, instead of the plain flour bin. Realising what I'd done, I nervously approached my teacher at the front of the class with my unusable bowl of flour. As soon as I told her, she pursed her lips and glared as she shouted across the room, "I just don't understand why you're in this class, Rebekah, when you obviously can't cook!"

Memories of Agnes raging at me flashed across my mind. I froze out of habit.

She'd yelled so loudly the entire class stopped what they were doing and stared. The blood drained from my face, and her words winded me. I had my back to the class, and I couldn't bear the thought of facing them. I wanted to burst into tears and run out the door.

But the new part of me that was taking some control didn't want to give her the satisfaction. "Um, I don't know," I told her, swallowing back the threatening tears.

I kept my head down as I dawdled back to my workstation, too mortified to see anyone's face. A few students approached and asked if I was okay. I nodded, grateful to know they cared.

Her words pierced right through the parts of me that always wondered, *why me?*

Her words also affirmed what I believed about myself and about my life. I was useless.

I couldn't do anything right, and my mistakes were always treated as heinous crimes rather than harmless errors. Perfection was the only path to acceptance, love, and worth, experience taught me that.

That teacher's words stuck with me for many years. Any time the urge to bake rose, my thoughts wandered back to that day, her emphatic words blaring in my head, "You can't cook, Rebekah." So I avoided it. Like so many other tasks I'd tried and failed, I added it to the list of things I couldn't do. The list sure was getting longer.

As I cowered from teachers who berated or criticised me, I leaned towards teachers who greeted me with warm, friendly smiles. The teachers who paid attention to me, who openly boasted about my strengths and skills, got my best work. I never believed much of what they said for long, but when their praise reached my ears, it briefly fed a yearning to be validated, before smashing against a mountain of evidence proving otherwise.

I'd become accustomed to my life being void of nurturing or warmth beyond Mum's vacuous "morning", and afternoon "hello, darling", followed by a meaningless smile. That's the best she had to offer, and I think she thought that's all she had to do to fill my cup.

Besides, my worth didn't matter, anyway. Which is probably why I clung like a magnet to my teachers, doing anything I could to attract or coerce more praise and positive attention. I worked extra hard on assignments, taking more opportunities to seek their advice, or implore them to read my draft just so I could hear their glowing feedback. And it wasn't just on assignments, but personal comments they made about my diligence, enthusiasm, dedication, and the wonderful student I was. I never realised how desperate I was to know someone saw me. I had been screaming for so long, for someone, anyone, to recognise me.

My relationships changed completely in senior school. Most of my friends from high school left at the end of year ten to get jobs or start apprenticeships or found different groups. Most I never saw or heard from again.

Somehow my new group grew to thirteen teenagers. A mixture of boys and girls from different walks of life. Some were alternative and grungy; others, like Danielle, were more conservative, like me. Some switched over from private schools for more independence, more subject choices, and the casual dress code this school offered. Even Amy, from primary school, became a part of our clan. Despite our eclectic personalities and styles, the group worked. We gathered on the city's vast park grounds at the foreground of school, during recess and lunch. We mingled, chatted, swapped funny stories, and shared cigarettes. I could forget about home life and my Cinderella relationship with Mum and be as much of a teenager as the rest of them. My friends filled a void, and for the first time in a while, I was happy.

However, as those friendships deepened, signs of dysfunction and emotional instability slowly surfaced. As we became familiar with each other, the initial buzz of getting to know everyone disappeared. Most had tested parts of their personalities—their weirdness, their funny quirks—on the group, like an initiation test for acceptance, and now they could let their pretences go to reveal more of their true selves. Now they talked about their families, their successful, career-driven mums and dads and the bonds they shared. They began to share tales of the stuff they did together as families too: sweet moments clothes shopping together or lunch after a sports win. Occasions like these were completely foreign to me.

Perhaps I was in too deep.

I'd not been in a friendship group long enough or meaningful enough to get to this point. For most people, this was probably normal. A natural pathway to deepening human connection. But not for me. No one except Anna knew me beyond the surface stuff, and that was only because she'd proven I was safe with her. How could I go deeper without exposing my dysfunctional family, my history? How could they accept me at a deeper level if everything below my surface was broken? What if they asked questions I couldn't answer?

None of these friends knew my story, and while I liked them all, I was afraid that if I shared the real me, or even parts of myself, that they'd reject me as the weird, broken girl with too many problems. Now, instead of feeling more secure, I was terrified.

I felt more comfortable with those protective layers on, like a mask or a disguise, just playing to the fun, light-hearted stuff that purposely kept a reasonable distance from my problems. I learned long ago to hide myself away. When I thought there was a chance at stripping the layers, the walls went straight back up, like when my family so callously rejected my truth. Nothing good came from being me. Nothing good came from the truth.

Those walls of mine were permanent now, and nothing anyone could do would tear them down.

Though I yearned for connection, I couldn't manage the emotions that came with it. I didn't know what lay beneath, and I feared exposure. But I still needed attention, a place I belonged. So rather than discovering deeper ways to relate, I unconsciously devised more creative ways of making sure the attention was solely on me but only at a surface level.

One day, as the bell signalled break time, I strolled over to meet my friends who were already sitting in the park, laughing and chatting. Suddenly, without knowing why, I started to panic. *I can't do this!* Not even knowing what "doing this" was.

My chest tightened so much it felt like my airways were closing in. I became faint, and dizzy. My whole body tingled, and I slowed my pace. As I stopped and leant forward to breathe, Danielle saw me in distress and dropped everything to run over to me. While I gasped for air, she lowered me to the ground. Despite my best efforts to relax, I couldn't stop the quick, short bursts of breath huffing out of my mouth. She comforted me in a soft voice, her hand rubbing my back, and slowly my chest relaxed while the tingling around my legs and face subsided.

I had no idea what caused this. Maybe my asthma had come back, I'd briefly wondered. Mum took me to the doctor when I was twelve, when I kept complaining of a tight chest and having difficulty breathing. Her younger brother died at fourteen of an asthma attack, so the doctor diagnosed it as a genetic condition. That was the easy answer, without provoking further investigation. But something told me this wasn't asthma. I hadn't used a puffer in years. Whatever it was, it didn't matter because I discovered it gave me what I really wanted: attention. Subconsciously, it spurred me to repeat it.

And I did.

Sometimes I hyperventilated so much I was taken to the emergency room with a friend by my side. This, I discovered, was a whole other level of attention, with not just friends but doctors and nurses. A whole team of people focused on me.

As my 'episodes' escalated to bigger and more dramatic performances, it at times strained my friendships. I didn't want to drive them away, in fact, I wanted the opposite; but sitting amongst my friends and watching someone else take centre stage made me feel unimportant and worse still, invisible. My game had to be bigger than theirs, so I could steal the focus for a moment or two.

I didn't care if their reactions were angry, sad, or happy, as long as there was a reaction. The silent treatment worked a treat. I'd become grossly offended for some slight that no one else would've given a second thought to, maybe I didn't get an invitation to a friend's place after school, or I didn't get the last drag of a cigarette going round the group. It didn't matter. All I had to do was let it be known I wasn't happy and enjoy the following hours having one of my friends beg me to tell them why I was mad. If I played it too long and my friends became annoyed with me, I would switch and point the finger at them, blame them for being mean.

Guilt over my pettiness notched up in my stomach. I knew my behaviour was stupid, but, rather than apologise, I'd shrug it off, or pass it off as a joke, downplaying or ignoring how it affected them. I wondered how many times I'd get away with it before they did the one thing I truly believed I deserved: abandon me. After all, it was the natural course, wasn't it? People who said they loved or cared for me eventually abandoned me. Why would my friends be any different?

As the end of grade twelve approached, conversations shifted once again, and a contagious buzz of excitement filled the air as friends shared their future plans and ways to keep in touch once the shackles of education were removed. I felt nothing but dread.

Uncertainty shrouded my bleak future. Soon there would be no more school to keep me in a routine. No more distractions to avoid an adulthood I wasn't ready for.

Instead of enjoying the final months of year twelve with my friends, I withdrew out of fear, unable to cope with the forced separation approaching. The night of my year twelve graduation came around, and instead of gathering with friends to celebrate, I spent the night alone in my bedroom, feeling the weight of abandonment and neglect even though I was the one who had pulled back from them.

Everything that led me to this moment was my own doing. When it came to embracing connection and enjoying my achievements, I abandoned it all in favour of the dysfunction I knew.

Chapter 14

For ten years, school had been my one consistent place of safety, away from abuse, a break from control and captivity. Somewhere I could go to just breathe. It was the only sanctuary I had to be with friends and try to be normal like everyone else. Where my teachers, who often felt more like parents, would wait expectantly for me to waltz through the door and then greet me with a smile. Everything I depended on was now gone. While my friends couldn't wait to burst through the school gates one last time, I only wished I could stay here forever.

School was my sanctuary, not a pathway to 'being' something, and now it was officially done. What would I do now?

Mum never had any pearls of wisdom except the one meaningless go-to phrase she repeated: "Just do your best". I rarely sought her counsel on anything, and that included what I would do for a career. I had no idea.

I didn't want to have to make hard decisions. I just wanted to retreat back to school and bury myself in assignments and hide away in libraries. I missed my teachers already.

I was offered a place at Rushton University to study business. Routine was once again in my sight. Avoidance, the major player, could resume its part. But after looking at the course subjects, I convinced myself there was no way I was capable. Frightened by failure and scared of facing another grilling from a teacher who might announce my stupidity to the class like last time, I deferred my university plans to save myself the anxiety and potential shame of enrolling in a degree I wasn't smart enough for. But I hadn't thought ahead to the next step. *Now what the hell am I going to do?*

Stone broke and five months away from being eligible to get my driver's license, I needed a job to save the money I'd need to move out of home. It was a catch-22 situation. I'd need a car to get the job, but I didn't have money or a license. As much as I didn't want to live at home, I didn't see any other options.

Since most of my friends had moved away to go to university, or found jobs in Melbourne, or travelled abroad on their parents' dime, there was nothing to do and no one to catch up with. With so much free time, I'd often wonder how my life was meant to work out. As days of nothingness passed, a mix of emotions swayed in and out; depression and then loneliness, followed by anger. Anger screamed the loudest. I was angry with myself for not having a clue, and not 'doing something', like everybody else. I was moping, and it wasn't healthy.

I craved an easy solution to magically appear. But nothing came.

I spent hours looking for work from twenty minutes to two hours away, even interstate, still without knowing how I'd be able to do it anyway. But fear and anxiety crept in, questioning every single ability or skill I thought I had, and I'd quickly talk myself out of sending an application. I was too afraid to put myself out there. Too terrified to face questions about myself, especially positive ones.

Sabotaging beliefs, whispering thoughts of uselessness, and hopelessness trapped me in fear and seclusion. I deliberately avoided seeing the friends who had stuck around, ignoring their phone calls and invitations to eighteenths, too embarrassed to admit I was fucking clueless with no direction and no money. My perceived problems overwhelmed any chance I had of letting go for a night to celebrate.

As I repeatedly declined invitations to meet, the phone eventually stopped ringing. They moved on. I didn't blame them. I didn't have the courage to face them and pretend life was great when it wasn't. Hearing about their wonderful lives made me feel like the biggest loser.

A few months before graduation I'd started dating Derrick, a friend of my older brother's. They worked together in the local mine. He was twenty-one, risky, and immature. If I had a type, he wasn't it. He wore clothes too loose for his scrawny build. He liked fast cars, fast bikes, and often showed a careless attitude towards road rules, sometimes speeding dangerously down the middle of the road. I didn't like that side of him. He thought it was fun. I thought it was idiotic.

Derrick lived about a kilometre down the road from Mum's house, a convenient option to home, particularly after I finished Year 12 and needed space away from Mum and the boredom of sitting in my room all day. He offered his company willingly, showering me with compliments and alcohol. With him, it was easy to ignore my non-existent plans and depend on him to carry me through. That's all I needed: company and attention, something else to focus on. Someone to take care of me.

He was my first consensual sexual experience. During intimate moments, my trauma was hard to hide and occasionally I'd freak out or freeze at the slightest touch. Sex was a constant cause of my inner conflict. A part of me knew it was natural in healthy, adult relationships, but the other part of me still thought it was the vilest, most degrading act. Drinking copious amounts of alcohol blocked the flashbacks, masked my shame, silenced the voices telling me I was a disgusting little girl, and released a side that allowed sex to be fun.

Sometimes in a drunken rage Derrick would threaten to hurt Pop for the things he did to me. Seeing his eyes narrow to a menacing glare worried me, and the more he drank, the more erratic and unpredictable he became. Was it just words, or would he follow through? I knew he owned a gun, but would he actually use it?

Though I never believed violence was the answer, a part of me felt vindicated when he'd offer to fight for me. From a family where no one stood up for me, it was nice to know he was willing to, even if I didn't necessarily want him to follow through the way he said he would.

Even though I could rely on my boyfriend for everything I didn't have, I wanted to be *doing* something. Every time he came home from work, I made sure I could list everything I'd done that day and all the jobs I'd looked for, just to mask my shame and embarrassment. But that charade wore thin, and I decided I'd need to do more than hang about the house all day and make excuses. It was time to move.

With a packed bag, I moved to Melbourne, a city with endless opportunities and a sea of people to hide in so I didn't have to answer the elusive question of "what are you doing?" Armed with high hopes and romantic ideas of 'setting up house', this was chance to get a job and get on with life. I'd been offered a super cheap room with another girl in a heavily subsidised unit through a women's outreach accommodation and support service for troubled girls. She was hardly ever there, so most of the time I had the place to myself. I loved it. The unit was clean and uncluttered, the total opposite of Mum's messy, dirty house I'd be too embarrassed to ask people over to.

This unit was *my* space. I loved keeping my kitchen clean, vacuuming, and mopping the floors. Often, at night, I'd nestle on my uncluttered couch and proudly admire *my* clean home.

Cynthia was assigned as my job case manager to help me find work. She embodied the perfect picture of the life I wanted. From her pretty, professional clothes, all the way to her own office with her chosen knick-knacks and plastic plants; she was warm, friendly, and compassionate, especially when I shared my fears around getting a job. Her encouragement felt like a warm hug. A comforting substitute in place of the teachers I'd relied on at school.

Months went by without finding a job. Every interview I sat, I managed to stuff up somehow. Feedback from potential bosses mainly made mention of my lack of confidence, avoiding eye contact when they asked me questions, and lack of experience. I was starting to really miss school, my teachers, my friends, my old predictable life.

What future did I have when there was virtually nothing to fill the gap between my seventeen-year-old self and my old-age self? Seventy potential years of nothingness yawned before me. My chest tightened at the thought of how bleak and empty my future looked. What was I going to do? Pressure to escape my own thoughts, my meaningless life, crawled up my skin. I suddenly felt like I was choking and struggling to breathe.

Every time fear came close to suffocating me—which it did on a daily basis—I'd race to the bathroom and drop to the shower floor, holding my knees hard against my chest, burrowing my head inwards and sobbing as the scalding water rushed over my bare skin. The heat washed my fears away until the suffocating grip on my chest loosened and I could breathe again. The steam created a protective layer to keep me safe and grounded.

To fight off boredom and fill my yearning to be looked after, I took the train to see Derrick at his mum's house, mostly on the weekends. After he'd lost his job at the mine back in my hometown and moved to another small mining town, catching up at his mum's house was more convenient.

Every time I visited Derrick's mum's home, a cold shiver would run up my spine the moment I stepped inside, causing flashbacks of The House to sucker punch me. An eerie silence clung to the frosty air as I scanned the room. Every piece of furniture was positioned perfectly, without a trace of dust or mess. In the distance, his mother barked orders to his younger siblings. She sounded like Agnes. My body tensed up as she approached to greet me. I sidled up closer to Derrick, sensing I'd need to watch out for myself here. Something told me she ran this place like a captain runs his ship and discipline would be doled out for the slackers.

But sometimes I forgot to pay attention.

On one occasion, while lazing in her spotless lounge room, I picked at my toenails absentmindedly, carelessly discarding them to the floor.

Moments later she walked in, pointed to the toenail pile on the carpet, and screamed, "Who did this?"

Oh no!

My jaw immediately clenched shut with terror. I stared down and began twitching my fingers, trying to avoid her glare, not daring to confess. *What were the consequences? What would happen to me?* I prayed time would speed up, for someone to change the subject, or do something worse than I had.

She huffed loudly as she swept it off the carpet and stormed off. I let out a sigh of relief, knowing I'd need to watch myself more carefully next time. *Mistakes were not welcome here.*

Spending weekends with Derrick filled the emptiness of my uneventful life, begrudging the thought of returning back to my unit alone. Hours before dropping me at the station, I'd cling obsessively to him, following his every move. Holding him tight on the couch and not letting him out of my sight, before begging him to let me stay and even move to where he worked now, just so I wasn't alone.

But his whole body tensed up at the mere mention of such a big step in our relationship. Suddenly feeling pressured and suffocated, like I was trying to pin him down, he withdrew from me and pushed me away, throwing hurtful remarks he knew would sting me.

When we arrived at the station, he wouldn't even look at me. He just stared straight ahead, stone faced, his mouth clenched shut. I pleaded with him to let me stay while tears streamed down my face. "Get out of the car," he shouted at me when I refused to leave.

The cloud of dust behind his car as he drove away seemed so final. Once I'd boarded the train, I slumped in my seat and stared blankly out the window, wondering if I had just lost the only person in the world who made me feel something other than fear and loneliness.

As the train clickety-clacked, my despair quickly turned to desperation. Panic gripped me as I imagined an even emptier life without Derrick. I needed to get him back or face a lifetime alone. I jumped off at the next station and begged him to come pick me up. Furious and refusing to get me, he demanded I get back on the train and hung up. The phone was still pressed hard against my ear as my mouth gaped open in shock. *What am I going to do?*

Dragging my heavy body back onto the train, I collapsed into the seat and sobbed the whole way. Now I was completely on my own. Tossed aside like a useless old rag.

How can I possibly go on if no one gives a damn?

I had no job. No money. I'd deserted my friends out of embarrassment. Mum would have no advice. Jack would listen, at least, but he'd only tell me I'd be okay. But I wasn't, and I didn't know that I would be. There was not a single prospect in my future to salvage.

Arriving home to an empty unit, my stomach rumbled loudly, reminding me I'd not eaten all day. My head heavy with anguish, my gaze paused on the knife block on the bench. I slowly shuffled over and drew out the longest blade and sat on the floor with it. I raised the knife to my chest with both hands while I imagined driving it deep into my heart. My eyes burned as I held the knife and wondered how I'd got here, to this point.

I didn't want to die, but the pain was just too much. I didn't know how else to stop it. I missed school, my teachers, the friends I'd discarded. I wanted to go back to my old, imperfect life and curl up in it. I dropped the knife, sunk into my bed, and cried myself to sleep, praying tomorrow would bring me a solution.

Living in the unit was a short-term arrangement until a more permanent home was found. Soon enough, a room became available with a girl named Sandy, who I discovered, never left the apartment. She was similar in age to me, a frumpier figure with long, golden blonde hair that frizzed around her shoulders.

Sandy parked herself on the couch, glued to the TV unless she was obsessively tidying up, vacuuming every square inch of the place or fawning over her boisterous bird. She controlled the heating to save money, so the unit froze like an icebox. I didn't feel comfortable there, too scared to make a mess or make a noise that disrupted her attention from the TV soap operas. Her penny-pinching habits stopped me from escaping to the hot, soothing shower I depended on when my anxiety gnawed at me. Even when I tried making conversation with Sandy, she only replied in one-word answers with her eyes still fixed on the TV she hogged all to herself. There was nothing left to do but sit in my icy cold room.

As my eighteenth birthday approached, I thought more of moving back home. I hated living with Sandy. Her constant presence and lack of motivation depressed me more. Any time we did speak, she prattled on about her grand plan to start living and working when she turned thirty. Her words lingered as I imagined my life on that path. Despite my current shitty existence, I still dreamed I'd be in a completely different space at thirty. I wanted what I thought most people wanted: friends, a husband, children, a career.

Watching her wait out her years reminded me of what I *didn't* want for my life and I worried her lack of motivation would be contagious. So I packed my things and moved back to Mum's, knowing a warmer room would be waiting for me.

I turned eighteen a week later, celebrating my first legal beer at the local pub with Jack. Not exactly how I imagined spending my eighteenth. But still, sharing this milestone with him, a man more like a real father to me, meant something.

Most days at home were spent either looking for work or helping Mum clean and organise her untidy house. Not only did it distract me from my non-existent future, but it gave my days some purpose. The more time spent with Mum, the more invested I became in trying to change her life. I lectured her with such gusto, like some Tony Robbins guru, running through plans and options and choices she could make. For brief moments, I wondered why I couldn't apply the same advice to myself. Even though Jack was there by her side as a supportive husband, he didn't get bogged down with all that 'clap', as he called it, that I tried to teach Mum. Not that I ever lectured Mum in front of him. If he ever overheard me preaching, he'd tell me off for nit-picking her.

"Let it be," he'd say. As long as his farm clothes were clean and there was enough grub in the fridge to make a meal, he was happy. "Why ruffle feathers and create a stir that doesn't need bothering," he'd say. Jack protected Mum like that.

How would she know how to stand up for herself and budget her money and be more independent and confident if no one helped her learn how? Still, I wanted to rescue her, and a part of me still hoped she'd return the favour one day.

At night, boredom and isolation kicked in, sitting alone in my bedroom where self-sabotaging, defeating thoughts crawled out of every crevice and magnified. The year was dragging on and I'd still not done a thing worthwhile or productive.

Too many nights alone in my bedroom, with nothing but blackened memories and dark emotions hovering, thoughts to escape my empty life rose up again. Maybe Melbourne didn't work out because it wasn't the right place, I pondered. Maybe Melbourne was the easy option and God was challenging me to be bold and move somewhere I'd never been, and then He'd reward me with a more exciting life with even more possibilities. So I decided to move again, somewhere completely new, believing a fresh start was waiting for me.

Dad lived in Brisbane. I'd kept in contact with him over the years, mostly during the holidays and birthdays. Out of God-driven courage, I spontaneously rang Dad and asked if I could live with him. I'd not lived with him since I was six years old. Maybe this was our chance to reconnect. He agreed, sounding almost as excited by the idea as I was.

I was optimistic things would be different in Brisbane. A new environment and a new city meant new opportunities. Opportunities perhaps I'd missed in Melbourne. This had to be what I needed. A chance to start fresh and sort out my life. A friend from grade twelve had moved to Brisbane six months earlier, so there was at least one person I'd know there.

Leaving Mum was the only part that bothered me. I worried she wouldn't cope without my encouragement to keep the house clean and spend her money wisely. Jack wouldn't nag her about it. The state of the house never bothered him like it did me. Nor would he encourage her to do more than sit in front of the TV all day. My stomach knotted up as I left, assuring her I was only a phone call away if she needed me.

As the bus pulled into the Brisbane bus station, my father was already waiting with a wide grin stretched across his face. My stomach flapped like a bird flailing its wings as I stepped off the bus. Dad paced over and hugged me tight, his warm embrace easing all the worries I'd had about staying with him.

Dad's house was as neat and orderly as I remember he liked it being. He hated untidiness, too. He showed me to my room to drop my bag before ushering me back into the lounge room to join him for a cold drink. While we caught up, every so often he'd shake his head from side to side as though he was grappling with the memory of his little girl compared to the almost woman in front of him.

We kept our conversation light over dinner. Nothing too deep. I didn't confide to him my dismal year so far. I shared my plans to find a job and eventually move into my own place. We weren't close enough to share anything beyond surface stuff, and I still remembered his temper when things set him off. Even when the abuse came out, Dad never approached me. He, like Mum, vehemently denied it to anyone who would listen, and then the subject was closed. By now, that well and truly suited me.

The next day I woke to silence. Dad had left early for work, leaving a note beside a bowl of muesli on the kitchen table. It read, 'Enjoy your breakfast. Have a good day and I'll see you tonight, love Dad.' I picked up the note, carefully repeating every word. *Love Dad, love Dad, love Dad.*

A wide smile stretched my lips. His gesture warmed my heart. *Is this how it feels when a parent takes care of their child?* I couldn't remember the last time Mum ever made breakfast for me or told me she loved me. I looked around, familiarising myself with my new home while I munched on my cereal, feeling the weight of uncertainty lift around my decision to stay with Dad.

I left the house that morning, determined to find a job and cement my life here. Luckily, my experience in hospitality from the few part-time jobs I'd had during high school quickly landed me a job at a city café. It wasn't the career job I'd been seeking in Melbourne, but it was good enough for now to save some money and think about a more 'grown up' job later.

Sometimes after work, I'd meet up with my friend at a local pub. *See, this is what I'm meant to be doing. Just like everyone else.* Independence, earning money, and socialising. Listening to music, kicking back, and having a great time. Everything I imagined my new life should be.

But after returning home past 5:30pm for the third night in a row, Dad wasn't having it. I cheerfully waltzed in like a carefree teenager, greeting Dad as I quickly threw my bag in my room, and casually turned on the TV. Dad immediately stormed in and switched it off.

"Who the hell do you think you are! You don't just walk into someone's house and turn on the TV! You ask!" he shouted.

Why is he so upset? I didn't think this was *someone's* house. Wasn't this my home now too?

His angry outburst triggered earlier memories of his temper. His major reactions to minor things—just like his father and the women in The House reacted. He hadn't changed at all. My dream of having a cool, loving

Dad was squashed. We wouldn't have the father-daughter relationship I craved.

I stormed off to my bedroom, threw myself onto the bed, and burst into tears.

Soon after, he called out for dinner, but I was still so upset I couldn't face him. I brooded over the incident, angry he couldn't relax and just enjoy our time together. I didn't want to live with Dad if it meant being yelled and screamed at.

The next morning, I sat silently in my room until I heard his car leave. He'd left breakfast for me again, this time with a note apologising for his outburst. My heart sank. I wanted to be close to him, but why did he have to be so angry over something so trivial? I wanted to connect with him, but I was afraid he'd blow up again. Why couldn't he just love me and be my dad? I worried if I stayed, he'd try to control me, just like they had in The House, so I decided to leave before he came home that evening.

I flipped through the Yellow Pages, phoning cheap crisis accommodation places, something similar to where I'd stayed in Melbourne. Nothing was available. Eventually, a man answered with rooms available immediately. I asked how much it cost, even knowing I couldn't pay, but I had nowhere else to go. There was no room at my friend's house, and I didn't have enough money to catch the bus back to Mum's house in Victoria until I got my pay cheque.

With no way of getting there, the man offered to pick me up.

I phoned Mum to let her know where I was staying before I packed my stuff, tidied up my bedroom, and locked the door behind me.

Forty-five minutes later a middle-aged guy rocked up in an old, beat up rusty ute. Just the sight of him made my stomach churn. Nothing about him or his car looked legitimate. A part of me wondered if I was willingly walking into something dangerous. But I didn't have the guts to back out, and I worried what he might do if I refused to get in the car. Against my better judgement, I got in and prayed my rash decision wouldn't be my undoing.

We arrived sometime later to a decrepit weatherboard house. No signage, no other young women, no other indication this was a legitimate accommodation service, just this strange man and me.

Inside, the curtains were drawn, the dark floorboards almost blended perfectly with the dark dusty furniture. A dim light flickered from the kitchen, casting shadows on the blackened room. He led me to a small bedroom just left of the front door. A mouldy smell clung to the icy cold air like the room hadn't been used in years. Everything about this place sent a shiver down my spine. Dark and dreary, this appeared more like a dungeon than crisis accommodation. *Who would choose to stay here?* But I was broke and starving, and I had nowhere else to go. By the looks of the bare kitchen and a thick lock and chain around the fridge, I wasn't going to get a meal here either. *At least there was a lock on my door.*

I huddled on the sunken bed, freezing, starving, and alone, realising my plans for a new start had failed, just like Melbourne. *How did I get here, again?* I'd tried a few times to make a life like I imagined my friends from school had. I tried to re-connect with Dad and that failed. It was September, and I'd wasted almost an entire year with nothing to show. If this was my first year out of school, what the hell was the rest of my life going to look like? My chin trembled as I buried my head into the pillow to muffle my cry from being heard.

I didn't want my life to keep going around in circles like this! I wanted so much more. I'd fantasised my future self as successful, happy, free of torment. Normal. Whatever the hell that meant. But everything I'd tried so far, failed. Like the answers to life was a combination and I didn't have the right numbers to unlock the secrets.

What am I doing wrong?

Anguish quickly turned to injustice. *It isn't fucking fair!* There was no one to help me. And I didn't even know what I was meant to know. Maybe

God was punishing me because I wasn't good enough, just like he kept reminding me in The House and after. *Was this my punishment? A shit life and never-ending fear?*

A knock at the door interrupted my thoughts. A lady had phoned to speak to me. Must be Mum, I thought. I needed to hear her voice right now. For all her faults, her soft voice could still sooth me at times.

"Hi, Mum."

"Hi Rebekah, it's Rita."

Rita was Dad's second wife. They'd separated recently, and she'd moved back to Melbourne.

I wondered how she'd got this number. *I'd only given it to Mum.*

Dad was worried and just wanted to know I was okay. Holding back tears, I assured her I was. She tried justifying Dad's behaviour, like she'd done a few times over the years when I stayed with her and Dad in Melbourne when I was a teenager. She'd been on the receiving end of his temper many times. She understood my fears. A part of me wondered why she was so quick to defend him when she knew how much his outbursts hurt. She pried further, wanting to know my plans. I let her know I was heading home to Mum's the next day.

Exhausted, I locked the bedroom door and huddled myself onto the musty smelling bed.

I woke as soon as daylight seeped through the curtains, packed my bag, and tiptoed out, unlatching the lock on the front door as quietly as possible and zipping out, before the man had a chance to see me and ask for money or question where I was going.

Once I'd escaped farther down the road, I let out a loud sigh of relief. I couldn't help but look over my shoulder every so often, in case he lurked behind.

I'd called my friend the day before and told her I was going back home to Mum's. She offered to meet me at the bus depot to see me off. Combining what little money we had, we bought a hot bucket of chips to share while

I waited to board. As we devoured the chips, Chrissi paused mid-sentence, "Hey, let's move. There's an old man coming over."

I turned around to look and there was my dad walking towards me!

Dad dragged a chair over and sat. He leaned in and grabbed my hand. His eyebrows furrowed as he fumbled his words, trying to find the right way to apologise. "Please don't go," he begged. "I overreacted and I'm sorry."

The genuine remorse in his voice made my heart hurt. "Dad, it's okay. I need to go home," I assured him.

I stood up to leave, but his hand was still firmly gripping mine. Looking up at me with a strained look on his face, he repeatedly promised he wouldn't react like that again. For the first time, I got a glimpse of a young boy behind the eyes of my father. A boy, behind the tough exterior, who just wanted another chance at loving me.

As I waved goodbye to Chrissi, Dad pulled me in to his arms and hugged me tight, not wanting to let go. But he had to. I couldn't stay. On the bus ride home, I reflected on my short time in Brisbane. Another failed venture. Brisbane was meant to be my new life, and yet here I was again, returning to Mum's. To do what?

Stepping back into my bedroom, with memories firmly anchored in every shadow and crevice, reminded me of all the sadness and solitude, the tears and torment this room had seen. A witness to so many things; things only I knew. A sanctuary during the good and bad times. Despite everything, I was grateful for this room that often felt like a dear friend. I dropped my bags to the floor, lay down on my bed, and stared at the ceiling.

Everything in my room was as just as I'd left it. Had Mum even changed the sheets? I presumed not. A stack of mail on my desk caught my attention. I sifted through for anything of interest. At the bottom, I spotted an

envelope with a university logo. I'd forgotten about my university place-
ment I'd deferred at the beginning of the year. Tearing it open, it was a
reminder to notify the university if I still wanted my place for 1996.

Just the thought of having plans for next year renewed me with op-
timism, brief though it might be. I phoned the university to ask about
any other degrees I could apply for that didn't seem quite as difficult
or overwhelming. My only option was Bachelor of Education, Primary
Teaching. I grabbed the university book to look at the topics. They looked
far more interesting than business, accounting, and statistics. This was a
new path I was going to give serious consideration to.

Moving back to Mum's, I slipped right back into my guardian role, like
we hadn't missed a beat. During the day, I kept busy hustling Mum and
directing her, but at night, the same fear-fuelled thoughts emerged, as if
lurking behind the curtains, waiting for darkness to fall. Just like they had
before I escaped to Brisbane.

In the solitude of night, with nothing but my thoughts to keep me company, silence echoed every single one of my failures. I over-analysed every
shit part of my life, every failed venture throughout the year, reminding me
of all my faults, my inabilities, my empty bank account.

An inner voice began to visit on those nights. It would taunt me with existential questions I had no answers for. *What are you doing with your life?
You've failed miserably. You will never amount to anything. Your friends
have left you. Your boyfriend dumped you. You have nothing. There's no hope
for you.* I would press my hands against my ears to block out the voices, but
they only echoed louder, trapping tortuous whispers in my mind that I was
a failure and I'd never amount to anything.

My thoughts plagued with constant anguish and defeat, I pulled the
covers over my head to try to sleep, the only solution to wake to new
day where life didn't seem quite so hard. Fear and hopelessness twisted
every stomach muscle. *How long can you really do this, Rebekah?* the voice
whispered. *It's too painful. Let go*, the taunting continued.

Tears fell as I succumbed to the words filling every moment my eyes were closed or I wasn't busy. Maybe this voice was right? Maybe it was time to give up? Besides, if this year has taught me anything, I can't make it out of school on my own. Nothing had worked, no matter where I went, no matter how hard I tried.

I would not spend my years suffering in this room.

Ending my life would solve my problems. No more anguish, just peace. Peace I deserved after all the shit I'd been through. Peace I wanted more than anything.

An opposing voice gnawed at me, pushing through the pain, overshadowing the voice of death, demanding to be heard. A new, yet powerful feeling, urging me to hold on and not give up. Like some angelic messenger whispering in my ear, the word **purpose** flashed bright and clear across my mind, flickering like a neon light. The strength of this enlightened voice coursed through my veins like a strong torrent of water I couldn't hold back. Was there a higher purpose for my anguish and suffering? Perhaps it all would be revealed in time if I just gave myself a real chance?

One thing I knew for certain, it was time to take my life back. This was my opportunity. I gave in to it with everything I had, not knowing how or why, but I trusted it. I'd battled the long and grinding path of misery this year, surely this path of hope was worth exploring? I didn't know what I was going to do with my life, but there and then, I decided this bullshit had to end. No more aimless wandering.

Whatever cards life had dealt me, it was my choice as to how I would play my hand.

As I gave into this new thought, it was like someone had painted the darkened sky with stars and every star was a possibility that glowed with hope. It was all there, and it was all possible.

I'd never experienced this before. I'd been plodding all year, fleeing at every dead end, waiting for the universe to hand me everything I needed. But in this new world of bright possibilities, I could grab it myself.

The next week, I enrolled in a primary teaching degree at the local university. Right now, it was something. It was routine I loved and missed. Now at least I had something to keep me busy for the next four years, and I wouldn't have to think about my life. I'd even decided to get my license—not that I had money for a car—but in the spirit of doing and not overthinking, it was time to get shit done. No more sitting around waiting for the opportunities to fall into my lap.

For the first time ever, I fell asleep with a mind so full of possibilities, I knew for sure better days were ahead of me.

Chapter 15

I t was 1996, and I began my Bachelor of Education studies which would run for four years. I got my driver's licence, but without a car, I moved into a unit on the fringe of Rushton's city centre to be close to university and walking distance to the shops. After a long week of classes, I'd often go to the nightclub, down a few drinks, and head straight to the dance floor without any shame or self-consciousness over my dance moves. I could let loose and release that rigid, moralistic, uptight girl I presented to people in the light of day and just have a bit of fun. Scores of men hovered likes hawks around the edges of the dance floor, waiting to catch their prey. I usually ignored them, and they ignored me.

One night I noticed a guy staring at me from across the room. He threw me a cheeky smile as our eyes met. I smiled back and continued to dance. He moved steadily towards me, still staring, still holding that cheeky smile. This was more than a momentary glance. He'd been eyeing me off for a few songs. With booze-fuelled confidence, I skipped over to him.

He was tall and handsome and overdressed in long creased pants, a white long-sleeved shirt, vest, and polished black shoes. The other guys wore t-shirts, jeans, and sneakers. I sensed he was a few years older than me, not just by his formal clothes, or receding hair line, but his more grown-up mannerisms than the boys I'd met at university. He was kind and sweet, avoiding clichéd pick-up lines and cheap compliments that might typically garner a quick score. We exchanged numbers and parted ways soon after. His name was Adam.

We went on a couple of dates, but after a few weeks our relationship fizzled. I figured we'd moved to the friend zone and were not a couple when he invited me to a gathering at his friend's house. While we waited at the door, I became jittery, pumping myself up to sit in a room full of strangers. Meeting new people scared me. Just the thought of striking up a conversation, to appear cool and calm, left me tongue-tied. What do I say? How do I behave this time? Adam sensed my nerves and wrapped his arm around me, giving me a reassuring squeeze.

Michael, the homeowner, greeted us and walked ahead to the lounge room, where the rest of his friends were already chatting and drinking. I kept close to Adam, waiting to be guided by him, hiding behind his ease around friends. As I sat stiff and stone-faced on the couch, I noticed out of the corner of my eye that Michael was staring at me. I pretended not to notice, but every so often our eyes met, and I blushed.

Why is he staring at me like that?

His glare felt intense, like he could see right into me. Suddenly, I felt very self-conscious, and my body tingled.

I had to investigate what this guy was about.

When his friends began leaving, I planted myself firmly on the couch and hoped for an invitation to stay. I didn't want to hurt Adam, but I didn't want to leave, knowing I might not see Michael again. I stayed. Adam left, disgruntled and rejected.

Alone in the house, Michael and I moved to the floor, our legs crossed, facing each other, my back warmed by the heater behind me. He continued his long gaze, trying earnestly to lock eyes with me. My gaze darted around the room, but I'd throw him a glance every so often before burying my head and giggling nervously.

"I one hundred percent desire you," he professed. His seductive voice captivated me as I unconsciously leant forward to hear more.

If this was a tactic to add another notch to his belt, I didn't see it. Nor did I care. My inner child snatched at his words, clutching them tight against her chest, not daring to let go. *Someone cares,* she whispered.

From thereon in, I made it my mission to keep doing whatever it was he desired, to keep his attention solely on me.

Had I judged Michael on his appearance alone, I would never have stayed. He was balding at a rate far beyond his twenty-four years and his average height pronounced his plumpish build.

But Michael seemed to be the whole package. He was self-employed and owned his own house. He had dreams, goals, and ambitions. He seemed so confident and self-assured. Not in a cocky way. More charming and easy-going kinda way. A trait I found irresistible. Time flew while we chatted. His soft, charismatic voice commanded my attention for hours, as I found myself hanging off every word he spoke. Never wanting our conversations to end.

Five years older than me, I could tell by the way he mingled with people, his natural charm, even his self-renovated house and growing business, he knew so much about life and he could be someone I could learn a lot from.

Most weekends, his house was a buzz with friends and music. He understood social cues and rules and knew how to read people far better than I did. In larger groups, where there was no pressure for me to engage, I'd watched in awe how he interacted, how easy-going and popular he was. People surrounded him like a magnet, drawn in by his stories, conversations, and quick-witted jokes. I'd never met anyone like him. I was as giddy as a schoolgirl that someone like him wanted to be with someone as naïve as me.

But the more time I spent with Michael meant his effortless confidence just magnified the big gaping holes in my innocence. He quickly noticed my apprehension and discomfort as I loitered in the background, making very little effort to join in conversations with his friends. He noticed certain quirks in my behaviour, like storming out when he invited friends over to watch a movie with themes of drug use in it that ran contrary to my rigid Christian beliefs, as well as conversational language that revealed my ignorance and sheltered life. Gross assumptions and idle judgements I made while we were alone about the people he hung out with and their lifestyle choices were cause for looks of confusion from him.

Sometimes he'd pull me aside and encourage me to talk to people, to let loose and have a good time. His advice hurt. Like a scorned child, I pulled away, folded my arms, and sulked. The more he mentioned the weird things I said, or knew nothing about, the more imperfect I felt. *Why am I not good enough for you? Can't you just love me? Why does it matter that I don't speak to your friends? You said you desired me.*

I didn't understand.

His advice screamed an even stronger undertone I perceived as *you're not good enough*. Something I'd been shown in so many ways in my life already. Despite what I thought I heard in his words, the risk of abandonment was too great if I didn't at least pay attention and try to improve.

Michael embraced people. He respected different values, lifestyles, and beliefs. He had a broad perspective on life and avoided narrow-minded judgements that boxed people into a specific class or stereotype. Around Michael, my rigid beliefs and religious morals made me look stuck-up and standoffish.

Being in Michael's world was like stepping into an alternate reality, a wild and rebellious place. A world my grandfather at The House warned me about. This world was full of a rainbow of colours, freedom, self-expression, acceptance, fun, and exploration. No fixed rules or dogmatic religion. A world diametrically opposed to the one I had been raised to expect and accept.

My world was black and white and devoid of colour or anything in between. No freedom to express myself, no permission to be me, not that I knew who me was yet. My world was good and bad, right or wrong. Definitely no grey. Rules must be followed. Even after leaving The House,

I felt bound by a strict Christian ethos, and a watchful, judgemental God who influenced everything I thought and said and who'd scrutinised my behaviour since I was six years old. Acceptance was only gained through perfection in the eyes of God.

Trying to uphold the image of perfection I thought I should be, to appease God and yet still appeal to Michael, exhausted me. I ignored bodily functions that showed humanness for fear I'd appear less than perfect and therefore be promptly discarded. I pretended I was never hungry around him, too scared to be seen as a pig or die of embarrassment to find something stuck in my teeth. Sometimes I'd hold off going to the toilet an entire day and hid away like a diseased rat when my period came. I had associated cleanliness with perfection, and bleeding and pooping were far from that vision I had of myself and how Michael might see me.

But Michael was far more observant than I gave him credit for as he gently challenged my rigid worldview, encouraging me to let my guard down and break free from every staunch belief that held me captive.

Sex and intimacy still triggered so much childhood trauma. Paralysed with fear, I'd curl up beside him, half naked in the sober darkness, waiting for a gentle touch down my goose-fleshed arm to signal he was ready. Questions anguished my mind. I worried I wouldn't satisfy him, fearing my performance would be graded, or worse yet, rejected completely. Even in The House, Agnes told me whether I'd made my grandfather 'happy', or if I 'did a good job' after visiting his bedroom.

Any forwardness from me, even in my adult relationships, was too risky, too immoral, and slutty. *And what if my advances were rejected?* I'd frantically try to pinpoint what I might have said or done that was displeasing or gross to him. Or worse. *Was it my body? Was I too unclean? Did I look fat today?*

The more I revealed, the more it explained my 'odd and peculiar' ways. Flinching, questioning his motives for romantic gestures, and my inability to express my feelings. My brokenness scattered like tiny shards of glass whenever I was around Michael. Instead of withdrawing or pushing me away, he nurtured me more. As my tough internal walls slowly crumbled away, I could feel myself falling in love with him. Believing he was the one who would be gentle whilst encouraging me to release the ways trauma had damaged me.

For the first time, I got a glimpse of a man who would do anything to protect me and keep me safe.

Six months on, my feelings continued to deepen for the man who welcomed me in, nurtured me, helped me make sense of a foreign social world I was afraid of but curious to understand and explore. Each time, nudging the parameters of his world just a little more and gently guiding me in. Why else would he bother if he didn't love me back?

Saying anything loving to him in a random moment or holding his hand or resting in the nook of his arm on the couch terrified me. A lump formed in my throat when I held back the very words I yearned to express, like a boulder holding back a torrent of water. It pained my heart not to tell him, but fear of rejection and exposing myself without the certainty he'd reciprocate was just too great a risk.

Instead of saying how I felt, I'd write him long, loving letters and poems, pouring my heart and soul into every word, making it crystal clear how much I adored him. Then I'd discretely drop the letters off and bolt like a scaredy cat before he had a chance to read them in front of me.

Sometimes, I'd buy him expensive gifts I couldn't afford on a student budget to apologise for faux pas I made in front of his friends, desperately hoping my gestures would be enough for him not leave me and love me that much more. Since he'd never rejected my grand gestures or my desperate acts to keep him, I assumed he felt the same way.

Michael worked at home from his shed, so I often visited between university lectures. Strutting in with a giddy smile, I would watch him as he worked. When he mentioned his uncle in Northern Territory had died and he'd be attending the funeral, I thought, *no problem. It's only a week.*

When he returned a week later, he called and asked me to come over.

I knocked impatiently, eager to see him. He opened the door and smiled with so much affection it sent my heart aflutter. After the requisite small talk, he cleared his throat but then paused again. "We need to chat," he finally said.

"Okay," I blurted. I grit my teeth and forced a smile, all the while a bundle of nerves swirled around my stomach like a ferocious tornado. My mind was frantic with questions. Was he breaking up with me? Did he meet someone? Or perhaps his absence revealed his true feelings? Something in his tone suggested otherwise.

"I've been offered an opportunity," he started, but then filtered off.

I dropped my chin to my chest, not daring to look, predicting where this was headed.

"The job's in Northern Territory..." Another pause. He looked apologetic as he continued. "I'm going to take it."

His final words crushed me like a tonne of bricks. I gasped for air, wondering what this meant for us and quickly clenched my mouth shut to hold back my sobs, but it was no use.

I bawled like a baby. Tears poured down my face. Gut wrenching pain rippled my entire body as I grappled with the reality of this decision he'd made without talking to me about it first. *This is not happening. We're meant to be together! Please don't leave me! I have no one! I need you. Who else will love me?*

"What about us?" I cried, instead of the other questions I wanted to scream at him.

"Beck, I can't stay for us. This is an opportunity I really want." He sounded sorry, but it did nothing to ease my pain. More tears flowed as I imagined an uncertain future without him.

"How long will you be gone?" I asked with a wild sob.

"For at least a year," he told me, explaining how he'd be travelling for a bit before settling in Northern Territory.

We spent one last intimate night together in his kitted out travelling van. In the relative safety of darkness, I nestled into his embrace, wishing I could stay within his arms forever. Someone I loved was leaving; an all too familiar feeling. How would I cope on my own again?

I rarely let a day or two go by without contacting him, needing to stay connected. He had to know that despite the distance, I was still committed. But my calls often went unanswered. Sometimes it would be up to a week before he'd call me back.

When we did speak, I eagerly shared my hatched-up plans to travel the vast distance to see him. But he always came up with excuses to put me off the idea. Way too costly, he'd say, or it was too far to travel, or he was never sure he'd be available when I was hoping to visit. His excuses niggled at me. A sign that things weren't as they seemed. But I quickly dismissed my concerns, believing he was merely trying to protect me, not brush me off.

When Michael returned after ten long months. Excitement and nervousness whizzed in my stomach as I walked towards his shed where he was still unpacking. In my head—the space where I played out my fantasies—I ran up and hugged and kissed him just like they do in the movies. When he saw me, he stopped what he was doing, strolled casually towards me wearing his charismatic smile that I'd missed so much, and stretched his arms out to embrace me.

Inadvertently, I stopped and jumped back.

Immediately I realised what I'd done, wishing I could redo the moment. But I couldn't. I was too afraid. Inside I berated myself, screaming to the girl within. *Why can't you give yourself to this man? The man you say you love.*

His face dropped in despair as he too took a step back.

"It's hard to think how we can be together if you can't even hug me," he said.

I dropped my head, not daring to look up, fearing he'd see all of my shame. My heart was heavy and anguished. *I love you*, I whispered inside. *Please let me love you this way until I am brave enough to break down the wall.*

I repeatedly apologised, begging him to understand. He stood silently, as if this incident prompted memories of all the ways my trauma overshadowed our relationship. I knew in that moment he wondered whether he could keep nurturing my wounds.

My heart sank.

I needed to shift the mood quickly, not give him the chance to dump me there and then when I'd missed him desperately. So I did what I always did. I made light of it, reducing the matter to nothing but his own childish overreaction.

"Come on," I said as I slapped his arm playfully. "It's not a big deal. So what! Don't be a sook. I'm here, aren't I?"

I continued visiting him, but there was a definite shift in our relationship after that day. I was way too scared to ask the status of it. As usual, I waited for permission, a sign, or to be invited to stay over. Something to tell me we were still together. But it didn't come. Was he punishing me for holding back or waiting for me to initiate affection for once?

Soon enough, I got my answer.

Visiting him, I waltzed in as he greeted me warmly and threw me a smile. *God, I love his voice, his face.*

"So," he said. "I need to tell you something."

It was strangely familiar to our last serious chat, but his tone didn't suggest anything too serious.

"Oh, what's that?" I responded casually, hoping he would tell me we were on again.

"I've met someone."

Time stood still as a large lump blocked my throat.

"What?" I blurted out before I could stop myself. *How could this be? What the hell is he talking about? He has a girlfriend? When did we decide we weren't together anymore?*

I summoned all my energy, inhaling deep to hide my heartbreak. Falling apart wasn't an option. Not now that it really was over. My throat ached as I swallowed hard to suppress the avalanche of tears while he told me of his new love and their magical connection.

"Beck. I think she's the one."

A stabbing pain pierced my heart. I couldn't breathe. I staggered backwards, trying to remain upright. Nothing made sense. My whole world shattered into a million pieces.

But didn't we also have a connection? How could he be so compassionate to my needs and my past and not be 'the one' for me? No-one could be this kind and not truly love me.

Despite my best efforts to woo him back, more gifts, more time, more affection, his girlfriend moved in. Having Michael within reach and not being able to visit or call physically pained me. Another person in the chain to let me go. Abandoned yet again.

I pushed through each day and night alone. Sometimes a sea of tears spilled out as I mourned the deepest love I'd ever felt. I would hunch over in a tight ball, holding my stomach in agony, cradling the immense agony and loneliness I felt. The love I imagined and believed with all my heart was mutual was gone.

In his absence, over time, the veil that hung over our relationship began to lift, and I saw things more clearly than I ever had. The truth of what was really a one-sided relationship. One I chased and was never equally reciprocated.

I'd never noticed our relationship was predominantly confined to his house. We never went out to dinner, to the movies—anywhere. With all the friends he had, he rarely invited me out with them. Instead suggesting I wait in bed for his return. He intentionally distanced himself from my birthdays, including my twenty-first. Justifying his presence would distract from the more important people there. I never questioned his disinterest, because I was so tied to my view of our relationship that I didn't even see it. He justified his reasoning in such a way that he was doing everything for my own good, and I believed him.

I invested my hopes and dreams into a man who had no intentions of committing. I misjudged his kindness, his compassion and sensitivity towards my trauma, and interpreted it as genuine love. He did care for me, but it was never love.

Deeper reflection revealed where my true feelings stemmed. I'd latched on to the first person who expressed sincere compassion of my childhood trauma and understood my brokenness like no one else had. A man willing to be with me despite my scars.

My grief exposed this as the loss of someone who did genuinely care for me. Someone who brought light to my darkness. That's what I would miss.

Michael and his girlfriend moved out of the state and out of my life. I would be relieved not to run into him again, but I would miss him, knowing that that part of my life had ended.

The God I still trusted had to have a good reason for removing Michael from my life. A lesson to be learned about myself, He wanted me to understand. The lesson wasn't clear yet, and I wasn't sure I was ready to see it. But there was a purpose, and my relationship with Michael was a part of this journey I needed to walk.

Whatever the lesson was, it wouldn't be revealed until I met the real man of my dreams.

Chapter 16

My second year in teaching would be more practical than my first. Applying all the observations I'd made in first year and theory I'd learned, to preparing lessons and actually teaching. This was the year we'd undertake two lots of practicum rounds—or work placements, as they're known. I purposely avoided thinking too deeply about having to teach, instead choosing to focus on the study part that kept me buried in library books. I would have remained a student forever if I could, then I wouldn't have to put myself out there in the real world.

The first time I taught, my nerves bubbled up through my legs as I walked to the front of the room, twenty-five eager sets of eyes following me. My thoughts scattered like a puzzle dropped from a great height, shattering into a thousand pieces. I had a script that I'd been rehearsing, but I was so worried I'd mess up, my mind went blank. All I could hope was that the words would come out right when I needed them.

Having the real classroom teacher critique my performance worsened my anxiety.

What will she think of me? I have to be perfect. How am I going to do this? I can't avoid doing this lesson, otherwise I'll fail; and I can't risk being seen as a failure. What the hell am I doing this stupid degree for? This is not hiding away. My mind was riddled with questions and worrying thoughts.

To mask my nerves, I pulled out my best self-protection strategy when I didn't want to lose face. Pretending to feel completely indifferent to the task and convincing myself I really didn't give a shit about the outcome.

It was my secret superpower I'd used many times over, and it worked to hide my nerves. When the lesson finally ended, I sighed heavily, releasing the burst of air holding my chest tight. It hurt like hell.

Of course, I dissected every part of it later, pinpointing my mistakes, torturing myself with everything I *should* have or *could* have done. But despite the inner critic taunting, much to my surprise, a part of me enjoyed teaching. Even my supervising teacher congratulated me on a job well done. For the first time, I could see a career path instead of using this degree as an escape. To my surprise, I could teach, speak confidently, and enjoy it. It was like I'd pin-pricked the bubble I surrounded myself in and got a taste of a real grownup life.

Beyond the teaching component, what I really loved was the connections I formed with the students. I'd rove the room, not out of requirement, but genuinely wanting to help students one-on-one and take the time to listen to their questions. The quiet students—the ones appearing to struggle in silence, like they were afraid to admit they needed help—those were the kids who stuck out to me. Their solemn faces tugged at my heart. Perhaps I had a sixth sense that detected their need to be nurtured the way I needed to be nurtured when I was a little girl in school. Often as we chatted, I couldn't help but wonder what kind of home life they had. *What are they going through? Are they neglected as I had been? Are they not loved, as I was not?* Remembering that I was that quiet little girl in class too, coming to school with the weight of the world on my shoulders, made me especially empathetic.

Now that I was a teacher in the making, I didn't just see students; I saw children who needed love and validation. As I roamed around the room each day, I couldn't help but wonder if I was the one person who could make them feel special or at least acknowledged? My energy went into helping students not just understand they were worthy but remind them by offering words of encouragement and highlighting all the great things they did. Seeing their wide, beaming smiles made my day.

Sometimes I think I was speaking to my own inner child as much as I was to the students when I would shower them with compliments.

I practically sailed through my first week of teaching rounds. But with two more weeks to go, my interest waned. It was all the other monotonous stuff, taking notes, observing, sitting through lengthy staff meetings that bored me and overshadowed the measly one lesson I was assigned to teach. I approached my supervising teacher to air my feelings, worried she'd judge me for not enjoying the rounds like I 'should'. But my discontent gnawed at me, and I couldn't ignore it. She suggested I go away and think about it but encouraged me to finish the final two weeks. I didn't have the courage to admit my decision was already made.

The next day, I deferred my rounds until the second semester.

I felt like a quitter for bailing out, but I reminded myself I wasn't at university to teach, but to hide. To bury my face in books and not deal with the outside world. I knew I couldn't avoid the rounds forever, half wishing I'd picked another degree without a practical component. Would I ever be brave enough to emerge from the shadows and show myself, my abilities to the world? I wasn't sure. But for now, I could avoid it and face that hurdle later.

When the second semester began, the enormity of requirements, plus an extra teaching round, daunted me. This would be a very full semester. But deeper, darker feelings lurked and began to surface. Existential questions became far more important than simply hiding away and keeping busy. *Who the hell am I? Why am I here? What's the point?* These questions gnawed at me, vying for my attention, wanting answers I just didn't have.

I sought advice from the university career counsellor, hoping she'd help me decide if teaching was right for me. We met regularly to try to chisel away at my battered self-esteem to find my strengths and help link them with teaching or an alternative career. But with each session diving deeper into my past and what motivated me, the direction of our conversations changed to revelations of my childhood trauma. I didn't see the connection between the pain of my past and my uncertainty now. To me, the issues were separate. The abuse, my parents' neglect, disconnection from my own identity, had absolutely nothing to do with my life now. How could it?

But while I denied any association, cracks began to appear on my tough exterior as I struggled to keep myself composed. Questions previously whispering in the background now screamed at me everywhere I turned. *What the hell am I doing with my life? Who the fuck am I? What the hell am I good at!*

These questions terrified me as they led to deeper, unstable beliefs. *Well, if I don't know what I'm good at, then I mustn't be good at anything. How come everyone else knows? What's wrong with me? I must be useless.*

Most mornings were a struggle just to get out of bed. My body was weighed down by overwhelming sadness, and I'd suddenly burst into tears without reason. *What's wrong with me? Why am I crying? You fucking idiot, what are you doing? Pull yourself together, you are acting like a fucking loser! Just get up and get your arse to school. You'll be fine. Get over it!*

I dragged myself to lectures, tuning out as I slumped in my seat and stared off into the distance while the voices murmured around me like white noise. When I came to, a surge of grief and sadness consumed me. As tears savagely tried to break through, I'd quickly gather my things and bolt for the door, my determined strides long and purposeful until I reached my car. I'd close the door, light a cigarette, and then release the floodgates.

What the hell was wrong with me?

Motivation to continue the second semester waned, and I started to avoid lectures, fearing I'd cry unexpectedly, like the last time. Teaching rounds loomed, but in my current state, I worried I'd not be able to even attempt it this time. If I deferred my rounds again, I'd be forced to defer the whole degree and be left sitting at home doing nothing. Again. That wasn't an option. I'd need to summon all my strength and continue.

But just three days into my teaching rounds, tears forced their way through the façade while I sat observing in the classroom. It was no use.

I couldn't do it. There was nothing in me I could have used to get through the next three weeks. I was running on empty.

I headed straight to my supervising class teacher and unapologetically blurted out, "I can't do this." I then withdrew from university. Just eighteen months in.

What am I going to do now?

Depression hit hard. I barely got through each day without collapsing in a heap. Whatever I did to avoid and suppress my problems in the past now seemed useless. Like an unstoppable force, my issues refused to lie dormant any more. The darkness in my body and mind merged, compounding my anguish. I dragged my body around like my ankles were chained to boulders. I smoked more and ate less, to the point where I lost a significant amount of weight.

Most days I wore a smile, never letting on to anyone how troubled I felt. If friends asked why I'd deferred, I just told them teaching wasn't right for me and I was "busy looking for another career". Which was half true. I told Mum I deferred, but I never revealed the real reason. She wouldn't have done anything, anyway. It was easier to pretend everything was fine, like we always did in this family.

My demons didn't bother waiting for nightfall any more. They came at all times of the day and night to magnify my hopelessness, my worthlessness. Dropping out of university was confirmation of how bloody useless I was. Just being in that place of defeat again, despite my efforts, set off a cascade of tears, while rocking backward and forwards trying to soothe myself didn't help like it used to.

I searched the blackened sky, the once glittering stars, looking for hope, praying another solution would appear out of thin air. This time, my fears dragged me closer to the edge of the cliff; and even though only a wall separated me from Mum physically, mentally and emotionally, I couldn't reach out to her for help. I knew needed something, someone, or I feared I wouldn't make it through the night.

I grabbed the phone book that propped my bedroom phone off my floor and searched through the pages to see if there was some kind of twenty-four-hour counselling hotline for pathetic two am callers.

When someone answered, I choked. *What am I meant to say? Do I just pour my heart out? What the hell can they do for me? Talking's not going to fix it! Someone just needs to take this pain away so I can be fine again.*

Something in the phone counsellor's comforting tone helped to lessen the anguish, loosening the vice-like grip around my chest. Just hearing someone's voice instantly made me feel better. I liked too that I could remain anonymous. Still, I felt ashamed that I even had to ring someone for help in the first place.

Maybe I'm fine. Maybe I'm just overreacting. This is silly. Hang up, Beck. Just hang up the damn phone, you fucking sook! I ignored the voice in my head. I just wanted one god-damn person to pretend they cared.

"I don't know what to say," I murmured down the line.

He asked me how my night was. *What a ridiculous question! How the fuck do you think it is if I'm calling a fucking counselling line at two am?*

I played it cool. "Yeah, I'm okay, I guess."

"What made you call tonight?"

I don't know! It's not one thing. It's everything. Um, I'm a fucking loser, who can't get her fucking life in order, and I don't know what to do, so I want out.

Admitting out aloud I wanted to die was too much, even for me. I spoke a bit and pretended my problems were only minor, keeping a lid on the avalanche of emotions behind my words. He couldn't label me a loser if I didn't reveal the truth.

Late-night phone calls became more frequent when I realised it filled a craving to be heard. Someone to hear what I'd held onto for years. Maybe that's all I needed. After all, nothing ever seemed so bad the moment someone answered. Sometimes, after my tears dried, I'd call so late, but their voice was all I needed to fall asleep.

I pretended I was okay for several phone calls before I divulged deeper. I briefly mentioned my history of childhood abuse and Mum's neglect, as a minor issue unrelated to my current situation. The counsellor made such a big deal, suggesting there was a definite link between my childhood and my current emotional state. I still refused to make the connection. Blaming this on past events was an easy cop-out.

The phone counsellor suggested I make a face-to-face appointment with a counsellor who specialised in sexual assault. I was reluctant at first, but perhaps it wouldn't hurt to give it one chance?

While I sat in the waiting room, I wondered if this appointment was really necessary. *Do I really need to do this? I'm not crazy, am I? I'm just a bit depressed and confused with my life.* I worried I'd made too big a deal of the childhood stuff. I couldn't back out now. I kept my head down while I waited for my name to be called. When I heard my name, I looked up and saw a man standing in the doorway. Was this the man from the phone?

Oh, God, what do I do now? How do I act? Do I look pathetic? Do I look like I need a lot of help? I panicked as I followed him. *Okay, just act indifferent. That always works. Act strong, tough, like you don't really need to be here. Pretend like you've got it all together.*

He began with small talk. But no sooner had I relaxed, his manner shifted unexpectedly.

"You're afraid, aren't you? What are you afraid of?"

His remark hit me like a smack in the face. *What are you talking about? I'm not afraid. What is that supposed to mean!?*

I threw him a menacing glare and said, "I'm not afraid of anything! What do I have to be afraid of?"

He ignored my firm tone of voice, which I hoped would make him ease up on me. This wasn't what I signed up for. *You bastard, you're not getting me. You won't tear down my wall. You think you can get me here and tear it down! Fuck you! I'm not coming out for anyone!*

A lump formed in my throat as my body tensed up. I had to leave. My gaze darted around the room for a quick escape. But if I ran out, would I prove him right? *Was* I afraid?

The pressure to stay became too unbearable. I couldn't take it anymore. I abruptly stood up and ran, not slowing down until I was safely in my car. What happened, I don't know. The room seemed to close in and suffocate me.

I sped home, screaming, ranting, and raving, tears streaming down my face. Home was twenty-five minutes away, giving me time to vent before I could dry my tears and walk inside with a smile on my face, like nothing was wrong.

"Why am I here again?" I screamed at my windshield. *What the hell am I meant to do with my life? Am I meant to be this miserable? It isn't fair! Why is this happening? I don't understand what I'm doing wrong. Why are you punishing me, God? I just don't get it! What the fuck do you want me to do! Give me a fucking sign!*

I felt like life wasn't giving me a chance, and it didn't seem fair. I desperately wanted God to point it out. *You're so all-powerful, you say! You love me, you say! Where's the fucking love now? Where's your power now! You don't give a fuck about me! I'm not one of the special ones! I've done something wrong, and you can't even tell me what it is! What's the point of me being here? Is it suffering you want? Because that's what I've got! You are NOT a loving God. You are a cruel God! Where is your love now when I need it the most?*

Fuck you!!

Retreating straight to my bedroom, I flopped myself on the bed and let the pillow soak up my tears. Seeing a counsellor left me feeling worse than I did before. With no one to confide in, no support from family, no future, no prospects, what was the point? I wondered whether suicide really was my only option. I'd tried life, but couldn't cope. Suicide would end my pain. I'd be free.

I looked around my room, wondering if I'd still be sitting here year after year, having achieved nothing and feeling the same. *Is this really how I want to spend my life? I'd managed twenty-one years of living. That's more than some.* If I'd tried everything and nothing worked, maybe this was God's way of telling me it's time to come home. *This is as good as it gets. Whatever your purpose was, you've achieved it.* My outbursts fell on deaf ears. I'd pleaded with God night after night and heard nothing in return except for reminders of my failures.

I rocked myself back and forward, trying to soothe myself. Sadness overwhelmed me as I cradled my knees tighter to my chest, knowing within me was a little girl who deserved to come out and live.

But crippling pain overshadowed any hope my inner child clung to.

At my lowest point, at peace to let go, a familiar voice emerged at the eleventh hour, like it had before. It whispered for a chance to live, to be heard. *But why? I'm ending this, I have to. There's no need to try and fail anymore. I won't put you through any more pain.*

We—my inner child and I—deserved to be free.

As I wrestled to silence her, she fought back with equal force, guiding me to hold on. Trying angrily to shut her down, I yelled out. "But how? How can I go on? What's the point? What possible reason would there be for me to hold on? I HAVE NOTHING! I have nothing left!"

"Please, please," I begged her. "Just leave me alone to die. We don't need to be here anymore. Go away! Let us go," I wailed.

Fatigued, her warm voice emerged beyond the tears. "*It's okay, Rebekah. There is a reason for this. A reason will be revealed in time. We are not yet done. This is not the end for us. It will get better, I promise you.*" I had no reason at all to believe her, but I did. As her words lingered, I wondered. Could I do this? Am I really strong enough?

As I searched my mind for evidence of this supposed strength, a stream of memories appeared where I showed courage, despite all opposition. I thought back to The House and all the times I was courageous enough to stand up for myself, knowing I'd be beaten for fighting back. I remembered all the times I'd spoken up at school, knowing people would hiss and avoid me. I remembered when I disclosed the abuse to Mum, knowing she might not believe me, yet I spoke up anyway.

Was there a reason these moments appeared so vividly now? Why show my courage when it only got me into trouble. *Yeah, I stood up countless times, but at what cost!? I'm sitting here alone. Courage doesn't get you anywhere!* I didn't want to be strong or courageous anymore. It sucked!

Too exhausted to battle my own thoughts, I fell asleep.

The next morning, I woke to the light of day, relieved my suffering had vanished with the rising sun. This time was different. The voice of reason's words from the night reverberated in my brain, only now I wondered about the purpose it kept repeating to me. I wondered why my memories showed me courage. What did that mean? Deeper questions emerged. Why do I keep suffering, particularly at night? Why do I feel so miserable? There must be a cause. What did courage have to do with all this? Was it time I figured it out?

My mind wandered to people in my life at university, friends, and strangers. How were they living? Did they wrestle with their own turmoil, keeping them up at night as well? Did they constantly want to end their own lives every time life got hard? Maybe the purpose in my suffering was to discover I had the power to change it, or at least figure out where it was coming from. I owed myself that much. Maybe it was time to find out why and get to the bottom of it. Maybe the reason examples of my courage appeared were to show me I possessed the courage to face whatever it was I hid from?

This realisation was one of the biggest epiphanies of my life thus far and I'd already had a few by now, smaller ones, easier to ignore or brush away when it suited me.

But this one was different.

It wasn't a Band-Aid to mask my problems. It wasn't a tactic to keep busy and avoid whatever problems I didn't want to deal with. This was a proactive solution that I hoped would end the unending suffering that tormented me—even more so at night. One that would help me learn to be a part of the world without the heavy load I carried trying to defeat me.

Whatever it was, the time to face the cause of my anguish was right now. I had to get it sorted.

It was time to seek professional help.

I phoned a local service in Rushton specialising in helping sexual assault survivors. It was the same service the police had suggested after I made my statement. Despite feeling apprehensive, given my last attempt, I forged ahead. Unfortunately, there was a waiting list, but I didn't hesitate to sign up when a vacancy arose.

In the meantime, I needed to be doing something. It wasn't good for me to sit idly. I knew that now.

I booked an appointment with my university counsellor to discuss other courses I could do instead of teaching. A course in Interior Design and Decoration piqued my interests. Given the many times I'd helped rearrange and decorate Mum's house, I thought it was a better option.

I travelled to Melbourne to enrol, but I immediately freaked out when I saw the student's designs on display as I walked into the arts department. There was so much flair and artistic vision. I wasn't sure I was *that* good. Mum's house was easy. This was so much more than what I was doing at home. The thought of being subpar to everyone's natural ability, was too much for me to bear. Thankfully, I discovered the course could be done by correspondence.

During the day I studied, burying my head in a book. It was where I felt comfortable, and it was an easy distraction from what I might face when darkness reappeared. I thought this renewed sense of purpose might keep the depression at bay, but as usual, with the night came the darkness. Every time the same pattern continued. Once again, rather than sit in my turmoil, I believed another location was the sure-fire solution I needed.

I packed my car and drove to Anna's house, four hours away. It was a good amount of distance between me and my troubles, and my relief at seeing Anna was immediate. I wouldn't ever have to do a lonely night again.

Within two days of moving, I was offered two hospitality jobs. I purposely took the night shift job so I could study during the day. Now my nights were occupied, my depressive episodes would disappear.

But an interesting thing occurred. The same emotional distress I experienced at night—the intense depression, feeling overwhelmed by where my life was taking me, big existential questions—surfaced in the daylight. I didn't understand this either. At Mum's it was easy to hide since she never checked in with me, but Anna would have noticed something was wrong if I stayed in my room all day. Now I'd have to force myself to go out just to pretend everything was fine.

This town had a branch of the same counselling service as Rushton. Maybe if I walked in and asked for an emergency appointment, they might give it to me.

"Um... Hello, is there someone I can speak to now please?" My voice shook.

"Do you have an appointment?" the receptionist asked.

"No, but I'm on the waiting list back home. I don't feel good today and I was hoping I could get an emergency appointment. Please?" I tried to hold back my tears.

"No, I'm sorry, but we also have a waiting list. Would you like me to register you on this list also?"

My heart sank. *I didn't want to be on another waiting list. I fucking need help right now!* "Please," I begged, "is there anyone I can see? I'm not coping. I'm really struggling, and I'm scared."

I'd never uttered those words aloud before. But I was past fearing judgement and embarrassment. I was in trouble and I knew it.

"I'm sorry," she continued, "but we don't have anyone available now, and our earliest appointment is eight weeks away."

"Eight weeks!" I screamed, tears pouring down my face. "I don't have eight weeks!"

Unfazed, she replied, "I'm so sorry, there's nothing we can do for you here."

I shuffled towards the waiting room and slumped into a chair.

The receptionist saw me and yelled from her desk, "What are you doing?"

I looked up, no longer caring about my tear-stained face. "I just need to sit here until I feel better."

"I'm sorry," she said. "But you can't do that. You don't have an appointment, so you'll need to leave now."

"Please," I sobbed. "I just need to sit somewhere safe until I feel okay."

"I'm sorry, but we don't allow that. You'll need to leave now."

My god, if I can't get help here, where else can I turn?

I grabbed my bag and slung it over my shoulder. I wiped my tears, dropped my head, and walked out the door. I paused on the footpath outside. I had absolutely no idea where to go.

Why was nothing working? Every time I tried to pick up the shattered pieces, it never stuck. I just ended back where I was: miserable, defeated, depressed. So what the fuck was wrong? My mood shifted to anger. *No one can say I haven't tried. I haven't just been sitting and wallowing. I moved away. I tried to go to university. I tried to get a job. I tried everything I could. Why can't I escape? Why do my problems, my fears, my anguish keep fucking following me? Why can't they disappear and leave me alone?*

I got into my car and sped off, determined to slam into the first tree that came along. I was done. Done with life. Done with trying.

"This is such bullshit," I screamed, pounding my fist into the steering wheel. *Take me out, so I don't feel a goddamn thing. Fuck you, God. This is not supposed to happen! I'm trying to make a life, and at every corner, you keep fucking me over!* I screamed and ranted as I pressed the pedal to the floor and picked up speed on the long, open road, waiting, hoping I'd lose control and finally end this!

But rage turned to sadness. Once I'd exhausted myself, I sobbed, crying out to God again. I begged for a sign that there was still hope.

What surfaced was not a voice from the clouds. It wasn't an inner voice, not even a sudden bolt of strength. This time, like a movie playing across the screen of my mind, something different appeared. An insight to a cycle I had not seen before. It was the same pattern each time; feeling lost, falling into depression, an urgency to escape or die, the eleventh-hour presence of some forgotten child within or sense of God's purpose for me.

I'd been doing this since I finished year 12. Now it was happening more frequently than ever. No wonder I was exhausted.

If this was something I needed to see, what could I do to break the cycle?

The following morning, I sat with Anna, but I didn't tell her the events of the day before. Anna knew I was troubled, but I never revealed just how far my dark thoughts wandered. I certainly never fully disclosed how much I wanted to die. And I didn't openly sob to her. I just couldn't let myself go that far, not even for her. She was the one person I couldn't have see me as a loser or a failure.

I realised I couldn't escape anymore. Moving to new places to avoid pain clearly wasn't working, nor did using work or study to distract myself. I'd believed my problems wouldn't follow me. Instantly morphing into a 'normal' person was fantasy, a delusion I'd created to avoid something deeper I didn't want to face.

Now it was blindingly obvious. The pain was *within* me, and it would continue to haunt me wherever I went. It wasn't going to go away just because I wanted it to.

The pattern was now obvious, but I didn't know how to resolve it, or even if it could be resolved, but it was time to break the cycle and confront the pain head on. There was simply nowhere else for me to go. I could stay in this exhausting loop and know eventually I *would* die, or I could figure out why I kept finding myself in this mess.

I knew in my heart that I deserved a chance at life and there was still some fight left in me. Each time I tried to give up, a new voice, a wave of courage, appeared. It couldn't be a coincidence.

So living became my only other option.

Maybe it was time to stop avoiding and running away?

I knew I could survive whatever truths came to the surface. It couldn't possibly be more painful than what I was already suffering through.

That seemed like a far better solution than facing even one more cycle of pain and anguish.

I was done with that.

Chapter 17

I moved back to Mum's to pursue counselling in earnest. This time my decision was made with clarity and with purpose. No obligation to change. I wanted it. My mission was to find out why life kept getting harder, not easier. Why darkness and silence brought up so much and why it was so hard to cope. Fortunately, it wasn't long before an opening for counselling became available. Whatever help I needed, I was ready to stay put and hear it.

I was assigned a counsellor I'll call Sally. She was a short lady, like me. In her early forties with short mousy brown hair, she swayed into the waiting room in her long beige pants and collared short-sleeve shirt to greet me. Her warm voice and casual conversations immediately made me feel at ease, and I got the feeling I was going to warm to Sally very quickly.

I approached my first session rather pragmatically. This was not about emotion but resolve. A quick fix solution to an array of problems. Why did I feel so awful, so lonely, so depressed, so hopeless? And why night-time in particular?

I showed up, not like a girl struggling to cope, but neatly dressed, with my hair tied back. I sat, legs crossed, hands loosely clasped together, straight-faced, and without a hint of the turmoil I'd experienced all morning.

Sally mirrored my poised position as she asked general questions. I answered with clarity and confidence. *This shouldn't be too hard.* I was already performing much better than last time. She etched slowly and casually into my childhood. *Here we go.* I played the game, as I thought I ought to, telling the story of an abused little girl abandoned by her mother. I spoke, still convincing her as much as myself the abuse was past tense. Sally nodding every so often and added, "That must have been hard", or "Sounds tough".

I shrugged it off and didn't allow emotion to reach the broken girl within I'd locked away years ago to protect. I quickened my pace, skipping past details, stopping any further opportunities for Sally to delve deeper.

The first few sessions I left feeling no different. My life hadn't changed. No further answers. What was the point? I'd replayed my history, the good, bad, and ugly. Why hadn't anything changed? I craved ending the day peacefully instead of with uncertainty. I yearned to wake up feeling different, lighter, happier, or at least content.

Counselling soon became a world the broken girl and I safely entered, just to be heard. Exclusive time giving life to my voice buried under shame and ridicule. In the beginning, opening up was difficult. Scarred by family I trusted, scared whether my truth would be ignored and mocked here as it had been there. How much could I reveal before my story would be questioned and discarded as lies?

With each session, Sally nudged a little further into my childhood. Questions that tugged at my heart. "How did that make you feel?" caused an immediate physiological reaction. My body froze, trying to shield myself, locking my wall in place. I kept my head down and avoided eye contact so she couldn't see the effort it was taking me to keep my emotions hidden. Not a single adult had asked me how I felt about anything that had happened to me.

Buried so deep, it felt like I had cut the emotion connected to it all, like it was a clinical retelling of a girl who'd lost her innocence to someone she should have been able to trust.

As more details of my story surfaced, the pressure to keep the fractured little girl safe behind my wall mounted. Cracks appeared. I fidgeted my fingers and shifted in my seat, restless and terrified. A hard lump swelled in my throat as I tried to swallow to keep the tears from surfacing. I couldn't let her out and risk being destroyed again. This was years of damage that a few hours could never undo. I was twenty years old now. I'd hidden her away for so long. The wall was strong. It had to be. With courage we could tell our story, but we couldn't let out the pain. It was too much. I wasn't sure if I could ever let her out ever.

What is the point to all of this? It didn't matter. No one's going to care anyway.

Pain wasn't relevant, but the details were. I wanted to be heard, to tell the story as it happened. Tell my side. I wanted Sally to believe me so she could tell me how to fix it so I could be fine. That's all I needed: an outlet and a little acknowledgement.

I never understood why Sally wanted more emotion from me. It didn't make sense. Every so often she'd ask me what I would have liked to have gotten from my mother. A question that instantly caused the back of my throat to ache from trying to swallow the gut-wrenching pain wanting to surge its way to the surface.

"Nothing," I'd reply as my mind flashed back to all the times she'd abandoned me. "Mum never did anything. That doesn't really matter, anyhow. That's not what I'm here for."

Sally sat still; her lips pressed together. Her gaze dropped a little. "What *would* it have meant to you if she'd protected you, Beck?" she asked softly.

There was no way I could answer that without bursting into tears.

Had Sally unearthed the core of my pain?

I took a deep breath and shifted in my seat. My voice cracked as I replied with subtle defensiveness. "Sally, it doesn't matter what I wanted. She didn't do anything. She never did anything. It doesn't matter. Can we please just move on to now?" I glanced at the clock, praying our time was nearly up so I could bolt out the door. The dark cynic in me wondered whether Sally enjoyed watching me struggle.

She called my reluctance to connect to my emotions disassociation.

I called it irrelevant.

I warmed to Sally despite the truths she revealed that I may not have been ready to accept. Like my schoolteachers, she nurtured my need to be cared for, to be visible to someone. As I slowly emerged from my shell, revealing snippets of my personality, she chuckled at my light-hearted jokes and quick wit I'd purposely start each session with to ease into the tough stuff I knew was coming. The beginnings of the sessions were my favourite part. She witnessed a side of me most people didn't. I often wished the sessions could all be light-hearted. I'd largely abandoned the Interior Design course I'd started, so appointments with Sally were the only company I had outside of Mum's house.

On rare occasions, I was given a substitute counsellor in Sally's absence. I hated it. I'd preferred to have missed my appointment altogether. The substitute's approach was much more direct. There was no rapport, no gentle tiptoeing into the deep end. Just straight into it. She pushed me into areas I wasn't ready for and, if I wasn't coping, I'd be left high and dry without any safety net for my emotions after the session. Sally was gentler and would guide me through difficult topics with care and compassion. I knew she'd only let me go as far as I could handle. She noticed when I was comfortable or strong enough to tread into traumatic areas and would slowly lead me in, or skirt around the edges, before drawing my attention away to ease me back into the present moment. I trusted her guidance.

One day I arrived at my appointment to learn Sally was absent. The receptionist, seeing my disheartened look, assured me this counsellor was very competent. I shrugged and dragged my feet to the waiting room.

There'd be no light-hearted banter, no chitchat today. No rapport. Whatever layers of my wall that had fallen away with Sally reattached as I reverted to protective mode. *Just give them the basics, Rebekah, something to chew on for the session.*

The counsellor, who appeared over-dressed in her black suit jacket and matching skirt, asked how I was in a dead-pan voice, like she was following a script and didn't want to be there any more than I did.

I mirrored her apathetic tone. "Yep, great." *That's why I'm here, because I'm just fucking fine.*

"So, what's been happening? How are you getting by?" she continued.

Okay, fine, if this is how the session's going to go, let's keep it all about what I'm up to. Let me bring you up to date!

I sighed apathetically, ready to roll out my own scripted response, "I deferred my teaching degree last year because I kept crying. I tried to find another career path, but I got bored, tried to move away, and that didn't work. So I'm here to try and sort through some stuff so I can go back and finish my teaching degree."

I leaned back, hoping I'd satisfied her inane questions.

She leaned forward. "So you finished high school then?"

"Um, yes." I wondered where her question was leading.

"Oh." Her eyebrows raised. "So you're doing a teaching degree now?"

I frowned, trying to comprehend her words. "Yes, well I was, why?"

"Well," she said, relaxing back in her chair. "Most people like you don't finish high school; and they certainly don't get a degree!"

Angered by her gross assumptions, I unglued my tongue from the roof of my mouth. "Okay, why people *"like me"*? What am I meant to do then?" My fury brewed.

Inside, I exploded into a tirade. *How fucking dare you? People like me! What's that supposed to mean? What, because I was abused, I have no right to a future like everyone else? I'm not supposed to do anything with my life because I was abused? What AM I supposed to do? You just want me to be some loser of society so it looks better on your reports for whoever reads these things? I'm just a no hoper because of my past? Really? How dare you automatically assume I'm destined for nothing. What kind of hope is that for people like us!*

My whole body stiffened, trying to remain calm.

She quickly tried to backtrack. "Oh no, I didn't mean it like that. I just meant it's unusual to see someone who's been through what you've been through, doing what you've done, and I think it's great. You must be really strong."

I took it as a backhanded compliment, still insulted by her degradingly low expectation of 'people like me'. That's all I kept hearing. *People like me? Weirdos? Losers? Pfft! How dare you pigeonhole me as a loser, destined for nothing?* She might not have said it, but that's what I fixated on.

I spoke and tried to keep my tone even. "Well, I don't know what is expected of me. I'm just doing what I want to do. I don't want my past to dictate my future. I'm trying to make something of myself, so this doesn't end up being the story of my life. Why can't I achieve what other people have achieved, simply because I didn't have the best start? How does that make me different and incapable?"

But as she tried to back away from her statement, surprisingly her words became even more absurd. "It's okay. I understand. I just don't usually see people who've been through what you have until they're at least sixty."

Woah! Was this conversation even happening? I wanted to scream and tell her to fuck off with her bullshit. I wanted to run out the door. I was so furious with her short-sighted ignorance. She may as well have written *No Hoper* on a big neon poster and tacked it on my back.

Though rattled with rage, I calmly replied, "What am I meant to do?" I threw back at her. "I'm here because I don't want this to be my future. I'd rather deal with it now than screw up the next forty years of my life. I want help now. Is that okay?"

She mentioned how remarkable it was I had such insight into my life at my young age. As she rambled, I tuned out. I resented her bullshit labels and ageism. Did she really think being abused meant I couldn't learn to live a normal life? I couldn't strive to achieve what others had because of my past? How were people encouraged to heal if these were the opinions and beliefs held by so-called professionals?

I wasn't doing this for her! I was doing this for my life. In my mind, there was absolutely nothing I couldn't achieve. I just needed help to figure out how to actually make it happen when all I wanted to do was stay in bed and not face the world.

And if I couldn't make it, I at least had to try. I'd done the shitty side of life. I knew what was on that path. But there had to be a flip side, like two sides of a coin. I had to at least explore the possibility that perhaps I didn't have all the answers, answers that could give me a better life.

If I learned pain, couldn't I learn joy?

I learned depression, couldn't I learn happiness?

If I learned what it was to be abandoned, could I also learn to relate and connect? In the present, I was a product of my past, but now I had an opportunity to change. And I wanted that chance to try.

I left the session angry. Did other counsellors feel the same way as this one? Did Sally? I had to know someone believed in me. There was no way I'd continue with therapy if she didn't.

Thankfully, Sally was back for my next appointment. She quickly noticed I wasn't my usual self, playing short with the normal chit chat. "Is everything okay, Rebekah?"

My eyes burned, knowing the tears weren't far away. Rarely, if ever, was that question asked of me. It was hard to hear, and not because I didn't like it. But for once it mattered to someone if I was okay and I liked the sound of it. But was it sympathy? Empathy? Something else?

Sally was the only person I'd let into my shattered world. The question I knew I needed to ask sat on the tip of my tongue. I couldn't let on how important it was, fearing I'd fall apart if her answer echoed Mum's abandonment. I warned the girl within not to get her hopes up. *It doesn't matter, Rebekah. Just keep it casual. You don't need her approval. Remember, you didn't get it from your mum or your dad, and you don't need it now.*

The girl within pushed, begging me to ask.

My voice trembled as I spoke. "Do you think I'm capable of achieving anything I want? Do you think it should matter what happened to me?" As I blurted out the questions, I nervously fidgeted my fingers, looking anywhere else I could to avoid eye contact.

Please let someone believe in me. I just need one person. Please. Don't let me down. I can't do this without someone to believe in me.

As I glanced up, our eyes met briefly, before I quickly looked down again.

"Rebekah, I absolutely believe in you. You are more than capable. You are such a strong and courageous young lady who's willing to be here and talk about your incredibly difficult life. I admire your strength and bravery in being here. You have so much to offer, and I absolutely believe you can do anything you set your mind to."

It was everything I'd ever wanted to hear. The little girl within collapsed to the floor. Tears spilled from my eyes. *There you go*, I whispered. *We have one person. Finally, someone believes in us.*

This was step one. Confirmation I needed to hear. One step on the road to recovery and a chance to let someone in who I was sure wouldn't hurt me. This would allow the girl within to slowly heal.

I kept Sally's words close, a wide smile beaming across my face whenever I replayed them in my head. Her belief fed the part of me starved of love. I didn't know if I'd ever fully believe her, but I knew hearing those words gave me hope I hadn't known.

Six months of counselling revealed how the abuse was only a small part of a bigger problem. More than emotional neglect, the role my parents played, my family's dysfunctional culture, were all interrelated and slowly everything made more sense. I did not understand life. Mum didn't have answers. Our trust was so permanently damaged, I didn't bother to ask her anything. I assumed I was supposed to know how to act, how to solve problems, how to approach challenges, and how to make decisions. But it was so much more than the art of navigating life itself. More than being handed a compass. I realised safety, worth, and connection were not things we were born with. These biological needs were woven like threads through repeated experiences and relationships with our primary caregivers.

No wonder I felt lost. Both my parents had ripped the safety net from beneath my feet and left me hanging. I had no grounding in a safe and secure world.

For all the times at school I thought kids 'knew' what to say and do, I could now see that they were being shepherded through life by their parents. They were having conversations about life, problems, friendships, and their likes and dislikes. They had someone to go to for help with boys and crushes and cat fights at school. They were given opportunities to connect, building a strong foundation to go out into the world. Most kids had their parents to fall back on, unlike me.

In many ways, I surpassed my mother's knowledge of life. I had not had the steady implicit or explicit understanding I was capable, worthy, valued, through the experiences I faced and overcame. Mum never reinforced that I was loved no matter what I did. I wasn't taught to get up and try again, no matter how many times I fell. I'd been left to try to join the dots on my own. My resulting picture was a mess rather than a masterpiece, the solving of a puzzle.

Each session with Sally revealed how Mum removed herself from her primary role of caring and nurturing me. That I had every right to expect she would protect and support me. That's what mothers do. Sometimes it seemed like Mum just gave up, leaving me to fend for myself, packing my own lunch, frequently cooking my own dinner. She did all the basics to provide food and shelter, but the massive gap in between was entirely up to me to figure out. But how could I?

There were no deliberate opportunities to build a relationship. No cleverly disguised 'Mum and daughter time' passed off as clothes shopping trips or casual walks to chat about stuff that kids ask about life and look to their parents for answers. No moments to sit on the couch together and bring up things that weighed on my young mind. Not even coming together at the dinner table to share stories from our day that might have helped me understand things about life and difficulties and how to handle them.

Because, as I discovered, Mum didn't deal with life. She brushed problems under the carpet. Or worse yet, pretended they didn't exist, or hoped someone else would deal with it for her—like her dad. She'd run from The House to him, and he'd rescued us. Sort of.

It was little wonder I expected life to just happen and work itself out.

Mum never imposed any boundaries as to how I spoke to her or others. I was never pulled aside and reprimanded for my behaviour, even when Mum witnessed it. So I got away with a lot. Respect was never expected, and consequently, not given. If I didn't want to do something, I'd refuse, regardless of how it affected others. If I didn't want to go to school, or I hadn't finished an assignment, I'd order Mum to ring the school with an excuse for my absence or to seek an extension. And she did.

The number of ways my parents failed me mounted so high that in some sickening way of looking at it, being abused no longer shocked me. Not if I saw where the trail of neglect began. They had put me in that situation and then had done nothing about it. Feeling lost and clueless made perfect sense. It perfectly explained the world I floated along in and why nothing stuck. Why everything seemed too hard.

Mum's neglect shaped my whole life. I was the person I was because of her.

Now I could release the guilt and shame surrounding a false identity that wasn't me.

The walls within could slowly come down.

It isn't my fault where I am today.

It isn't my fault I'm in this mess. There is a reason.

I was not to blame.

This helped me to free myself and feel the raw pain. I could grieve for the abuse, for the loss of my innocence, the loss of Mum's attachment and parenting. Knowing for once I damn well deserved to have had parents who would stick up for me, to protect me and keep me safe. It wasn't a privilege I needed to earn. It was a child's goddamn right, and it was something I should never have gone without.

Once I gave myself and the girl within a chance to emerge without fear, more tears flowed. I'd been in this position before, but this time was different. Before, I'd not known why I felt so hopeless and why the tears wouldn't stop.

Now I knew why.

This time, release came with an end in sight. All the years of built-up pain, agony, and anguish were now purging from my soul. I gave myself permission to let go of everything that weighed me down. And as pieces of the wall crumbled away, for the first time in my life, it allowed something different to enter: love. Self-love. To fill my soul with what I needed and what I deserved. To give myself the love I'd missed out on. The little girl within deserved to be loved too, and now I could release her slowly, showering her with love instead of shame.

Now the process of healing could finally begin.

Chapter 18

Once we'd left The House, my strict, religious life all but ended too—much to my relief—except for a brief stint shortly after, when Mum took us kids to church, probably out of habit. The handful of times we went, the experience was so different from what I knew. The children gathered in a separate room to sing happy songs and colour religious pictures while listening to the teacher promise us that He was this happy, loving God. This wasn't the same God I knew at all. My God taught me I was naughty, a bad child. My God was a Supreme Critic, a real killjoy. When Mum stopped taking us to Sunday School, I never knew the reason, and I never asked. I was glad to erase that part of my life.

When I was eighteen, religion came back into my life again. My friend Anna converted from Catholicism to Christianity. Christianity focused more on a relationship with Jesus, rather than Mary. That was the only difference I understood.

Anna wasn't new to religion, though. She'd come from a Catholic family who attended church every Sunday and went to a Catholic school. Their house displayed Jesus and Mary statues. Plaques with religious verses hung on the walls. I purposely ignored all the religious symbols dotted around the house whenever I visited. The mere sight of a Jesus statue, or a woven verse that read "God is Love" reminded me too much of The House. *God is Love! Yeah, right. How the hell do they believe that crap?* I'd always hoped Anna's mother, Jill, would never ask about my faith, uncertain I'd be able to hide my contempt for their 'loving' God.

Anna was so excited by her newfound faith that she repeatedly tried to convince me to believe as she did. While I respected her new beliefs, I wanted nothing to do with her God. There was nothing freeing in her God's cruel, judgemental, perverse so-called love. I was constantly beaten, punished, isolated, and abused beneath her God's eyes. Scars remained and the pain was still raw.

His teachings robbed me of my childhood, my innocence. His veil of unworthiness draped around me wherever I went, at school, my friends, and my non-existent self-esteem. It was always an underlying factor in why I felt so undeserving, because God and his bastard servants constantly reminded me that I wasn't good enough.

The more she spoke of Him, the more resentful I became. Couldn't she understand why I hated God so much? It was okay for her. She hadn't been destroyed in His name like I had. "A loving God would never hurt you," she'd say. It was only because I trusted Anna the most and knew her intentions were genuine that I decided to give her church a chance. At the very least, she'd back off if I tried and it wasn't for me.

Just entering the church gates took me straight back, like I was six again, walking the path towards the doors of damnation like I used to at The House. As if on cue, my shame, my imperfections, and unworthiness surfaced like a rash. I felt myself cowering before I'd even entered, shrinking inward to avoid being God's target here as I'd been elsewhere. Why was I voluntarily walking into condemnation? I spoke nothing of the anguish I felt inside.

Inside, people gathered before the service, filling time with small talk, laughing, and chatting. *Why were they so happy?* Perhaps they'd already paid for their sins? I wondered what had they done to be accepted? Maybe they didn't screw up as much as I did?

The service hadn't even started, and already I wanted to bolt. I hated church and everything it represented. Why had I put myself in this position just to appease Anna?

I didn't run. I reluctantly followed Anna. I sighed heavily as I sat, ready and waiting for the finger pointing to begin. For someone to label me as a sinner who was unworthy.

As soon as the pastor began, I dropped my head and tuned out, just like I used to do. I couldn't wait to leave. Something distracted me from withdrawing into myself. It was the pastor speaking. His voice sounded warm and charismatic. Bewildered, I looked up. He smiled as he spoke to the congregation, sharing a story that drew parallel to the theme of the day's service. *Is this a church service?* I wasn't trusting it. My face stiffened to disinterest rather than outright hatred. I held my scepticism and distrust close to the surface, ready to pounce on the bullshit he was about to spin.

It didn't come.

The pastor spoke calmly as if he was speaking to a dear friend as he gently led us from one story to another, often pausing midway to laugh or to throw out a question encouraging deep reflection. His stories were delightful, compelling, and sincere. What was this? Was he luring us in before he damned us?

I looked around the room, waiting for someone to admonish the crowd. But there was no such person. This was nothing like anything I'd experienced before in the name of God. I kept looking around, waiting for something else to happen, something negative or bad. And yet everyone's attention was glued to the pastor and his gentle words. There were no shameful looks, scared expressions, or fear. Their faces were relaxed and there was an occasional nod, almost like they were grateful to be hearing his sermon.

This is not church as I know it.

How did people welcome God into their lives and look so happy about it? It raised more questions, which only stirred up more resentment and anger. *So you love them more? What did I ever do?* I pouted like a petulant child, now feeling even more undeserving of His love. The happiness of those around me magnified my insecurities. In that moment, I hated Him more than ever.

Leaving the service, I vowed to never return, no matter how many times Anna would try to persuade me. I couldn't go back to a judgemental place where my shame felt amplified. It was too much. The pain was just too raw. My resistance still didn't stop Anna from talking non-stop about God, more bible passages, more stories, and healing for the broken.

"But I'm not broken," I'd say, and if I was, it was God's fault.

The more Anna talked of God's love, the more I wondered if another version of His love did exist. Her incessant preaching bothered me, but there was something about her chats that niggled at me too. That peeved me even more. Was it possible I was not taught the truth? Would Anna work so hard to convince me if there wasn't something more to it?

I decided to attend church again, but this time with an open mind, without the lens of past experiences clouding my judgement. I observed the congregation more intently. I'd hear the pastor's message as if I were hearing for the first time. Was he offering His love, or was he about to condemn us all?

Without bias, his message echoed grace, forgiveness, and acceptance. There was no condemnation. No shame. No punishment. No angry voices or threats of punishment. No one forced to lie down on the carpet and beg for forgiveness. Most importantly, there were no conditions attached. There were people from all walks of life here, too. People brought their pain, their torment, and their imperfections here for release, for resolution, for healing. Not to be punished, but to be free from them.

But could all be forgiven? Could all shame and brokenness really be re-moved? Why would God take all my damage? Why would he do that for me? I had nothing to offer in return. I hadn't earned any of this. All I felt was shame for the abuse and endless punishment. I was hurt and scarred, damaged to the core. How could I trust that this God would freely accept me as I am?

I wasn't ready to offer myself to this God, yet a shift in my mind was occurring. This experience was slowly proving vastly different, loving yet terrifying at the same time. Going to church more regularly, I became more open to what was being taught and this different ideology. To surrender myself into a community of people willing to accept me, enticed me. But years of damage taught me to protect and keep myself guarded. To not trust those who said they cared until they could unconditionally prove it.

People openly wept and comforted one another quite often at church. How did they do that? I'd fall apart if anyone tried to hug me. I couldn't show how damaged I was or allow myself to be vulnerable, to open up or to weep for my past. To attempt to release my pain would be petty, anyway. It didn't matter. It shouldn't matter, because the abuse was over, and I couldn't let it be a factor in why I had been so broken. *Why would you openly weep in front of everyone? That's weak.*

Usually, a soppy tear-jerker service prompted a dash for the door. Someone seeing me tear up was too great a risk. I could act apathetic for a brief moment, but if I stayed and mingled, I might come undone. The people who broke down during the service appeared just fine after. They weren't embarrassed by their tears at all. Other people walked past them and offered a gentle touch and sometimes an invitation to speak privately over a cup of tea.

Their vulnerability was embraced rather than scorned.

Was it okay to be vulnerable? This space suggested it was. To depend on someone? To be comforted? How was I to know people if would accept my particular past? Would they use it against me? Would they abandon me as my mother had when I spoke up? I wanted to know more, but I was too afraid.

Sometimes I pretended to begrudge going when Anna invited me, but secretly, church became another place like counselling, where I was accepted, troubles and all. A place to at least dwell within a community that seemed to care for people. A place where, if I dared, I could let my pain surface. I wasn't ready yet, but just knowing I could, comforted me. I couldn't risk trusting in a God who'd already proved he could break me. Instead, I'd wait until church finished and run out, my tears drenching my shirtfront on the drive home.

But I couldn't hold it all in forever.

On this one occasion, Anna and I went together. I smiled, greeting people as we took our seat. The first song played. The songs were familiar by now. Some were fast and upbeat, designed to raise the energy or lift the mood that a slow Sunday brought. Others were slow, reaching for our deepest emotions. I learned to hold it together for the slow ones, purposely breathing more and focusing on the words rather than on the intensity of emotions trying to push their way to the surface.

But this time was different.

As the melodic voices of the congregation filled the room, I became so wrapped up in the song, I forgot to keep my heart in check and my tears flowed without warning. Instead of trying to hide or flee, I extended my hand to Anna and looked to her, blubbering mess and all. For the first time, I was unashamed to openly cry, for strangers to see me and for someone to comfort me. Dropping the weight of old teachings, my upbringing, my shame, the constant earbashing that I was bad. For all the times my needs were ignored, I let go, shedding the layers that held my pain captive. A warm sensation tingled through me as if draped by a warm blanket. The realisation something bigger than me existed became a major catalyst in my healing journey.

Everything I'd been taught about God changed as I discovered He was love and not control. He never expected perfection. God's truth revealed the deceit and perversion of my paternal grandfather's lies and debauchery. His ways were never of God but of his own sick and twisted agenda. My new faith comforted and guided me through hard, lonely times from that day forward, knowing someone greater than me cared.

I dedicated my life to church, seeking friendships and a sense of family within the community. Church became another healing space for guidance and support I'd missed out on from my own parents. I bought Christian-related books to further understand how God worked in all aspects of my life. I soaked up the teachings from pastors and bible groups, learning as much as I could.

People I hardly knew welcomed me into their homes, giving me so much I realised I needed. A place to belong.

From the moment I met Jo at a new church in 2001, I immediately noticed how at ease she made me feel. Her tall frame and genuine smile radiated warmth that rippled throughout the church room. Her dark, wavy brown hair and the black lounge wear clothes she often wore were in complete contrast to her colourful and charismatic personality.

Every Sunday, I found myself scanning the room trying to spot her and to find a way to speak to her. From a distance, I could see people gathering around her, smiling, hanging off her every word, before a chorus of laughter echoed loudly. She was funny and light-hearted and so genuinely interested in people that it wasn't long before I felt comfortable and safe enough to drop my guard quicker than I normally would, to reveal my sarcasm and quick wit, a trait she took a fondness to, as she laughed along with me.

The more time I spent around Jo and watched how compassionate she was to complete strangers, nodding her head while people poured their hearts out to her, the more I wanted to learn how she related to people the way she did.

By now, I'd had a lot of counselling to process the abuse and abandonment I went through. I'd had time to deal with the pain of what it all meant.

Now I wanted to understand how to behave and relate to people without the trauma behaviours I'd picked up. Without my overbearing judgement of people and rules and criticism. At twenty-five years of age, I was finally ready to shed everything I saw that I was in response to my upbringing. I wanted better basic social skills, to be more empathetic and understand people. I wanted to be someone other people wanted to be around. I was done feeling sorry for myself and blaming the world for my problems.

I had enough self-awareness now to see that my behaviours weren't my fault. It was all survival and protective behaviours. The person I had become was distrusting and demanding. I didn't deal with conflict well. I slammed doors or gave people the silent treatment until I got my way. I played mind games and had a bank of manipulative tactics I'd used throughout school and beyond. I'd lost friends behaving like this and struggled to make new ones. I was narrow-minded, harsh, judgemental, and overly critical of others. My ways were immature, childish, and very underdeveloped, not at all how I wanted to behave now. I was way too uptight, too black and white. My views were narrow-minded, and I constantly squawked at other perspectives, like they didn't matter. I didn't like who I was. I wanted to behave like Jo. People liked her and I wanted to be liked like she was.

When I approached Jo, asking if she'd be willing to mentor me and teach me how to be more relatable to people, she humbly accepted if I agreed to a few conditions. I wasn't allowed to storm off, slam doors, play the silent treatment, or hang up on her if we had any kind of disagreement.

Around Jo, I was a curious observer. I watched everything she did and banked so many questions. How do you know what to say to people? How do you keep yourself composed when someone clearly deserved a set-down when they said something I thought was so idiotic? Rarely did I see Jo frustrated by trivial things. She just seemed so level-headed at times when I'd typically go bat shit crazy in the same situation. I wasn't afraid to ask these questions, even if it seemed completely obvious. I didn't just want to know; I wanted to understand so I could learn to behave more like her.

The journey to personal development was slow, with many hiccups, childish tantrums and stuff ups along the way. Most of the time, my emotions got the better of me, and I reacted aggressively if I only saw things as black and white, right or wrong. I'd still escalate issues to be so much bigger than what they were. I still judged people as harshly as I judged myself. I'd fire up at the slightest injustices against me, exploding into anger at the absurdity of people's ways that didn't align with my own narrow views. Like the time I failed my driving test and rang the transport department and let 'em have it, insulting the tester for daring to fail me. I pissed off so many people at the local office that I had to wait six months to go for my license again.

And yet, as I ranted about life's unfairness, trying to justify my angry outbursts, Jo remained calm, nodding and listening, never criticising. She'd gently persuade me to see another point of view outside of my tunnel vision of the world. She helped me to understand people; she gave me books to read to understand my own behaviours and where they may have stemmed from. She gave more specific strategies to solve a particular conflict, to learn how to relate with and to people.

There were many times Jo needed to be firm with me, reminding me of the conditions I agreed to. But sometimes it was so challenging I'd revert back to old habits, yell and curse at her, as I stormed off and slammed the door behind me. Or I'd just be plain rude and completely ignore her, not even saying hello. After all, that's what Mum always did. I resented having to have a conversation and talk through problems, when all I wanted to do was run away and avoid facing the issues. But Jo wasn't having it. She'd wait until I'd calmed down from my ranting and raving, before explaining her reasoning and remind me that she'd no longer mentor me if I kept behaving this way.

"Beck, this is what you said you wanted," she'd say.

Despite it being so hard, I knew this was for my own good. Jo's mentoring was a time of tremendous personal growth. Of intensely shifting unwanted behaviours and beliefs I was attached to for so long. With her mentoring, and my own reading beyond her recommendations, I started to learn about healthy boundaries, respecting other's opinions, learning to listen instead of reacting, and how to relate to people and deal with conflict. I learned to come down from my moral high ground, to be more open-minded, more understanding, that my perspective wasn't the only one. She helped me to notice my own strengths and the likeable parts of me. Jo guided me to use my voice, that part of me willing to speak up, but to use it in a way that wasn't divisive or hurtful towards others. I'm not so sure anyone else would have had the patience to help me as Jo did. I was so stubborn at times.

Jo is one of the people I attribute my recovery to in shaping me into the person I am today. Being taught these skills growing up would have made the next part of my journey so much easier.

Chapter 19

On the morning of the 5th of January, sunlight streamed through every pinhole in my old, weathered curtain. Half asleep, I heard an ambulance speed past, its siren piercing and loud. It wasn't unusual. Mum's house edged the main road, so I often heard sirens go past from my front bedroom. Usually I ignored it, only to briefly wonder what happened.

I dragged myself out of bed to an empty house and started making coffee.

The phone rang. It was Mum's sister, Samantha.

"Hello, Rebekah," she said.

"Hi," I replied, intrigued by her early call.

"Um... Rebekah, Uncle Harry's been killed."

My jaw dropped. My mind spun so quickly; my vision caused everything to blur. "Wha—?" I must still be dreaming. I pinched myself so hard, it hurt.

I screamed down the phone, "NO, NO, NO! What do you mean?"

Samantha refused to explain over the phone, suggesting I drive to Nana and Pop's house, where everyone had gathered.

I jumped in the car and raged to my windshield. What happened to my uncle? Killed meant he was dead, but that wasn't possible. I tried to resolve it in my head, but I couldn't. What the fuck is going on? I fucking saw him three days ago. Tears streamed down my face as I recollected our last moment together. It was still fresh in my mind.

Three days earlier, I'd driven over to Uncle Harry's house, picking Mum up along the way. After completing my Bachelor of Teaching in 1999, he was the first person I wanted to share my achievements with. I knew he would be proud of me. He'd always encouraged me to do my best and strive to finish what I started. When I deferred eighteen months into my degree, he didn't hold back in letting me know he wasn't happy with my decision.

He never knew the real reason at the time. How could I tell him it was because of his father that I struggled to show up to class? How could I tell him that all I wanted to do was die to stop the pain?

"What can you do with half a degree?" he'd said when I told him.

I knew he was right, but at the time I couldn't hold myself upright and concentrate on studies at the same time.

Now, eighteen months later, I could proudly tell him I'd done it. I finished what I'd started, just like he'd taught me to do.

While driving, I vividly recalled the way he used to greet me. "How ya goin', Ugly?" That was his pet nickname for me. A sign of endearment.

Never in a million years would I have ever thought that I'd never him hear say that to me again.

When I told him I'd finished my degree, a wide smile beamed across his face.

"Congratulations. That's great. I'm glad you decided to go back and finish what you started. And now you have a degree that no one can ever take away from you. A degree you've earned, and you can now do what you want with. Now, what are you going to do?"

I couldn't help but smile as I remembered Uncle Harry dive straight into proactive mode. I hoped to bathe in his glowing praise for a little bit longer, but that's not what he was like. Strike while the iron's hot was his motto. It was advice I wouldn't get from anyone else. Sharing his wisdom was his way of showing how much he loved me and wanted the best for me. And I soaked it up.

Early that same evening as my aunty, Mum, and I sat in the lounge room, Uncle Harry picked up a guitar and treated us all to a session of music and singing. A passion so clearly laced through everything he did and was proudly displayed around his modest home. The walls were lined with cassette tapes and old records. His stereo took centre stage amongst the tower-sized speakers, while the tv I rarely saw him watch collected dust.

While he played and sung, I asked if he'd consider teaching me the guitar, despite worrying my short fingers would ever reach the strings. He warmly agreed, assuring I'd pick it up in no time.

As the night drew to a close, he and my aunty walked Mum and I out to the car. I wound down my window to thank him for his encouragement and capture his proud smile on his face. "Congratulations on finishing your degree. You'll be fine, kid. You've done the work, now it's time to get out there. You can do this!" he said. These would be the last words I'd ever hear him speak.

Now as I pulled into my grandparents' driveway, somewhere I never thought I'd ever be again, I wiped the tears from my face and took a brief moment to compose myself.

Summoning all my courage, I finally got out of the car and walked slowly toward John, his eldest son, who was standing on the veranda smoking a cigarette. Not knowing what I would say, I took a deep breath and tried to hold back the tears. I wanted to be strong for him. He stood frozen with a long vacant stare, like he had no idea what had just hit him. Everything seemed so unreal. Nothing made sense. He leant forward and buried his face into my shoulder and wailed as I held him tight.

"I'm sorry. I'm so, so sorry!" I cried with him.

He pulled away and looked up to the sky, shaking his head in disbelief, before letting out a heavy sigh. "Dad was run over by his own ute."

Uncle Harry had stopped at the local tip to dump some rubbish. He'd left his car running without the handbrake on. As he threw the rubbish in the skip bin, the car slowly rolled forward. Without thinking, he jumped in front of the car to stop it but lost his footing on the loose gravel, pinning him under the wheel and crushing him.

His death puzzled me. I tried to imagine the scenario. I had more questions as I tried to accept the truth, and yet I couldn't.

I looked towards the front door, wondering what the hell I was about to walk into.

Ten years had passed since I'd been here. So many memories sat on the other side of that door. What would my reception be? Would my grandfather publicly banish me? My stomach churned as I turned the round wooden handle.

Entering the house, an eerie silence draped the air as I looked around a room full of stunned faces. The same roast smell I remembered from Nana's Sunday night roast dinners wafted through the air as if it had absorbed into the walls. My attention, as though directed unconsciously, looked straight ahead to a familiar chair in the dining room. The one where Pop used to sit me on his knee as a little girl and molest me. Now Nana sat silently while Pop sat across from her. He too was dazed. I couldn't help but remember sitting there as a young girl, and a sick feeling rippled through me.

I quickly turned to my left to see my aunty slumped in the recliner, her chin rested on her fist. A vacant stare across her face as well. Seeing her like that confirmed the truth.

My uncle was really gone.

I wanted to throw myself at her and openly sob for our loss. *Does crying and pleading with God bring someone back? Can time be rewound? Can we do this morning again? What if my uncle knew how much I loved him? Could he come back?*

I stared at her, knowing I had to say something, but what? What could I possibly say that would make any fucking difference? I couldn't openly wail while everyone sat in silence. I swallowed hard to hold back my tears. I knelt and hugged her. I mustered up the courage to whisper, "I'm so sorry.

He was such a good man." I pulled back and watched as she continued to sit, frozen with disbelief.

A few hours later, I left my grandparents' home exhausted, retreating to my room and lighting a cigarette. There were still so many unanswered questions looping my mind. I had no idea where Mum was. But like any other tragedy this family incurred, silence, avoidance, and denial were still her chosen method. Don't talk about it. We don't do that.

Pretending I was fine when I wasn't now felt more uncomfortable. I'd much prefer to talk about it rather than letting it fester in my head and my heart. So I rang my closest friend, Anna, knowing she'd make me feel better. She always did. She'd always been a friend I could rely on.

When her mum, Jill, answered with a cheery hello, I burst into tears. Jill listened while my grief poured out, offering wisdom and comfort I wouldn't get from my own mother. I leaned on Jill for answers while I struggled to comprehend God's hand in this. I questioned why God would take away someone I loved and needed in my life. I reflected on the last time we'd caught up, wondering if I'd blown my last opportunity to tell him I loved him.

"Would he know, Jill?" I asked while I sobbed.

Warmly, she encouraged me to view our last meeting as a divine blessing, a special way of saying goodbye in the most perfect way. "Cherish the memories of your uncle and know he will never be too far away," she told me.

It was everything I needed to hear.

In the weeks and months after Uncle Harry's death, I still struggled to come to terms with it. Beyond my grief, so many things in my life showed big gaping holes without him. After all, our relationship had come full circle since the abuse was revealed to the family. He, like Pop, had sworn never to speak to me again for making such an outrageous statement against his beloved father. But as time went on, my uncle slowly came back into my life again. We'd reconnected almost like nothing had ever happened. I was puzzled at first, but I was so happy to have him back in my life again, I never dared to question it or raise the topic, ever.

Every time I walked down the city streets, I was reminded that I'd never spot him a mile away in his trademark jeans, grey jumper, sneakers, and pilot-shaped sunglasses he always wore perched on his thick wavy hair. Never again would we pass each other in the street, pausing to throw sarcastic, insulting comments at each other and then chuckling as we went on our way.

Every time I'd hear his favourite band, the Eagles play on the radio, I'd burst into tears; while slowly over time, I would laugh whenever I heard the Bee Gees playing. Remembering when Mum and Jack married, Harry arrived looking like the fourth member of the Bee Gees, sporting flared pants, a brown leather jacket, and his trademark wrist bangles. The bangles, I was told, kept his arthritis at bay while his pilot-shaped sunglasses held down his thick, black wavy hair, which he purposely kept long to cover his Dumbo-size ears.

As soon as my uncle swayed into the room, I snickered from across the room. "Hey, when are the Bee Gees touring? Are you gonna sing *Stayin Alive*?" Pointing a finger in the air, I mimicked John Travolta's Saturday Night Fever dance moves.

Memories were all I had now. Memories of the past that, unless I held on to and reminded myself of every day, would slowly fade, and I wasn't ready for that. I wasn't sure I would ever be.

The prospect of living life without going to him for advice, knowing I couldn't rely on him when my car broke down on the side of the road and he'd tow me twenty kilometres home, was a harsh reality I didn't want to face.

There were very few people who showed me I mattered. The way we joked and laughed was special. How was I going to get through life without him and his presence reminding me I was important?

I couldn't do life without him. I needed someone to keep assuring me how good I was doing. I didn't have the strength on my own. My uncle validated my strength and my worth. Who would I go to now? Where would I get that reassurance from? Without him, my strength, my courage, my ability to keep going, to finish something, might not exist.

To imagine the rest of my life without my uncle devastated me. I threw up a barrage of questions to God, searching for a reason, a purpose to his death. I wanted to understand the timing. How could I have been led to this point, to accomplish what I did, for him to be taken away? Who would I share my victories with now? Who would I share my first day of official teaching with? Who would advise me on all the challenges along the way, through teaching, through life?

Through a constant wave of tears as I searched for answers that would make sense, that would give me some peace. I learned to remember the great times and to laugh at the trouble I'd get myself into with him and my loose tongue. I learned to reflect with sheer gratitude of how lucky I was to have had him in my life.

In ways he never knew, he guided me through some of my life's toughest moments. He was there for me when I needed him to be. Through his gentle guidance and reliance over my younger years, he invited me to see my own strength and determination when I thought it was never mine in the first place. He showed me, even after his death, that I already possessed all the courage and strength I would ever need and that I would be okay without him.

Chapter 20

In my final few months of study, on my uncle's recommendation just before he died, I dropped off my resume to local primary schools in Rushton, hoping to gain relief teaching work. Though I was terrified to put myself out there, with my uncle's sage advice still fresh in my mind, his words gave me the extra boost of confidence I needed.

My uncle believed in me. But it was up to me now.

Walking up the school paths, my mind spun with questions: *What do I say? How do I speak? Do I look like a teacher?* Still questioning myself even as I left my resume. This was the next phase of my life. *Is this what it feels like for everyone else? Is this what it's like to grow up and be an adult?*

Finally, I seemed to be doing what everyone was doing: living. No longer in my own bubble, struggling to find a reason to *be*, or wondering how everyone else was living "normally". I *was* here. I had survived so much.

Despite all the ups and downs I'd ridden on this crazy roller coaster called life, I was learning to face obstacles and move along the path with renewed confidence and new resources and abilities I never thought I had. Each time I overcame a situation, I discovered I could take these new coping strategies—and my new mindset that seemed to get me through—into the next situation. Nothing seemed as scary or potentially life-ending like it once had. Finally, I was in a better space, coping for longer periods of time without small hurdles taking me down.

The last couple of months of university were great. My timetable was flexible enough to teach casually at a local school in Rushton. The time, just like the end of year twelve, was coming where life would change again. Finishing our degrees, friends would move away to pursue permanent teaching positions, to begin new chapters in their lives. But instead of being terrified of the future and deliberately isolating myself, I was ready. I knew I'd be okay wherever life took me. A change I couldn't handle only five years earlier.

As a final 'hurrah' before graduating and going our separate ways, my friends and I hit the town one last time. It was the Easter long weekend—Easter Thursday.

We headed to the most popular nightclub in town, where everyone revelled in the four-day weekend. Despite a long line of people waiting to enter, we joined the queue, listening to the blaring music thumping against the walls.

My two friends, who were dating each other, stood behind me and, as I usually did, I scanned the line up ahead. I noticed a guy who looked to be alone in front of me, with his hands in his pockets. I blurted enthusiastically, "Hello!"

I was wearing my cheesiest grin as he turned around.

He smiled sheepishly. "Hi."

It wasn't bubbly, but it was sweet. He appeared nervous and unsure, and I had all this newfound confidence.

When he realised I wasn't going away, he turned to face me.

"What's your name?" I asked.

"James," he replied.

I didn't wait for him to ask my name, so I shouted out, "I'm Beck!"

"Hi, Beck," he replied with a grin.

I studied his face while we spoke, trying to determine if this was someone I might want to have a drink with inside. He had ginger hair, and clusters of freckles decorated his pale face. His smooth skin, without a hint of stubble, made him look boyish. Much too young for my twenty-two years,

I concluded, before wishing him a great night and turning back to my friends.

Once inside, my friends and I made our way towards the bar, squeezing through the jam-packed room before continuing on to the third floor, which played retro music. It was overcrowded, too. Deciding we'd had enough, we turned back to go down the stairs when I noticed James beside me. I yelled out to him, "Hey! What are you up to?"

"I'm still looking for my friends," he screamed back through the blaring music.

"Do you want to come outside with me?" I blurted.

He nodded and followed me downstairs. *That seemed an easy catch, too easy.* There was no intention to pick him up, but I was tipsy, and I wasn't quite ready to end the night.

Once my friends left, James and I stood outside the nightclub. Without music or more alcohol to talk crap, silence quickly filled the void.

We strolled towards the local food van, grossly known as the Dunny Diner, parked around the corner from the nightclub, waiting to dole out greasy hamburgers to hungry drunks.

James offered to buy me a burger. *Ugh!* The food van looked putrid. Thick oil stains smeared above the chipmaker and around the grill. Nothing about eating greasy food in the early morning enticed me one bit. Besides, I didn't eat around guys. That was embarrassing.

James devoured his burger like he hadn't eaten in days. *Was this a man who was trying to pick me up? Wasn't he meant to be piling on the charm?* Between mouthfuls, he described his treasured dirt bike and 'hotted-up, turbo-charged' car in a dry, monotone voice, like he wasn't even excited about his own life. Had he ever picked up a girl before? He wasn't good at it.

What am I doing talking to this guy? Could he be more boring? A young boy who loves bikes and hotted-up cars? Leave him here with his disgusting greasy burger! Go home! This is not the guy for you.

I wanted to leave, but I didn't want to hurt him. Though I wasn't exactly thrilled, at least he wasn't cocky, feeding me bullshit or making corny inappropriate gestures like other guys. He wasn't swearing or coming on strong. He was quiet and polite. Outside male friends and my exes, he was like no one I'd met. Despite not feeling any vibes, I couldn't walk away. His sweetness struck me.

"Do you want to come back to my place?" I hadn't intended to invite him back, but I didn't know what else to say to counter the radio silence while he chewed.

"Sure," he replied shyly.

As we hobbled into the taxi, I questioned my rash to decision to invite a stranger back to my house. I'd done this a few times before, but never with the intention to have sex. The thought of one-night stands made me feel cheap and used. I'd been lucky that none of those guys had ever forced me, but in the back of my mind, there was always a chance I'd put myself in a dangerous situation.

The next morning, I woke squashed up against the wall on my narrow single bed. The glaze of alcohol had worn off, and I was left wondering why the heck I was in bed with a guy I didn't know, or was even interested in. At least we didn't have sex, I thought.

I crawled over him and scrambled to dress before he saw my half-naked body in the daylight.

I had to be somewhere in a couple of hours, and my car was still at my friend's house. Most guys left before the sun came up. I didn't want to be rude and kick him out, but I had to get rid of him. *Do I offer him coffee?* This was kind of new territory for me.

As he emerged from the bedroom, he looked so young, like he had the night before. He approached timidly, like staying at girl's house was unfamiliar. Was he cute? I didn't know. He looked like shit—hung-over and weary, and with an even paler face than I remembered from the night before. There was something about him I liked, though I still wasn't quite sure. The red hair perhaps?

"Would you like a coffee?" I blurted out without thinking.

"Um, yeah, that'd be great," he replied.

Damn it! Good one, Beck! Make him stay longer.

We stood and sipped our coffees, each slurp filling the silent moments.

"So, I have to be somewhere in an hour, and I don't have a car, soooo..." My words trailed, hoping he'd get the hint and offer a solution that would make him leave quick smart.

"Oh, sure. Can I use your phone to get my flatmate to pick me up?"

"Okay," I quickly replied, relieved there was an end in sight to the most painful, drawn-out pick up in history.

While he arranged his lift home, I left the room to get organised.

"Can I leave my number?" he yelled out.

Ah, why? It must have been obvious to him we weren't compatible. Petrol-head, awkward boys were definitely not my type. Still, I didn't have the heart to say no thanks.

"Sure! Just write it down next to the phone," I called from my bedroom.

When his ride came, I shuffled him out the door. "Okay, nice to meet you. See ya, bye!"

"I'll give you a call," he said as he left.

Sure.

I sighed behind the closed door. Thank God that's over. Nice guy, but no. That's not going anywhere.

A couple of days later, on a relaxing Sunday afternoon, my older brother was visiting when the phone rang.

I heard a soft, unfamiliar male voice. "Hello."

"Who is this?" I asked.

"It's James," he said.

Who's James? I tried to stall the conversation as I searched my mind for someone I knew with that name.

"We met the other night," he offered into the weird silence.

"Oh," I exclaimed. *Holy shit, why is he ringing? How the hell did he get my number? I didn't give it to him.*

I tried to keep the conversation brief. I felt like I'd been caught off guard. James explained he'd gone to Phillip Island to watch a bike race. *Oh, great, the bikes again. Why am I letting this guy go on? I don't care!*

"Great," I said. "Sounds great."

"So, I was wondering if you'd like to go out this week sometime?"

What? You can't possibly be interested in me!

"Um, okay, sure." It wasn't exactly an enthusiastic answer. I hung up, uncertain if I'd made the right decision. I figured he was harmless enough to at least give him a chance.

James offered to pick me up. I was happy about that. At least I could have a couple of drinks beforehand to lessen the awkwardness. Besides, it was easier to ramble on if I was a little tipsy.

While I ran around getting ready, I heard a knock. As I opened the door, I was immediately reminded of how young he looked.

"G'day," he said quietly, wiping his feet on the mat before walking in.

Who is this guy? He behaved like a perfect gentleman. I didn't get it.

We hopped into his green, hotted-up hatchback. *Oh crap!* This was the car he'd bragged about the night we met. *What am I doing? He is so not my type!* And yet, he seemed a contradiction to the stereotype of a young guy who loved his turbo-charged cars and motorbikes. He wasn't fitting the car bogan type I imagined. He was polite, well-mannered, and sweet. He remained quiet as I rambled on to avoid silence. But just as quickly as I was trying to change my opinion of this guy, he changed gears and his car made this loud squirting noise. *Oh dear God, what the hell was that? This is not for me. Beck, let's get through this date and call it quits already!*

After dinner, we went to a nearby pub. It was hard to talk over the loud music and crowds of people; but it suited me as I was scrambling for things to talk about, anyway. He was just so quiet. Not knowing much about

James, apart from his obvious love of fast things, his electrical apprentice-ship he was finishing, and where he lived, I was relieved when he suggested a game of pool. Finally, something in common and a way to pass the time.

I'd played a bit of pool before. Anna and I often played pool at our local pub back home, honing our skills for hours when there wasn't much else to do in our small town to pass the time away.

James went first and broke while I strategised my game plan. *Will I be ultra-competitive? I don't even know him.* I had nothing to prove, and yet I wanted to him to know I was more than what I appeared to be. *I may be small, appear uncertain, but I can win. I can be strong and determined, and I can take you down.* I almost laughed out loud. *Lighten up, Beck, it's just a game of pool,* I mused.

As the game progressed, not only could he play, but he was good! Even better than me. He was easily two or three balls ahead of me. Watching him pocket multiple balls, I found myself quietly impressed and even a little bit attracted to this man and his pool-playing prowess. A smile stretched across my face. Normally I'd blurt something defensive out at this point to save face. But the usual embarrassment I'd felt at losing so convincingly wasn't there.

Instead of acting cocky while he kicked my arse, he seemed bashful, almost apologetic for beating me so easily. It was the sweetest thing. After over-analysing everything I didn't like about him, there was something I did like about James, and it went deeper than the surface stuff I naively scrutinised and judged him for.

We laid the pool cues down and headed to the bar. James walked towards me, instinctively grabbing my hand to lead me through the crowd. *Whoa! I paused momentarily, feeling* a spark shoot through my hand and my body, making me tingle. Something electric happened when his hand grabbed mine. Without a word, there was something so eternal in his grasp. His firm grip felt protective and strong, almost like he never wanted to let me go. But how could that be? We didn't even know each other. I wondered what it meant.

After our first date, James rang often, wanting to spend time with me after work and on weekends. The first time I went to his house, he asked me to join him for a quick drive to the shops for milk. I didn't understand why. My ex-boyfriend never took me anywhere outside his house, and certainly not for anything as trivial as a quick trip to the shops.

Instead of gushing at how sweet it was, I thought it was a tad pathetic. As much as I wanted to like everything about him, I didn't trust the ease at which James seemed to accept me. Never completely comfortable, I started questioning his motives, suspiciously looking for anything that revealed a flaw in his judgment. *There must be something wrong with him if he likes me like this. It can't be right. There's no thrill of the chase. Don't I have to earn my way into his heart? This is not the way relationships are meant to be. It was all too simple.*

After a couple of weeks, I convinced myself there was no future with James. "I really don't think this is going to work out. I'm sorry," I said as I left his house.

"Okay." He obliged, but I could practically hear his heart breaking.

I'd never broken up with a guy before. They either found someone better or brutally dumped me. On the drive home, I tried to ignore my conflicting thoughts by reaffirming out aloud I was doing the right thing. *He's clearly not for you. We have nothing in common. He's not charming. He's so quiet. He likes motorbikes. Come on, Beck, he has a friggin black FOX banner that literally takes up a wall in his lounge room! It's too easy, something is wrong with this picture.* Despite my best efforts, something still niggled at me.

Over the next couple of weeks, I intentionally kept myself busy, but it was hard to ignore the yammering in my head, begging me to reconsider James. When friends asked about him, I spoke of the obvious differences against my exes. They replied with annoying, thought-provoking questions. Stuff like, "They're exes for a reason, aren't they? How many of them were so devoted to you for no other reason than they liked you?" And, "Maybe it's a good thing James is different. Maybe you deserve this, Beck."

Their statements hit every nerve as they echoed the same sentiments as the rational part of my mind I was trying so hard to ignore.

As my inner conflict rose, the positives began to outweigh the initial objections I had towards James. Perhaps my beliefs of what a real relationship was, needed to be challenged? Maybe I'd learn what it's like to be with someone I didn't have to act in a certain way for, or feel I had to earn my love. Maybe I did deserve this.

Stepping back into a relationship with James was awkward. He never questioned my return, making it even more difficult for me to understand what was going on in his head.

The whole thing unnerved me.

Whatever happened to the thrill of the chase? Where's all the drama? What of all the demands and expectations from me? The scheduled time-frames to hang out? Where are all the cryptic messages I'd spend countless hours trying to decode? Surely, there's more to this? I'm just here with you, to simply be? What a bore!

With no little mind games to play, I'd dissect every part of our relationship again and again. My deep, inner beliefs and criteria about what relationships were meant to be like kept overshadowing the good times, and it meant I couldn't easily relax. I was always preparing myself for the inevitable discard. Eventually he'll realise I'm not worth it.

I associated love and relationships with drama, manipulation, storming off, distrust, silent treatments, trying to be perfect, hurling insults to mask my insecurities. What was I meant to do instead? There was a huge chasm, a void in the relationship that needed filling. I could not be content with just being myself, because something in my brain told me if I did, it would be over, that he'd leave me.

So I did the only thing I knew how to do: I created drama. I'd throw snide remarks at James to trigger an angry outburst for overt attention—negative or positive. I found trivial things to whinge about, a reason to throw an insult I thought might anger him into an argument, just so I could quickly pounce on him and retaliate. I'd purposely sabotage a planned weekend away by finding something to argue about, just to get back into the toxic cycle of hurt. I felt comfortable in that space. Love meant getting hurt, feeling lousy, being abandoned, and getting treated like shit. It meant getting my own way, demanding it, sulking when I didn't. It meant manipulating situations to make James look like the bad guy.

Love any other way just didn't feel right or normal.

James not only had to prove his love, he had to show me why he loved me too. I wasn't content with his sweet gestures of bringing me a coffee in the morning or giving me a hug for no reason. When he was loving and sweet, I'd misread it as cunning and sly and call bullshit. Even in movies and soap operas there was drama. The guy chased the woman and showed grand gestures of their love. Where were my grand gestures?

Without any hidden agenda or sexual exploitation that I could find, it was difficult to believe James genuinely wanted to be with me, so I purposely sabotaged moments and outings just to retreat back to the trauma I knew. My comfort zone.

I baited arguments for the pure enjoyment of watching James explode or hurl hurtful words and storm off. I made sure I incited anger and disruption just so he could come back and apologise. But that wasn't the end of it. Oh no, I wanted it to linger. I went hours and sometimes days purposely staying silent, ignoring his phone calls, sitting beside him in complete silence, just waiting for an apology that was good enough to make me speak again. If his apology wasn't up to scratch, he'd storm off, and we'd be in a new cycle of silence. James was screwed, whatever he did.

No matter what I threw at him, though, he kept letting me back in. He forgave me when I knew I didn't deserve it. I didn't understand why he continued to love me when I tried in so many ways to prove I was unlovable.

After dating for two years, we moved in together. This still didn't seal my commitment nor convince me anymore that we were right for each other. I still had to have an 'out', just in case.

Moving in, I imagined constant displays of affection, romantic trips away, breakfast in bed, romantic dinners. The 'Days of Our Lives' kinda life. Instead, we juggled our relationship with real life, work, household chores, appointments, friends and family. Living together wasn't measuring up to the fantasy I'd created in my head. It was so dull and boring. Another reason I added to my list of why this relationship wasn't right.

I used my perfect fantasy to compare and judge my reality, to draw criticism about every little thing that did or didn't happen to what I thought should be happening.

James couldn't quite understand why I was so adamant about making our relationship difficult. I barely understood it myself at the time. There was so much going on beneath the surface, battling my demons, trying to keep them at bay. Trying to line up the unattainable romantic fictitious story of a relationship in my head with the one I was actually having with James, the perfect guy who had to have a catch, a flaw, something.

Trauma continued to rear its ugly head. Even when I thought I'd banished one demon, another one surfaced, appearing to possess my body. Sometimes after sex my head would start shaking involuntarily, like rapid spasms. It didn't happen at the beginning of our relationship, but the more intimate we became, the more frequently it happened. In the dark, James could only hear a rustling of the sheets before he'd place his hand on my trembling body and ask me what was wrong when my head wouldn't stop shaking. Sometimes this went on for ten or fifteen minutes, while tears spilled out onto the pillow. The more it happened, the more I realised my mind was trying to shut down specific memories. Images of lying naked in bed with my grandfather.

My mind was remembering, and as an act of protection, it was trying to chase the images away. It got worse before it got better. All James could do, knowing the story of my childhood trauma, was to hold me and assure me everything was okay until I felt safe again and then my head would stop shaking. I never knew what to say in those moments while I battled feeling filthy. It wasn't him, that much I knew.

My whole idea of love was a complete contradiction. On the one hand, I wanted James's love and support. I wanted all the 'normal' things, the stability, the nurturing, and the security. But it contradicted how I had received love in my upbringing. To accept love meant being vulnerable and exposing myself to betrayal and abandonment, and that wasn't something I was prepared to do. As a child, every time I let my guard down, someone would hurt me all over again. It wasn't safe to be open and unguarded.

As I kept up my defence, I used the big arguments to threaten leaving and then storm off, hoping it was enough for an apology. But there were only so many times I could do that before I'd need to make good on it.

After yet another argument I'd deliberately escalated, I told him this time I was leaving for good. "Take down my bed!" I ordered.

His readiness to do what I ordered only fed my anger. *See he won't stop this. He won't prove he loves me and beg me to stop this nonsense, beg me to stay. Fine, I'll play this until the death and then I'll be right!*

I stomped around the house, collecting my belongings. I banged and crashed all the doors, throwing his things carelessly out of the way to get my stuff, not giving a damn what damage I caused. Every noise made a point. Still, I hoped he would stop me.

I loaded his ute, aware this was as far as I'd ever gone, as far as I'd ever pushed. *When would he stop my madness? Please, James! Come on! I can't admit I'm being a bitch.* It was up to him to make it all better, to fight for me, like they did in the movies. *See, you don't fucking love me! What kind of an arsehole are you, to let me walk out? To pack up and ship me off like we mean nothing! I knew you didn't love me. No one who really loves me would do this. I hate you. I hate that I believed you when you said you loved me, when you don't give a damn at all!*

With the last few things piled on, we hopped in and drove the thirty minutes to Mum's house.

James remained silent the whole way. Every so often I'd tilt my head to catch a glimpse of his face, vacant and solemn, like he had nothing left to give, like he'd finally had enough of the tumultuous roller coaster of the previous two years. Maybe he'd finally given up on me just as I expected he eventually would.

I looked at his hand and wished he'd reach out and place it on my knee. No words, just a simple gesture that always said so much. I desperately wanted to hold his hand in those final few kilometres to Mum's house, but I'd blown it with the only man who might have truly loved me. The only man who stood by me through all my bullshit, through all my petty fucking games. I had reached the limit of love. Because love did have limits, didn't it? My mum's had a limit, my dad's, my nana's, both my ex-boyfriends' had limits too. They'd all eventually given up on me. And now James had too.

I imagined I'd feel victorious. Proud to finally see what I was trying to prove from the start. But I didn't. I felt ashamed and remorseful for how I'd behaved. I never really wanted that point to be proven. Far from it. I didn't want James to ever give up on me. I needed him, despite everything.

When we arrived at Mum's house, I dawdled towards the door, wishing time would freeze and a miracle would appear. As I unlocked the door, James folded his arms, and slumped against the car, staring hopelessly after me. I stopped at the door and stared back like a forlorn little girl, wishing I could undo the consequences of my tantrum. My lips pouted as the tears fell.

Immediately, he rushed over and held me tight as I sobbed in his arms.

"Do you really want to end it?" I pleaded through my tears.

"No," he said, softly and reassuringly stroking my hair.

Wiping my face, we both got back into the car and drove home.

I didn't attempt to explain my behaviour, nor did James ask. We just drove back in silence, with his hand on my knee, and that was all I needed for now.

I had a lot of time to reflect on why I acted the way I did, realising this was another pattern. I didn't like who I was when I behaved like an entitled brat. It was time to understand why. What was I really afraid of? It was time to stop testing James, to stop running away and expecting some grand gestures to prove his love to pull me back, when the evidence was always there, that he'd stuck by me no matter what.

It was hard to break this particular pattern. I couldn't just give up the very behaviours that protected me from getting hurt. Those protections I wore like armour so no one could get inside my carefully constructed, but very fragile walls and take anything from me that I wasn't freely willing to give. No one deserved that part of me, not even James. I couldn't risk exposing my deepest vulnerabilities so someone could come in and destroy me again. I'd trusted my parents and my family to look after me and keep me safe, and they didn't.

The inner battle to resist and accept James into my life for good came the day we had yet another argument. I'd succeeded again in making it a bigger than it needed to be. Even as I screamed at him, I wanted to stop, but I couldn't. My ego, my habit, wouldn't let me. This time instead of packing up, I stormed off towards the back of the property that backed onto a shallow creek and trudged through dense bushland thick enough to camouflage me. I came to a small clearing where I could see directly through to the back of the house and watch James's movements.

I sat there for hours watching him, tightly grasping my mobile phone, waiting for him to call, then deliberately ignoring when he rang as he paced around the backyard. Watching him become more frustrated and concerned satisfied me. For once he was the one worrying, he was the one feeling pain and agony. For once I got to see him feel like shit, liked I'd felt so many times.

As the sun began to set, James's concern grew. My phone constantly vibrated. He sent multiple text messages. *Please tell me you're okay. Where are you?* He came out of the house more and more, scanning the yard, placing his hands to his head. I could see the worried look on his face and something inside of me clicked into place.

What am I doing? Seeing James hurting, that's gratifying to you, Rebekah, really? Look at him. He's upset. Why are you doing this?

I felt my conscience challenge my shameful behaviour. I could no longer ignore what I was doing. I could see my pattern so clearly. I felt the inner conflict flash across my mind and heart. A familiar voice emerged. Perhaps it was my inner child rising. Just at that moment when an awakening, a transformation, was present like she'd always done in the past.

She spoke to the frightened part of me, terrified to let my guard down. As I sat in the dirt, huddled with my head buried between my knees, a voice whispered, "Why do you keep doing this? How many more times are you going to keep running away from James? Why do you keep sabotaging this relationship? Haven't we had enough? All we've ever wanted was for someone to love us for real. James has loved us through every tantrum, every fight. He has never let us go. Please let him love us."

As the truth of her words sank in, I suddenly felt tired and exhausted. Tired of the games, tired of pushing James away. Tired of rejecting his love. My protective walls crumbled as I prepared to surrender.

Could I be brave enough to accept his love? Could I be courageous and let him in just a bit? Would I survive the risk of being hurt again?

I watched James without the sabotage in my heart, but with love. He emerged as a man who'd played all my games and won. A man who'd proven through every single storm, every breakup, that he loved me. He wasn't prepared to give up on me, like so many others had. James showed me he was a partner who was patient, loving, strong, and who offered love, pure and simple. He could have easily left, but never wanted to. Even when he had every reason to go, he chose to stay.

With emotion clogging my throat, I spoke out quietly, "Beck, you deserve this. It's time to stop running away. It's time to let yourself be loved."

I cried when I realised everything I ever wanted was right in front of me. I cried for all the pain I'd caused, for the little broken girl inside who just wanted to be loved. She would finally get her wish. Slowly, but surely, I would decide to be brave and begin letting the wall come down and allow James's love to reach us both.

I dried my tears and stood. My legs shook as I walked towards the house; for the first time choosing James and choosing to stay. No more back doors. No more leaving one foot outside, just in case. No more running away. I was going to stay put this time and learn to change my ways. Learn to open up.

I tiptoed into the darkened house and walked down the hall. I found him lying still on the bed, staring despondently at the ceiling.

I gazed upon him with sadness, so sorry for all the hurt and pain I caused him. I wanted to tell him how much I loved him. How much I needed him and craved the security and protection he always offered. I wanted to tell him how troubled I really was. How frightened I was to let him in. How scared I was of being traumatised again. I wanted to tell him I didn't mean it—I was just protecting myself.

But I couldn't speak nor open my heart so readily just yet. I curled up beside him. Without a word, he turned and wrapped his loving arms around me and held me tight. He wasn't letting go. And for the first time, I wasn't going anywhere.

Chapter 21

After dating for five years, James and I married in May 2005. Jack, the closest person to a father I ever knew, walked me down the aisle. A few months later, we found out we were expecting our first child. Though I'd imagined years would pass before the idea of motherhood was something I'd need to think about—much like any other 'possibility' in my life I'd push away to deal with later—the idea seemed too surreal and even more so, when it came to be.

So many mixed feelings surrounding this next chapter swirled around my head. With many choices and responsibilities ahead of me, I began to mentally prepare and probably even over-analysed my new role, questioning the type of mother I wanted to be. Probably more than most people.

What do I want to teach my children? What environment will my child grow up in? How do I want to see my child as a future citizen of the world? Every thought, every outcome that I could imagine, went under the microscope of my mind.

Given everything I'd gone through with my own parents, I needed to do this right. The benchmark really wasn't set too high after all. This was my chance not to screw up my own child's life and try to do it 'properly', the way it ought to have been with me.

My ambitions for my child's future weighed heavily on me. Sometimes a little too heavily. Knowing what I would have wanted from my own parents allowed me to imagine other possibilities and offer gifts of a good life and upbringing to my own child. This was my chance to really love and teach love. I knew I would give them every opportunity to live without trauma as their foundation and to know their self-worth.

As a mother, it was critical for me to be present and show up in every single way—emotionally and physically. Not simply saying I was a mum and it not meaning anything. My child needed to know and feel they were loved in every sense of the word. Often, I wouldn't let a moment of silence go by without badgering James through Q&A type sessions, trying to work out a plan for how we were going to raise our children. James obliged my need to dissect every deep question that would help us to figure out how we were going to do this *right*.

Every now and then, he'd say, "Why don't we wait until the baby's born?"

"*Pfft*! Yeah, what a plan. That's what my parents did and look how well that turned out," I replied sarcastically.

The more I thought of my growing baby, the more I was reminded of all the ways I'd been abandoned. All the things I wasn't taught. All the ways Mum *said* she loved me but failed to show it. All the times my parents failed to protect me.

Everything that was so wrong with my upbringing became so blindingly obvious now that I was to have a child of my own. It brought more pain to the surface as I connected with my own baby growing inside me. I thought I'd largely dealt with this, and yet here it was, battering me at all times of the day and night. I'd cradle my belly a little firmer, my heart sore at the thought of ever standing by and allowing my child to go through the same experiences as I had.

I felt an immediate maternal bond with my baby. I wondered how my parents could have failed me so spectacularly. Where was their maternal instinct to protect me? How could they fuck up so majorly and not just with me, with my siblings too? I just didn't understand. Was having children just a tick-the-box exercise with no thought to anything else beyond that?

I'd not even met my unborn baby and yet I felt nothing but the purest love and an unwaveringly fierce desire to protect my child. The very thought that I could ever turn away from my child seemed unbelievable. I would fight and die for my baby. There was no chance I would ever turn my back on my child. Parenting wasn't a half-ass job. Mothering wasn't a concept, it was an action of showing up and being there consistently.

My thoughts wandered to my family culture and the relationships within it. How certain family members protected and defended each other. How each adult in my family played a part in covering up the abuse and having each other's back. The hierarchy of power and control was made even clearer too, as though the curtain had been lifted and I could finally see the whole picture. Family who stood back, those who stayed silent, the ones who cowered and waited to be told what to do and say. The weird way my parents idolised their own fathers was part of that control. They never abandoned those perfect father images for a second to question their immoral behaviours, instead casting their own flesh and blood off as a liar.

Witnessing a family culture that allowed abuse to be swept under the rug and ignored made me sick. It was a system no one dare disrupt by speaking the truth for fear of being excluded from the pack. Or worse yet, expose the aiders and abettors who hid behind a career of duty and service, or the role of 'loyal wife'.

As a victim of this system, it hurt. But as a mother, it enraged me. How could they defend their parents against their own daughter? How could they leave their own defenceless child to fend for herself? How do you ignore abuse and never question it?

How could you not consider that I, your own child, needed you?

Never would I allow history to repeat itself with my own family. I discussed it frequently with James, emphasising my strong stance, declaring emphatically, "I don't care how much you think you love your parents; it will never be them versus our child. It will ALWAYS be my child. I will defend and protect my children with everything I have. Nothing will ever stop me from being there for my children. So if you ever think that I will jump ship and support your parents or my parents over our children, know I will never ever compromise my children's safety or welfare to be kept in the good books with your family or mine. I am not afraid of speaking up and standing alone. Nor will I pretend or protect any dysfunction. I will not be silenced to keep the peace, or show up at Christmas parties and play the 'happy family' role to mask truths that demand to be heard. Nor will I stand aside and allow my children to be brought up in the same dysfunction."

If this was my opportunity to stand up and stop the cycle of abuse repeating itself, then I would take it with everything I had, and nothing and no one would stop me.

While I adjusted to becoming a first-time mum, I began to think more of my relationship with my own mother. Questioning *my* role in it in ways I hadn't done before.

In the past, Anna had tried to slip her thoughts into conversations about how she'd observed the role reversal with my mum and I, but I usually downplayed it as 'just helping like any daughter would'. But now I knew what Anna had tried to help me see, giving new meaning to what I had been doing.

When I worked three nights a week to support myself while living out of home and studying, I bought extra food to put aside for Mum. I felt guilty that she couldn't afford to buy as much food because I wasn't paying board anymore. When she had a heart attack, I begged her to demand Jack stop smoking in the house. I put in so much effort to help her lose weight by writing out detailed food plans, trying to convince her to exercise. "Just walk around the block," I'd urge, hoping it would motivate her to change.

I'd sit with her for hours to help write goals, breaking each one down into smaller steps in the hope she would achieve something and get back on track to living a long life, beyond the days when her children would all leave home permanently. I frequently checked up on her to make sure she was sticking to any of the changes discussed at length. But no matter what I did, the many hours of talking, persuading, and buying the very things she needed to make it all happen, it never made a difference.

Now I was going to be a real mother to my *own* child, rescuing my mum had to stop. The penny finally dropped, like a punch line I finally understood. She was a big girl. It was not my job to look after her. It never was. She would never make any long-term, healthy changes while I continually picked up the pieces for her.

It would not be easy for either of us. I'd need to end Mum's dependence as well as liberate myself from the guilt of 'abandoning' her because that's what it felt like I would be doing. For a normal mother-daughter relationship to happen, changes had to be made. I decided to tell her next time we spoke. *Great things never came without fear and challenges*, I reminded myself every time I thought of chickening out.

My stomach churned when I answered the phone and heard Mum's voice. Mum was never a vengeful person. She wouldn't give me a mouthful. But I also knew she wouldn't understand. She'd be confused.

She gave her usual cheery hello. I paused, not mirroring my hello back in the same tone. "Mum," I said, launching straight in. "I can't do this with you anymore."

"Do what?" she replied.

I ignored her question and continued. I feared that if I stopped to think, I might change my mind and abort my decision. "I'm going to be a mum now. I can't keep looking after you. This is my time to be with my own child and learn to be a good mother. I just need some space."

Mum's voice rose. "Beck, what's wrong? What's going on? What are you talking about?"

She wouldn't understand this, coming completely out of the blue. I'd processed so much of my own trauma over the years, and this was just another moment of awakening that needed to be addressed. Everything seemed fine to her, but it wasn't for me, so I pressed on.

"Mum, I'm happy to chat when you're ready to talk about every-thing—the abuse, our dysfunctional relationship, and family. You ring me and let me know. Until then, please just give me some space."

"Beck? What's happened?" she repeated more urgently.

Instead of trying to explain, not even knowing where to start, knowing she wouldn't see how screwed up our relationship was, I hung up the phone. It felt brutal to end the call so abruptly. I burst into tears, relieved to have released the burden of responsibility I'd carried for so long, but I was scared, not knowing if I would ever speak to Mum again. I wished she understood how much I wanted something different for us.

Without her, I'd be learning about motherhood alone. I still hoped for the mother others had. One that would delight in being there during my own pregnancy and motherhood. She wouldn't be there to ask questions and share my excitement. We wouldn't shop for baby clothes together. She wouldn't watch my belly grow as my due date approached. And it was also very likely that Mum would not get to meet my first-born child.

The reality of my decision hit hard, but I knew the risk. There'd be moments she'd miss that couldn't be repeated, and I had to accept that. I believed with my whole heart that I was doing the best thing for *my* family. This was what it would take to break the cycle. This was me trying to decimate the generations of dysfunction in my family. To start afresh for us and my family. For future generations to come.

On the 13th of April 2006, my son was born with James by my side and Anna, who I'd asked to be there for support in place of Mum.

I cradled my new son with smile I couldn't wipe off my face. He became *the* most important thing in my universe.

As word spread of my son's birth, Mum's absence niggled at me. I had not seen or spoken to her since I was eight weeks pregnant. Even Jack stayed away when the birth was announced. His absence stung just as much as Mum's. Even though I knew his stance was more about protecting Mum than an act of vengeance. When friends, siblings, even James's parents visited and held my son, I cried inside, wishing I could have this same moment with her. Those were the times I questioned my decisions. Was it really worth it? To allow these moments to pass without my mum in it. Would I come to regret my decision years later?

Could I bend the rules, my rules, just this one time, so the memory would not be lost years later when our relationship repaired as I hoped it would be? Or would this only confuse her and show her what I wanted for us didn't really matter? My need to change our relationship outweighed relaxing my stance. I had to stand firm even during these precious moments. Maybe missing out might inspire Mum to want to sort our relationship out. I couldn't blur these lines with her.

As the months rolled on by, and my baby reached milestones I couldn't ring or meet with her to share, in the back of my mind I wondered what she was doing. Why was it so hard for her to come to me? How could she sit back and happily miss out? Does this mean she really doesn't care at all?

My end goal was far greater than some missed moments. When it got too much, I'd fall into James's arms and he'd stroke my hair while I cried for the pain my stance caused. Yet I believed in what I was doing. I was thinking about the future—a better future—and this was just another hurdle to overcome. I had to be strong and keep my purpose in the forefront of my mind. That's how changes are made. Not by repeating patterns, or staying silent, but by creating new behaviours, all for a better, healthier relationship. How can a new culture within a family be created if we don't address the changes that need to be made? If I caved in, then we'd be back where we were, and I didn't want the same for me or my children anymore.

Chapter 22

In September 2007, my second son was born, just seventeen months after the birth of my first. It wasn't a planned pregnancy, but I readily accepted it, naively assuming it would be as smooth as the brief time I'd had with my first son.

But it wasn't long before I realised two babies did not mean the same personality, feeding habits, sleeping habits, or even the same demands as one child. Having two children doubled my workload in ways I hadn't thought it would.

At first, the little thoughts that began to creep in seemed harmless. Wondering how I would keep up with the boys' constant needs, particularly while James was at work. *How do I give equal love and attention to my eldest son if I am constantly attending to my newborn? Would he feel abandoned? How do I keep up with the housework while continuously keeping up with the needs of two young children? How do I even consider my own needs over theirs, and should I even have needs now that I'm a mother?*

Mum still wasn't in my life, leaving so many parenting questions unanswered. The *how to*'s and *how do I*'s were all but left up to me and James to figure out, and often we had nary a clue while we walked blindly down this unmarked path.

That was until Jean turned up unannounced on my doorstep one morning as I rushed around, trying to get both boys into the pram with a cargo load of necessities to walk to the shops. As soon as I opened the door, frazzled and overwhelmed, she offered to look after the boys while I went alone. I cried like a baby on the spot. It was the first time someone had ever taken care of my boys and the first time I'd got to the shops on my own without waiting for James to come home since my eldest was born two years earlier.

I'd met Jean in 2001 at a school we both taught at. A tall, slender woman with short black hair and glasses. Jean was my supervising/mentor teacher, as I was at the beginning of my teaching career. She was direct but caring and nurturing at the same time, always willing to offer support when I needed it. She'd regularly pop into my classroom and make sure everything was going okay, offering tips as well as tried and true strategies she'd notched up from almost forty years of teaching. I quickly endeared to her help, which at times felt maternal as well as professional. Over time, her maternal nature extended outside our working relationship.

After I resigned from my job, I didn't see much of Jean. We kept in contact sporadically, catching up for a cuppa every now and then. It wasn't until I had my second child that she visited more regularly. Without Mum around, it was nice to have someone like Jean to step in. She willingly came over to help with my sons she adored, offering much needed advice along the way, having three adult sons herself. She filled that motherly position, not that we ever spoke of that being her role.

Over a short period of time, Jean became someone I could trust to air annoyances that occupied my mind—the situation with Mum, my boy's new quirks and milestones, plus the demands of being a mum. She would sit and listen to my long whinges and then tell me to get over it, but not in a harsh, dismissive way. More to motivate me to keep going and not attach to little things that often irritated me way too much.

"Just get on with it and don't worry about it," she'd often say, just like Jack's advice when I was younger. It was good, no nonsense advice I needed to curb my overthinking ways and get on with the job.

Jean's ways were so completely different to Mum's. When Mum was still in my life, all of her repeated baby stories told the dreamy side of raising children. The way she toilet-trained us so easily. How easily we slept through the night. Repeatedly spruiking how well behaved we were and how much she loved being a mum prior to moving into The House.

At least with Jean, she was real. Her stories were real too. She never glossed over the hardships and challenges that parents often face. I preferred that style over Mum's rose-coloured glasses version.

Mum never complained parenting was hard. The tantrums, terrible twos, sibling rivalry, different sleeping patterns, different personalities. Even when my siblings and I would scoff at her 'perfect child' stories, Mum still protested how good her children were.

Mum never showed any emotion, nor how difficult and demanding being a single mum with four children was. She behaved as if nothing bothered her, and I don't know if she was pretending or if her denial was strong in this too.

Now, as a parent myself, her earlier words confused me.

Mum's perfect version of parenting planted a belief that motherhood was meant to be easy and without challenges. If difficulties arose or things didn't go as planned, it said something about *me*. I wasn't good enough, or a natural. Mum's rose-coloured views lingered, following me around, whispering in my ear as I struggled at times to keep up with the demands of two busy boys.

Mum could do it with four children, so why can't I do it with two? How did she get her children to sleep without a hitch? What am I doing wrong?

Sometimes the simple monotony and never-ending tasks got to me and, for brief moments, I dreamt of escaping to do nothing on my own before the guilt of even contemplating such a thought crippled me. Stress to complete everything within a day to appease James and his subtle remarks of performing my homely duties as society dictated I should, plus looking after my boys' needs, began to drain me emotionally and physically.

Of course, I never expressed my real concerns to my mothers' group, which was the only outlet I really had outside James and Jean and I didn't admit it to them either. What sort of a mother would want to flee for a moment of privacy? It was too shameful a thought to speak aloud when all the other mums were still gushing over their new babies.

Sometimes I'd whinge to James about how non-stop my day was, while he did his best to help when he got home from work. At times, I hated to ask for his help after a long day at work. But I often wondered when my 'shift' ended so I could have a real break.

Like a well-rehearsed script, Mums' group started off with the usual whinge. We'd offload how much time our children took up, the exhaustion, the repetitiveness of our daily task. Nothing too deep though, before we moved on quickly to other light-hearted and happier topics outside the monopoly of time our children took up. Maybe for a moment, we just wanted to feel free again—the women we were before motherhood took over our lives

I kept my darker thoughts hidden. Never revealing to anyone in my inner circle—including James—of the unattainably high expectations I continually placed on myself to be the "perfect" mother. Seeing other mothers appear so happy and content, it must have been my problem, my inadequacies, so I kept everything inside, brewing and ruminating. My version of a 'perfect mum' grew further out of reach with every moment I stuffed up with my boys.

Sometimes my inner 'bad mum' critic got so loud I'd drop to the floor and sob. Slam the clothes on the clotheshorse while my sons continually demanded my attention with their loud cries and their little hands pulling at me. In those moments, I reached my limit. I'd had enough of the relentless demands of parenting, with virtually no support during the day while James was busy at work and no one else there to give me a solid break. And yet even as anxiety and depression increased, I never sought out help, fully believing I was to blame for the way things were. I compared myself to everyone around me and wondered why no one was complaining and struggling like I was. I desperately wanted to be 'good' at motherhood and enjoy every moment. And I cursed myself whenever I wasn't.

In January 2008, Anna called. As most conversations were a chance to catch up, I relaxed back into the couch for a long chat. "How are you?" I asked.

She muttered something inaudible.

"What did you say?"

"Mum has bowel cancer."

"Okay, um, what does that mean?" Questions bombarded my mind, but I remained silent while Anna explained.

Even after she explained it all, a burning question remained.

"How did she know?" I asked.

I expected Anna would tell me Jill had experienced blindingly obvious symptoms. But instead, she replied, "She knew something was wrong, but she didn't know what."

I desperately wanted to know what she meant, but I was too afraid to ask.

Hanging up a long time later, I couldn't shake Anna's words. I didn't realise they were busily planting a seed of fear within me. How did people know they were sick with something terrible like cancer? I'd managed to control most parts of my life up to this point—my behaviours, how I mothered my children—but an illness, a serious illness, that was one thing I couldn't control, much less predict. A burning sensation rippled through my body.

What if I was sick and didn't know it?

Irrational fears started gnawing away at me, over-analysing every little thing my body was and wasn't doing. Every single ache and pain provoked questions. *What's that? Why does that hurt? What's that coming from? What does this mean? Do I have cancer?*

Every feeling magnified a fear I had a disease I wasn't aware of. Bowel cancer was internal. How the hell would I know if I became victim to it? What would I need to see? Or not see? The unknown petrified me.

As I singled out one part of my body to forensically dissect, other symptoms appeared. The more I focused on an ache, the worse it felt, confirming in my mind that I was seriously ill. Every single day, the voice of fear became louder. The unknown and questions that followed multiplied and intensified.

From the outside, I appeared fine. Taking my boys to the park, hosting mums' group, laughing and chatting, grocery shopping and running errands. But on the inside, my whole nervous system boiled like a constant furnace, burning from the minute I woke, right up until bedtime. My thoughts became an obsession, taking on a life of their own. They slithered like a snake throughout my body, alerting me to any ache or anomaly. Voices inside my head taunted me. *Beck, what's wrong with you? You have cancer, that's what's wrong. You haven't been to the bathroom in days. That means you're sick. You've got the same thing as Jill. You can't go to the doctor because they'll tell you that you're dying.* I felt completely trapped, unable to control rapid thoughts multiplying every minute of the day.

Distracting myself from the screaming voices in my head telling me I was dying became increasingly difficult. Sometimes I'd muster up my own opposing voice, trying to scream back. *NO! No! Help me. Help me!* While my eyes scanned my environment, desperate for something or someone to interrupt the chaos in my mind..

Now that eleven days had passed since I'd been to the bathroom, panic seized my entire body, confirming my worst fears: I was seriously sick. I desperately wanted to grab on to James and blurt out my fears, but I worried admitting my demise out aloud would either make it true or make me sound crazy. Neither option could mask my shame. So I held it all in, saving my torture for a moment on my own, away from my family, to panic and hyperventilate.

Every day became more exhausting, more difficult to manage. Carrying around my burning body and the weight of my worries pressed against my mind. Sometimes my legs dragged like concrete pillars. My head was constantly dizzy from the non-stop voices yammering everywhere I went. Obsessive thoughts drained my energy, and I began to lose concentration midway through conversations. I became forgetful, wondering if I'd just done something or imagined doing it. I would check and recheck the boys had everything they needed. Menial tasks and the boys' daily routine became difficult, yet paradoxically, helped me pass the time until James got home from work. Even when talking to James about his day, whispers taunted in the background.

When James was speaking, I would stare at him and wish I could tell him how sick I was. *Beck, you have to tell him what's going on! He will help you. He will not abandon you.* But I couldn't. I knew I was finally going crazy. That was the downside of keeping my problems to myself. While it built up and got worse on the inside, I pretended to the world I was fine. What would he make of my sudden desperation?

James had to know somehow what was happening without exposing the full extent of my obsessive thoughts. Just enough to release the pressure valve on the ferocity of symptoms constantly plaguing my body. I staged dramatic performances; ones I knew would get James's attention immediately. Purposely I'd mention feeling light-headed, deliberately stand up, and drop to the floor. James would frantically rush to my side, shouting and tapping my face, urging me to open my eyes while he called an ambulance.

The ambulance would come, and I'd be taken to hospital for further tests to find the thing that was so obviously wrong with me. I needed these tests. I needed answers. There was no way they could miss something terminal now, with so many specialists and doctors around. Someone had to find something before it was too late.

For all the waking hours my mind spent hypervigilant over every ache and pain—reminding me not to miss a beat just in case my body was slowly killing me, and I was ignoring it—there, ever so quietly in the space between that space, shame flickered. Rational thoughts managed to niggle through a glimpse of space besieged by the villainous thoughts. Why was I going to such lengths to get someone's attention? Why did I put James through this? My sons were in the room. How could I do this to my children? As much as I wore the guilt of my staged performances, it was the lesser of the two evils. I was sorry on the inside, but I just couldn't admit to the health anxiety obsession increasingly controlling my life, when I honestly thought they would find something wrong with me.

I played the sickness, fainting, ambulance to hospital game no less than four times. Every time the doctors ran the tests, nothing worrying ever came back. No cancer, no gallstones, no heart attack, nothing. James was left puzzled, wondering why this was happening when there was no medical explanation for it. I pretended I was just as puzzled. Deep down on some level I probably knew I was okay, but my mind and body were still convincing me there was something terminally wrong.

Most mornings as soon as I woke and tried to eat, a sharp pain pierced my stomach. When my doctor referred me to have a gastroscope and nothing abnormal showed up, I was stunned. This was *real* pain. I could physically feel it. This wasn't in my head. I wasn't crying wolf.

Convinced I could do better than any doctor, I researched online for all stomach-related diseases and soon enough, I found Coeliac Disease. Bingo! Finally, a diagnosis that explained everything that was wrong with me. To be sure, I took all my 'evidence' of all the symptoms I matched up like a game of snap to my doctor and convinced him I needed the test. The results showed the probability of Coeliac Disease.

The relief was immediate. Now, instead of trying to explain my way out of every ache and pain, I had a real medical diagnosis I could announce whenever the pain surfaced. James was relieved to finally have an answer too. Everything would settle down now I had 'a condition'. Now my mind had something else to focus on and I had a plausible 'story' to tell people.

On 1 December 2008, Anna's mum, Jill, died of bowel cancer, almost a year after diagnosis. I was shattered, not quite believing she was gone. Three weeks before she passed away, her daughters and I gathered in her lounge room, laughing and sharing jokes. Seeing her frail body, I wondered how she kept a smile on her face, fully aware of her own demise. I left Jill's house believing in my heart I would see her again, not wanting to say a final goodbye because this wasn't it. Anna knew. Not that she said anything. Still, I held on, refusing to believe God would take away someone I depended on being there in the background. Besides, good people like Jill don't die. If good people die, then what will happen to all the other good people? Will I fall victim to the same fate now that I was a good person who had my shit mostly under control?

I didn't want to grieve. It only made her death real, and I wasn't ready to accept that she was gone. Besides, she wasn't my mother, and I didn't have the right to grieve as though she was.

Six weeks after Jill's funeral, James and I planned a car trip with our two young boys to watch the Tour Down Under in Adelaide. Not that I was interested in cycling, more to catch a glimpse of the event's star competitor Lance Armstrong in the flesh after reading his biography.

Planning the trip was a pleasant distraction from the non-stop internal chatter and burning sensations I tried to block out of every waking moment. Despite a diagnosis, chronic panic and anxiety continued to bubble beneath the surface. My tormenting voices weren't convinced Coeliac Disease was the real culprit, still provoking me to believe something more sinister was going on.

I tried to fight back with more vigour, trying to convince The Beast that was my dark thoughts, of my Coeliac diagnosis. I could feel The Beast was slowly overtaking again and it was becoming too much to handle. I was uncertain how long it would be before I was no longer in control, but I feared it would be soon.

We packed our bags the night before for an early morning start to Adelaide. All we had to do was eat breakfast, get the boys ready, pack some final things, and leave for the long drive ahead. Our aim was to arrive in Adelaide before nightfall, in time to feed the boys dinner.

As usual, I woke to instant mind chatter, followed quickly by a tight chest and shortness of breath. The aches, pains, and burning sensation fired up their usual ripples and vibrated through my limbs. Nothing new, it was familiar to me now. I was still adjusting to a gluten free diet, so I grabbed a banana. As soon as I swallowed, a striking pain ran throughout my body, like a knife was stripping my stomach with a sharp blade. I crouched over in agony and yelled out to James.

"I've just eaten a fucking piece of fruit! This is bullshit! What the fuck will I do if I can't even eat a simple piece of fruit? I have to go to emergency!"

I was terrified I'd been misdiagnosed. Proof the beastly voices inside me were right. There must be something far more serious than Coeliac disease. *See, I really am sick*, my mind tormented. I was starving and I couldn't keep anything down.

I rang Jean and asked if she could drive me to hospital while James stayed home with the boys. She was always good in emergencies. As soon as we arrived, Jean whispered a quick tip. "If they ask you what number pain you're in, always say ten. That way you'll get seen straight away." That wouldn't be too hard, I *was* in an awful lot of pain.

Thanks to Jean's hot tip, I was promptly ushered into another room to await the doctor. Jean quickly remarked, with a glimpse of pride, how this strategy worked liked a charm. While we waited, I glanced over at Jean when a massive revelation struck. The crippling pain which had me doubled in agony until I entered the doctor's room had vanished. And for once, I knew why.

I was sick, not physically, but mentally.

All the times I'd been rushed by ambulance to hospital, the fainting episodes, every frequent pain, every single time I ran to the doctor, the symptoms vanished as soon as I arrived. I'd made this connection before. I'd sit in emergency and watch handfuls of people around me genuinely suffering while my own pain dissipated. I'd never admit it, convincing myself I couldn't make myself this sick. It had to be real.

Now the connection was abundantly clear. The pain always disappeared as soon as the doctors or specialists were examining me. Every time I sidled up to James and told him I had an or ache or pain, it would suddenly disappear. Now there was a reason why doctors could never find a problem.

There wasn't anything to find.

There was no way I'd admit this to Jean or the doctor, so I played along one last time, promising myself I would never do this again. I had to tell James, though I didn't know where or how to start. There was so much to it, but now I knew the truth. And the only way to get better and stop this charade, which was impacting my family, was to admit to it. Even if it made me feel like a fool.

Because of my performance, we didn't leave for Adelaide until 2pm. During the drive I reflected on all the drama of the last year, feeling completely ashamed and embarrassed. I realised Jill's diagnosis and death had a profound impact and it contributed to my anxiety and panic. It's what started my health obsession. In a lot of ways, my own realisations were a huge relief.

I purposely waited for the dark of night to hide my shame before I told James.

"You know how the doctor thinks I'm a Coeliac?"

"Yeah," he replied.

I held my breath, knowing I was about to reveal everything, but not knowing how he'd take it. "Well." I paused. "I... I don't think it's that."

James turned sharply towards me. "What do you mean? You've been really unwell. Every time you eat gluten, you get really sick. All the pain and aches you've been getting, all pointed to you being a Coeliac."

"I know," I said, nodding as he listed off all of my symptoms.

"So what do you think it is, then?" he asked.

"I... I think it's all in my head."

For the first time I heard the words I'd been too afraid to admit out loud. The relief was instant. Despite feeling embarrassed, I had not expected the weight of my worries and anxieties to lift so quickly. Without any hindrance, air flowed effortlessly into my lungs. It felt amazing. Speaking out was the first step towards recovery.

James tried to make sense of the bombshell I'd just dropped. "What do you mean? How can you make this up?"

Driving the final thirty minutes, I explained everything from the moment I'd learned of Jill's diagnosis to her death and how it all snowballed into losing control of my body and mind. I felt lighter as I purged every dark thought, every deep fear, leaving nothing out, like every admission was a tonne of weight falling away from me. I wanted to apologise for all the pain, stress, and upheaval I'd caused. For raising our young sons in a chaotic and unstable environment. I assured James I'd get to the bottom of it and make it right for all of us.

"It'll be okay, honey," he assured me as he grabbed my hand and held it tight, like he always did.

Tears streamed down my face as I turned to him in the darkness and nodded.

Releasing all that I held onto didn't erase my problems completely. But whatever the next chapter brought, now that he knew, everything would be okay. Eventually.

Chapter 23

I hoped things would improve dramatically now that I'd told James what had been happening over the previous year. Now he could help make sense of my irrational thoughts.

But I learned quickly, it was one thing to have irrational thoughts and quite another to actually share them without the darkness to hide behind. Sometimes I did, while other times I kept those thoughts to myself, still far too ashamed to admit just how irrational they could be and how frequently they consumed me.

Jill's death crossed my mind often, creating new layers of fears that provoked deeper existential questions about life and death. Questions I rarely thought about, but now urgently needed the answers to. I couldn't shake it. I wanted to know why people died. Why some suffered and others who deserved pain lived. Why can't the people who inflict so much pain on others die instead of the good ones? It didn't seem fair. Wasn't God a fair God? Weren't his faithful followers, the true believers, meant to be the last ones standing? Where was the reward for a life of devotion if He was just going to cut it short?

Jill was a good person, devoted to God. She loved her family and showed kindness to everyone. She attended church and adorned her home with effigies, celebrating her faith. Why would God take her away? And so quickly and so painfully. It wasn't right.

Jill's faith supported mine. Her faith upheld mine, even in moments of doubt. Sometimes during a moral crisis, I often thought of Jill and her staunch faith, knowing as long as she trusted God, I could too.

Her death exposed the fragility of life. If God could take her away, my uncle away, then he could just as easily take me. It didn't matter that I had two beautiful boys and a supportive husband, my life could still end. That terrified me!

Somehow, I'd convinced myself both my uncle's and Jill's existence protected mine. By taking them away, my security blanket, my belief in a safe world, was gone. Would I be taken next? After all, nothing was guaranteed anymore. Good people died. How could I feel safe and protect my own family? Who's to say James wouldn't be taken away from me also? How could I keep myself from leaving this world when Jill and my uncle hadn't exactly had a say in dying? A ripple of terror swept through me.

Urgency to find the meaning of life bombarded my mind. My faith in God was no longer a "sure thing" for a long life. Wasn't there an unwritten rule in place? My faith in exchange for a long life? Faith wasn't enough now, nor was trying to be a good person.

Despite no imminent danger, life terrified me beyond my thoughts and pervaded my life as I searched relentlessly for purpose in the everyday, mundane moments. Get up to a new day? Why? Hang the washing out? Why? Clean the house? Why, oh why? Nothing made sense. No purpose attached to anything I did anymore. My mind continually looped, searching for meaning in everything, and wondering if I could be snatched away at any second. Every day was like playing a game of Russian Roulette. Was today the day I succumbed to a terminal illness, had an accident, was killed? *What is the fucking point of doing anything, or trying to become something, if we all just die anyway?*

One day, while James was at work, my young boys asked for water. I grabbed a couple of cups and suddenly a wave of heat radiated throughout my body. My nerves fired up like a furnace to alert me of imminent danger.

My legs turned to jelly as I struggled to stay upright. The cups became completely foreign objects. *What the hell do I have in my hands? What the hell am I doing? Why am I doing this?* The floor beneath me became unstable, like I was standing on a wooden raft at sea, trying to remain upright in treacherous waters. Everything around me seemed to be moving and my trembling body gasped for air.

My god, I'm going crazy. Where am I? Help, I screamed inside.

Frantically, I searched for something familiar to stop me from collapsing to the ground. But nothing around me made sense: the house, the kitchen, the chairs, the kid's toys. Where the hell was I? Something needed to ground me back into reality, and quickly.

Aware that my two young boys were off in the distance, busily playing in the same room, I forcibly convinced myself, *it's okay, Beck, your boys need water. This is a meaningful task. They're thirsty and that's why you're getting water. This has purpose, it's okay.* As I repeated this over and over, my senses slowly came back. The ground beneath my feet stabilised back to solid and the weight of the cups in my hands normalised. I walked towards my boys, handed them the cups, and flopped myself on the couch, stunned by this strange episode.

What the hell just happened?

That, I learned, was my very first panic attack. I didn't tell James, instead, convincing myself it was a once off. Besides, James would just brush it off. He had a logical mind and didn't over-analyse everything like I did. He'd just assure me I was fine, and I was. Sort of.

My health obsession and hyper-vigilance over my body never went away. Still stressing over every single ache and pain, continually monitoring my body, keeping abreast of any changes no matter how insignificant. Jill's stage four diagnosis constantly reminded me I needed to keep a watchful eye on anything that could be slowly killing me. I was constantly torn between not wanting to appear crazy by seeing the doctor for every pain, yet terrified I was ignoring a sign I was dying. Sometimes I'd deliberately ask James, what do you think this pain means? Or point to a new mark on my body and ask, "What do you think this is?" I always hoped he'd shrug it off as nothing or scoff at the ridiculousness of my own terminal diagnosis. When James compared my aches or marks to something he experienced, his stories acted like a strong dose of morphine, putting my mind and body at ease immediately. Secretly I'd promoted him to doctor. As long as James MD was okay with my aches and pain, so was I.

Most days my obsessive, intrusive thoughts were so intense I'd hold it together as long as I could until James came home. His presence was enough to ground me. Ask me to rate my anxiety today, I'd say to him, just to diffuse the ticking time bomb in my mind.

James still didn't know my anxiety had erupted into panic. Nor did I tell him of my new fear of living a meaningless, purposeless life. How could I admit this without worrying him again? If I could just get through each day, everything would be fine.

But things only got worse.

On Wednesdays, my one day off as a mum, both my boys went to child-care. When I got home from dropping off my sons, an eerie silence gripped the air and released my deepest fears, that I normally kept well-hidden. Silence often reminded me my dark thoughts were never too far away. With no distractions, no little people to care for, my obsessive thoughts now had maximum opportunity to dance and linger in the air around me, tormenting my unstable mind.

There's no safety net anymore, Rebekah. God has taken them away. There's no one here to rescue you. You're on your own. And if I can take Jill away, then I can take you away. Life is not safe for you anymore, Rebekah. Fear rippled through my body. Suddenly, a burning sensation rushed like volcanic lava through my veins. My breathing escalated into hyperventilation and my heart belted against my ribs like a jackhammer.

Oh my God. Oh my God. Help me.

I searched around for something to ground me. But I couldn't find it. Hysterical, I screamed for help into my empty house. I needed to call someone, and quickly. But who could I call? I tried Anna, but there was no answer. I couldn't call James, I just couldn't.

The only anonymous call I could make, allowing me to unleash my tortured mind, was Lifeline. The phone rang and rang as I repeatedly screamed out. *Please pick up. Please pick up. Hurry, please hurry!* As soon as someone picked up, I screamed, "Help me, please! I don't know where I am. Please, please, I need help!"

The lady on the other end tried to calm me down. Despite standing in my own bedroom, everything was unfamiliar. There was nothing holding me back from a black hole trying to suck me in and swallow me up. I continued to scream, begging for some evidence as to where I was.

She calmly asked me, "Have you got any children?"

Her question grounded me instantly, like I'd been thrown down a tunnel and thumped onto the ground. My bedroom and everything within it—my bed, pictures of my children, my hairbrush, my pillow—had a story, a purpose that came instantly back as my life.

"Yes," I answered, and then threw myself down on the bed and cried hysterically.

I wailed to the lady on the phone. "I'm a mum. I'm a mum. I'm so sorry, I don't know what's happening to me. How can I be a good mum to my boys when I'm going crazy? How can I look after them? They deserve a mum who has it all together, and I'm falling apart. What's happening to me?"

The lady stayed on the line, reassuring me until I was okay. I hung up, feeling more drained than I ever had. Lying like a zombie, trying to make sense of the most terrifying experience of my life, my eyes heavy, I succumbed to exhaustion and fell asleep.

The next few months became the loneliest and scariest of my life, even when surrounded by friends. As I tried to keep my anxiety and panic under control and hidden, at times an unexpected wave of panic would overcome me in the middle of a coffee date with friends, or a lunch date with James, and I'd have to get up and flee before I exploded into another full-blown panic attack. Sometimes the panic struck when out with my young boys. I'd have to breathe with such control and focus, like a Jedi Master trying to mentally keep a boiling pot from spilling over, just to fight off a panic attack.

I didn't know how to cope with the instability of life or the fear of illness taking me away, and yet I tried to find a purpose in a life that would end regardless of how hard I tried.

Nothing was safe or sure anymore. Knowing life could be taken away in an instant terrified me to my core. The more I obsessed, the more I struggled to silence the non-stop thoughts yammering in my head. Despite feeling exhausted at the end of each day, trying to disarm panic and look after my boys, my mind wouldn't quit. The only way I found I could sleep was to lay on the couch and glue my eyes and ears to every scene, watching *Friends*. That way I wasn't in my head. The actor's voices could drown out my own voices and eventually I would doze off. It was the only thing I could do to get my mind to rest so I could rest.

After a couple of months of sleeping on the couch while James had quietly supported my need to do anything to cope, he finally spoke up.

As I settled in for the couch—my new bed—yet again, James came to me.

"Will you ever come back to bed?" he asked, solemn.

I couldn't give the definitive answer he was hoping for. I knew he missed sharing the bed. He missed the intimacy. It wasn't completely gone, but the occasions were becoming few and far between. He never pressured me; but for once, I saw the sadness on his face, and I knew this illness affected him too.

"I don't know," I replied apologetically. I knew I needed to solve this if we were ever to have another child. We'd spoken of the possibility a few times by then. Every time I decided to sort out the baby clothes, my heart sank, like throwing them away was also throwing away the chance for another baby. Our youngest son was two-and-a-half, and though I was managing okay, I knew I was too sick to contemplate another child. My heart yearned for a little girl, but I just wasn't ready.

"I just need more time," I implored. "I promise I will do what I need to do to get better."

"Okay," he replied with so much love and trust. He kissed my forehead and went off to bed alone, again.

The next day I found out I was already pregnant with our third child.

Chapter 24

Now that I was expecting again, resolving my illness was an urgent priority. Any excitement was marred by my rapidly deteriorating mental health and the deadline loomed to sort this out before my baby was born. I'd decided against seeking my doctor's help because I knew I wasn't physically unwell.

I still made regular appointments, trying to be diagnosed with a new medical condition Google assured me I had. Despite requesting blood tests, or another scan or ultrasound, nothing ever showed up. By now I knew it was a mask for a deeper issue. I needed another kind of help.

Not only was my anxiety at an all-time high, intruding on every part of my day, but now my panic attacks were so frequent and unpredictable, I was losing the battle just to keep up a brave face out in public. Raising three children with an unstable, erratic mind weighed on me heavily. Trying to ignore the voices in my head and deal with my children's cries and demands stressed me out to the point I'd often lash out at them just to be able to silence one or the other. Sometimes it was easier to quieten the boys than the voice in my head. It was all getting too much. The viciousness of this constant cycle exhausted me. I became hostage to my own mental turmoil.

I searched for a psychologist specialising in anxiety and panic disorders, someone with a magic answer that would permanently stop the racing thoughts and physical symptoms that ravaged my body. Someone who could fill in the missing pieces that separated me, constantly tiptoeing around impending doom, from the people who weren't having panic attacks every day. I convinced myself I didn't know something "normal" people knew. That was all it was. Surely an anxiety specialist would provide the missing piece of the puzzle that would cure my insanity once and for all.

Scanning the yellow pages, the words 'Anxiety Specialist' leapt off the page in large, bold print with a big black frame around it. When I rang to arrange an appointment, I quizzed the receptionist to make sure the psychologist was indeed a specialist as the ad proclaimed.

"Yes, of course, Rebekah. She's dealt with hundreds of cases over the years." Just what I need, I thought.

Being thirty-six weeks pregnant, I had run out of time to sort this out on my own. This needed to be good. She had to know how bad my anxiety, my daily life, really was. I'd need to abandon my usual brave face that masked my struggles and force myself to be completely honest, so the psychologist wouldn't waste a minute digging into my psyche. I needed urgent click-of-the-fingers solutions.

When my name was called, I eagerly walked in, sat, leaned forward, and waited for the usual start. I'd done this so many times before, I could almost predict the routine without her even uttering a word. The counsellor would break the ice with general weather talk in a soft, yet warm and inviting voice that would melt away the protective wall between us. I would then open up and answer her scripted questions, blah, blah, blah.

But the usual warm, caring tone I expected never came.

"So, what's the problem?" She spoke as if she were bored to death, barely looking at me as she pushed one side of her mouth upward.

My gaze darted around the room, and I wondered if I'd sent myself to the right place. Was I to mirror her apathy, or try to show her how it's meant to be done? Or simply plead for compassion? I'd had enough therapy by now to know this was not a great start.

"Um, I have some problems," I stuttered. *Yeah, "some". More like an avalanche of problems. Good start, Beck!*

Stone-faced and dry, she repeated, "Okay, what's the problem?"

By now I wanted to walk out. *Fuck this shit. I don't need this crap from you. Do you know how much it took for me to just come here? At least pretend you give a shit.*

Bound by my urgency for help, I stayed. Perhaps, she needed time to warm up. Maybe I was judging her too quickly, knowing I needed time also.

I spoke in a calm and considered manner, rather than melodramatically, as I'd planned to, about how my anxiety and obsessive thoughts had become so bad that it had escalated to daily multiple panic attacks. The constant feeling of impending doom. The fear of managing three children and my own mental state. I detailed my inability to find any purpose in life after Jill's death. I spoke of the lightning speed at which my anxiety switched to panic and the multiple physical symptoms that savaged my body like wild animals on a fresh kill. The burning sensations perpetually bubbling beneath the surface of my limbs, the rapid heartbeat, hyperventilation, my shaky legs, and constant dizziness; how it all erupted in an instant at the mere thought—consciously or unconsciously—of anything that terrified me. Which by now, was just about anything.

I pushed on past the lump in my throat that usually seized the very words I would normally silence and bravely admitted, "I am struggling to exist."

With a sigh, I reclined back in my seat, relieved and somewhat proud I'd been brave enough to tell it like it was, despite not giving any emotion to it. Now I waited for her expertise and a solution that would save me.

"So, do you understand how anxiety works?" she asked, seemingly unmoved by my raw admission.

What the fuck? I silently raged. *Are you not even going to do reflective listening? The very basics of counselling? Demonstrating you've heard and understood what I've been saying? Not even an attempt at caring? No, "sounds like this is very difficult for you." Really? What the fuck is this style you prescribe to called, lady! Right now, I don't give a fuck HOW anxiety works, I just need a solution. Can you not see I'm 36 weeks pregnant? A lesson on the structure or the mechanics of anxiety is not really what I need to hear right now!*

"Um, no, not really," I muttered, all the while suppressing the rage wanting to surface.

For the next forty minutes, she rambled on, lecturing me on how anxiety trickles down from your brain to another part at the base of your neck, and travels through something.

I nodded, pretending to listen, jaw clenched, hands clasped tightly in my lap like I was pushing myself into the seat to keep me from fleeing the room. *How does this fucking help me through a panic attack?* I wanted to scream at her. *Have you EVER had a panic attack? Do you even know how it feels! I can positively assure you I am not concentrating on any GLAND or whatever in my body at that point! I am trying to find some ground. I am trying not to lose my mind. I am trying to find something that makes sense in my life so I can be okay and care for my children.*

After her lecture, she asked no more questions about my life, or what had started this whole thing. What specifically triggered my anxiety, or how I was coping. Nothing. She just blurted, "Ok, we don't have much time to deal with this before the baby arrives, so we need to get this sorted in the next four weeks." She spoke as if I was a deadline she needed to complete.

"Sure, okay," I replied, seething with rage inside. *You can shove your $150 lecture on anxiety. I will not be coming back.*

Leaving, feeling completely disheartened, I wondered if anyone could help me. I didn't want a lecture, a graphic explanation, a diagram. I just needed help.

I remembered Bryan, a psychologist I'd met at church. He was a tall, slender man with a brown beard and glasses. He'd run a relationship workshop James and I attended before we were married, so I was already familiar with his relaxed yet compassionate style.

His gentle voice felt like a warm hug. Exactly what I needed to help me. I wasn't sure if he'd agree to see me professionally outside of church, but I knew his manner and added insights into 'God's ways' was what I was seeking. Thankfully, he agreed.

In our first session, Bryan greeted me, in his familiar soft tone and warm smile, instantly allowing me to relax in the chair. I felt confident he would help clear the fog over my life and help me make peace with the war going inside my head.

Relaying my problems, my constant anxiety, my bewilderment as to how I had got myself into this mess, he locked eyes with me, nodding every now and then, listening to every word and emotion that lingered off certain words. Every now and then, a smile appeared on his face, which assured me he not only understood my fears, but I was safe in sharing them with him. He genuinely cared and seemed united with me in finding a solution.

He never showed any indication that he too believed I was in trouble. He simply replied, "You'll be fine." Not that I trusted those words right now, but his faith at least gave me some hope.

When I expressed how scared I was at the thought of managing three children, he explained how raising children only accounted for about ten percent of our lives. In theory, it seemed like nothing. The worries and high expectations I held to be a good mother seemed trivial in the grand scheme of *their* lives. But his statistics did nothing to relieve my turmoil.

He assured me of God's love, promising things would eventually make sense. Though his sage advice provided instant comfort in the moment, it did nothing to help long-term. It felt too simplistic. I needed a strategy I could take away to curtail the torture I was living through. Would he offer more practical advice if he knew just how close I was to a complete mental breakdown?

As if the universe aligned to provoke my fears, I had a panic attack at my next appointment in Bryan's waiting room. Waiting rooms were often my safe haven, knowing help was just on the other side of the wall.

But that day, sitting alone, silence provoked my mind to wander way into the future, inventing worries and obstacles and fears surrounding my children. It wasn't simply things I needed to get done today or how the boys were going in day care or what I would make for dinner that night. No, my mind dove straight to the deepest depth of life's unanswered questions, like every particle in the air had an urgent post it note attached to it with a list to complete and worries to sort out immediately.

Every part of my life magnified, like my entire life was flashing before me. I wasn't just trying to figure out today's problems, but tomorrow's and the next ten years beyond that. How would I live out my entire life in this very moment? Pressure mounted, like a boulder-sized weight crushing my chest, sending an instant ripple of terror through me, yanking the safety net from underneath as the floor opened up, swirling around, harnessing its power to drag me down and suck me in.

My breathing escalated and my heart beat like a crazy drum. *How can I do this? Help me. Where am I? I can't do this. I can't handle life. It's too much! What do I do at this point? Do I run out without any explanation? I can't let him see me like this.* My legs turned to jelly and I knew I'd fall if I tried to stand. I waited desperately for Bryan to call my name. A break in my torment would ground me in an instant. *Please, please, Bryan, hurry up, I'm going to lose it. I can't hold this in much longer.*

Bryan poked his head around the doorway and smiled as he prompted me to follow. *Thank God!*

Slowly I lifted myself up, trying to push through my shaky legs and hide the panic attack I was still in the middle of. Once I sat, I waited for him to speak. *Please lead me in,* I pleaded. But he just sat there, smile drawn, calm, and ready for me to begin. But what could I say? I didn't know how to play it, but I needed him to see how this was crippling me without me having to spell it out.

I glanced his way momentarily, while trying to appear calm and composed as my nerves bubbled at the surface of every limb, like a pot of boiling water. I hoped he'd detect something was amiss without me having to say it. I couldn't risk the humiliation to admit the state I was in. *Speak, Rebekah, shout it out. Scream out to him! Tell him how bad this is! Scream, we need to get it out, Rebekah. Scream!* But I couldn't.

Struggling to hide my shaking body, I took a deep breath and finally spoke.

"Bryan, I'm really afraid right now. I'm kinda having one of those panic things." My voice tremored with each word, trying to hold back the voice inside wanting to scream out my petrified state.

My body gave a preview of this little episode. My legs bounced up and down, and my breathing was shallow and loud. Tears fell as I relayed my panic attack in the waiting room. I tried to water down my symptoms, but my body decided not to play the let's-pretend-we're-fine game. I hung my head in shame, knowing I was losing the battle to contain my panic.

I became very aware of how my body was responding to fear now, hearing my words so clearly, just as Bryan was hearing me, as I described how much I feared living every single day. How much I feared not being able to cope. Still trying to find a reason for Jill's death that didn't constantly make me afraid to live. Still trying to find the reason why we live at all. Guilt for bringing another life into a world that made no sense, that had no purpose, ate at me. Especially now that I was not stable enough. I cried, not only out of fear, but sadness that I had got to this point. I was barely hanging on, and no matter what I did, nothing made sense.

Bryan very calmly passed the tissues. "You'll be okay, Rebekah."

"Will I? But how?" I urged. "How do you know?"

He asked me to close my eyes, a task which terrified me outside of the comfort of my bedroom. It was like being locked in a dark room I couldn't escape, with nothing but my worst fears to devour me like a pack of ravenous wolves. I didn't want to go there. I needed to keep my eyes open and look at something I could attach to. Anything was safer than my mind.

Still, he instructed me to breathe, to slow everything down. But each time I tried to get a full breath in, my lungs shut off from the neck down, which triggered more anxiety. I quickly gave up and opened my eyes. "I can't do this," I cried. "I just can't."

Bryan explained the exercise helped to increase relaxation and reduce my anxiety and panic by getting me to focus on the now. Peace is here in the present, he'd say. Learn to be in the now, he kept saying.

I nodded, trying to understand his point. But I didn't want anything to do with 'the now'. The now is terrifying. Now is horrible. I can't be here in the now, because I'm not coping. I want to go to *there*, wherever there is! There, the place where fear, anxiety, terror, and panic attacks don't exist. 'There' is where I want to be. Why can't you just take me there?

I left the session exhausted and without a concrete solution. Nothing, it seemed, could make the overwhelming fear and panic go away.

I continued to see Bryan for a few more sessions as my due date edged closer, but just to offload my mounting fears. Although I loved Bryan's style, I wasn't getting the practical help to quash my anxiety permanently. While Bryan helped make some sense of Jill's death, my anxiety was a living, breathing monster; The Beast who'd taken up permanent residency in my mind, bulldozing any rational thoughts trying to push through.

The Beast had me like a puppet on a string, controlling everything. Orchestrating a full body ripple effect after a thought was planted. The fear, the panic, the overwhelm, caused a tsunami effect on my body, and now I was powerless to stop it. I couldn't control it, nor stop the physical symptoms that cascaded through my body, affecting every cell that crossed its path. It was too powerful and strong to be stopped now. And no one could help me.

I tried to manage each day as best as I could, carrying a baby I was ready to give birth to physically, but not mentally or emotionally. My bubbling nerves, along with my head yammering with torment, followed me as I went about my daily routine, using all my energy to keep The Beast at bay.

Each night I prayed the demands of a new baby would starve The Beast into oblivion and everything would return to normal.

That was my only hope. The only solution I had left.

Chapter 25

In February 2011, the girl I'd hoped for was born. My initial assumptions were true; I had less time to think about my anxieties and fears. With three children under five, life was busy. Competition for my darkest thoughts was lost to their demands, and I thought The Beast had somehow just disappeared with my newest arrival.

Two weeks after my daughter was born, I settled her down to sleep for the night and went to have a shower. As I stood under the hot water, a sharp pain struck just below my ribs. Initially I ignored it, but moments later it came back, only this time, the pain lingered.

By now I was quite good at self-diagnosing my anxiety. Hyper-analysing every anxiety-related ache and pains over the last couple of years had made me pretty good at knowing if it was due to my worries or not. But this was noticeably different. The pain, even when I tried to ignore it or put it down to my monkey mind—which was the usual trick I used to test if it was anxiety or not—kept coming back. I sprung out of the shower, crouching over as the pain worsened. I wanted to tell James, but I worried he'd brush it off as anxiety too.

"There's a pain under my ribs, and it feels like it's getting worse," I announced, firmly hoping it was enough to command his immediate attention.

"That's no good," he replied with vague sympathy, before turning back to the TV.

Just as the pain stabbed my body, this time with ferocious intensity, I fell to my knees and screamed. James bolted over.

"Are you having a panic attack," he shouted, but only to be heard over my screams.

"No. No!" I screamed in agony. This was something completely new.

James rang the ambulance and then rang Jean to look after the kids while I was taken to hospital.

When I arrived, doctors poked and prodded around different parts of my torso, pressing on the skin and tapping in that way doctors do sometimes. The appendix was dismissed as the culprit because the pain area was too high. The only explanation left was gallstones, but that was impossible since they'd scanned for gallstones before I fell pregnant with my daughter and nothing showed up.

With preliminary testing done, doctors had no definitive medical answer for the sudden attack. A sickly feeling bubbled in the pit of my stomach, made worse knowing the pain, as if on cue, disappeared shortly after I'd arrived and been assessed, just like all the other times. Had I made this up in my head again? *Great! Good one, Beck, another fucking episode.* I didn't want to believe I'd created this. Feeling certain *this* pain was real. Really real. I hadn't pulled out that trick for a long time. Even so, I felt so ashamed of the possibility and avoided looking at James.

My heart sunk as I looked down from my hospital bed at my sleeping daughter, completely unaware of how messed up her mother was. She doesn't deserve this. A mum who couldn't sort her shit out. Surely God could have chosen someone far more stable for her.

An appointment was arranged the following morning to have my gall bladder scanned. Not that I wanted to. What was the point? James didn't say much except to suggest it was a good idea, 'just in case'. He needed the clarity more than I did, hoping the results would prove to me this was nothing more than another anxiety attack.

I nodded, knowing what this scan really meant.

I struggled to sleep that night. I knew how chronic my health anxiety was and questioned if I'd been masking it under the stress of being busy. These days I was the first to admit when my anxiety played up, and I'd stopped trying to hide it from James. I even shared my latest aches and symptoms with him, no matter how silly I felt freaking out about it, waiting for his opinion before I diagnosed myself with a terminal illness. But after this latest episode, it bothered me that I'd potentially missed it.

My issues before my daughter was born were not yet resolved. Anxiety and panic don't simply just go away, I knew that much. I was busy, but I didn't think I was so busy that I could ignore the signs my anxiety was playing up, or that an impending panic attack was on its way.

I wanted to get better and yet this latest episode had me feeling like I'd gone back to square one.

The next morning, the radiographer scanned for gallstones.

"Have you been experiencing pain?" she asked.

"Yes," I replied, briefing her on last night's episode.

She moved over my gall bladder and stopped immediately. "Oh," she said, "Look at that!"

"What?" I asked with curiosity, even though my heart rate jumped with panic.

"Your gall bladder is full of gallstones."

"What? Are you sure?"

"Yes." She pointed to the screen, circling around the white spots. "Those are stones. You have quite a few in there."

Instead of the throat-squeezing panic I'd usually experience, my anxiety fell away. I was over the moon that they'd found something. My gut instinct was right. I could barely wait to leap off the bed and phone James with the news, hoping he would trust me just that little bit more. As much as I knew I wasn't well, I knew my body now.

But it would take more than one incident to convince James I was okay.

A week after that scan, James and I with our three kids, attended a birthday party. A few hours later, white spots began popping up around my youngest son's mouth. When they became painful, James and I drove him straight to hospital. By then, he was screaming in agony as the spots kept multiplying. Without an immediate diagnosis, doctors advised he stay overnight. Reluctantly, I hugged my son tight and left. I'd never been away from any of my children. I didn't get much sleep that night, worrying about him.

When I returned to hospital the next morning, my son's mouth had worsened. His lips were bright red and had doubled in size, with white spots bigger and spreading to the inside of his mouth.

He stayed in hospital for the next five days. Doctors suggested I visit without my three-week-old daughter, who'd not yet been immunised, due to the high risk of it being contagious. But how I could leave my young daughter while she still needed regular feeds?

The thought of asking anyone for help, even Jean, didn't cross my mind.

My heart ached at the thought of my three-year-old son sitting alone in hospital, on top of the regular demands I already had with a newborn and a busy five-year-old.

Every morning, I'd have to pack my daughter up, drop my eldest son off at kinder and be at hospital to sit with my son, just so he wouldn't be alone. James spent most nights at hospital while I went home, too exhausted to cook, instead making a simple sandwich or instant noodles for my other son. As soon my children were in bed, I was alone with nothing but worries burdening my mind, wondering how I would continue to cope if my middle child was seriously ill.

Somewhere in the back of my mind, a niggling voice torpedoed through the chatter. *You can't just feed your son a sandwich for dinner. What kind of mother are you? You're not doing a very good job, are you? Is this how you care for your children?* I quickly turned on the TV to drown out the noise threatening to break me, while telling myself, "I'll do better tomorrow. I'll make sure I have a 'real' dinner for my son."

Things settled down in the weeks after my son was discharged from hospital. I was still racing around, juggling the feeding and sleeping times of a six-week-old, in between driving the boys to kinder and day care. Some days I couldn't get an hour at home just to sit without having somewhere else to be. Most of my time at home was spent in the kitchen, prepping food, cleaning, cooking dinner, or playing catch up with the never-ending washing and folding. There was never any break. The routine exhausted me, and yet still I didn't ask anyone for help. This was motherhood. *Suck it up, Beck, you wanted to have three children! Just be better*, I'd tell myself.

Innocent little digs at my subpar parenting began slithering their way into my mind, as I paced around the house day after day, trying to keep up with the endless list of tasks, provoking me to consider if I'd made a mistake having three children. *Maybe I had overdone it with three? Why did I have a third if I can't handle it? Was it pure selfishness just to have the girl? I should know what I'm doing by now. It's too much. I shouldn't be this exhausted. I'm such a failure.*

The very fact I was exhausted proved to my mind that I was useless and incapable of handling their constant demands. Yet I was determined to remain afloat, in charge and in control. *I'm okay, I'm okay*, I kept trying to convince myself. But the honest truth was, I wasn't sure how much longer I could ignore the taunting thoughts.

One day, as I mindlessly prepared the boys' lunch, I suddenly became hyperaware of the monotonous routine I was repeating every single day, when a realisation hit me: I was forever bound to the kitchen, to the home! I slid to the floor and burst into tears. My life's purpose was reduced to the kitchen and attending to kids. That was the sum of my life. Groundhog Day the Sequel. Cook, clean, children, repeat.

I thought back to my teaching days—out there in the world, enjoying a career.

Searching for memories of my old life, I could barely forge a clear picture. The days of being me, working, going out, seeing friends, didn't even seem real. Was I still the same person? I barely recognised her.

Was I just having another existential crisis? I didn't know. But I couldn't help question the reality of my life. Who had I become now? What was my value and purpose to the world outside of the house, outside of being a mum and a wife? Was this it for me? This mothering job was exhausting, relentless, and sometimes cruel. The days were long, never-ending, and so goddamn monotonous. There were no rewards, no accolades, no paid time off, no annual leave, not even a pat on the back for a job well done when I was acing it.

Why did I even consider having a third child?

The load felt so heavy. I didn't want to do it anymore. I needed a break from motherhood, but how? There was no possibility of that ever happening. Motherhood went on forever. No matter where I went, I would *always* be a mother! Even if I flew to the ends of the earth where no man existed, I would still be a mother! It was like being attached to a rubber band, and no matter how far it stretched, it would spring back. There was no escape.

I was trapped in this role of my own making with no end in sight.

Panic surged through my body. The Bastard Beast had returned.

Increasingly I begrudged going to bed, knowing I'd be rising to repeat the same damn routine. I tried expressing my feelings to other mums, some family members, but my words fell on deaf ears. My concerns were brushed off as a facetious or exhaustion. No one took them seriously. Even James passed it off as 'tired'. "You'll be fine," he kept saying. "I'm here to help when I get home from work. You know that."

But I knew I wasn't fine.

I envied watching James leave the house every morning, knowing he'd be getting a break. He'd get to have a coffee without a toddler or baby clinging to him, vying for his undivided attention. *Why can you leave, and I can't?*

I want to go out and do something I love, something I'm good at. You get to be you. You get to have adult conversation, use your skills, and be uninhibited by the constraints of demanding children needing something of you every second of the day. Where's my break?!

But I kept going, forcing myself out of bed each morning to parent against the heavy drag trying to pull me back in. More and more, I'd wake crying, feeling less like a person and more like a robot. The only way to function was to go on autopilot. I tried to keep talking to James as best as I could, expressing how tiring it all was. No matter how much I told him, I couldn't let on how anxiety and panic were slowly intruding into my days again. I knew the stress that would cause him. I had to be strong and manage our children while he was at work because that was my job now. How could I tell him I was sick to death of doing this gig already? How could I tell him I hated being a mum, and all I wanted to do was escape?

It was Sunday night, and the kids were all in bed when everything turned to shit again. Sitting in the lounge room, enjoying my hot cup of tea watching as James was getting organised for the working week, my thoughts jumped to waking up again to three children on my own. It sent a terrifying wave of fear and panic through me. A familiar feeling I'd had so many times before. This was not good, and I knew it. I purposely struck up a conversation with James to repress the panic brewing beneath the surface, but it wasn't working. Inside I began screaming, *help me, help me*. I wanted to scream out of sheer terror, but I could not expose how terrified I felt to be left alone with my children. Not even to James.

I ran to the shower in an attempt to thwart a panic attack, desperately wanting to expose me. As the hot water flowed over me, I cried out loud, *it's okay, Beck. You won't hurt your children. You'll be fine. You've done this before. You have survived before and you'll survive again. You're okay, Beck.* I was scared I was even having these thoughts.

Was having three children the problem? I'd never had quite such extreme thoughts like this before I had my daughter. Sure they were bad, but not this bad. Yet my inability to handle motherhood had only worsened since having her. My latest worries all seemed to stem from having a third child. Do I just need to offload my daughter and go back to having the boys? Life would be easier. I coped better when it was just my sons. This seemed like the most rationale solution I had, the only solution I had. But what would I do with my daughter? I didn't want to hurt her. I loved her so much. I just needed to find someone I trusted to raise her and be the mum I couldn't.

With that solution in mind, I started to feel better. I got out of the shower, wrapped the towel around myself, and scooted to the bedroom to make a phone call.

"Hello, Jean." I tried speaking without crying, but it hurt. I had failed. The girl I'd always wanted, I couldn't handle. I couldn't mother three children. I wanted to burst into tears, but that would only make Jean think I was being irrational. I needed her to take me seriously.

"Hi, Beck, how are you?" she asked.

I ignored the question. "Jean, I need you to come and take my daughter."

"What are you talking about, Beck? Take her where?"

"I can't look after her. Can you please come and take her? I can pack her things up for you."

"Beck, what's wrong," Jean asked, sounding really concerned.

"Nothing's wrong."

"Where's James?"

"He's in the other room. He doesn't need to know about this," I insisted. "Jean, please, just come and take her. You can raise her. Please, just do this for me. You can come and get her now," I begged.

"I'm coming over."

Quivering, I tried to contain my tears. "Jean, please don't try to talk me out of it. I just need you to come and get her, please."

Jean replied, "Okay, Beck, I'm coming over right now. I'll be there in a minute."

When she knocked at the door, James wondered why she was visiting so late. I sat frozen on the couch, not daring to look at either of them.

James offered Jean a cuppa as she sat next to me with a book in her hand.

"Now, Beck," she said with compassion, but also in her no-nonsense way. "What's going on?"

I burst into tears. "Jean, I can't do this! I don't want to do this anymore. I'm so tired. I'm sick of doing this every single day. I don't want to be here anymore. Please, just take her for me. I can't look after her. Please," I sobbed.

Jean rubbed my back while she listened.

James eavesdropped from the kitchen. "What's going on?" he asked with a puzzled look on his face.

"Beck, I think you have Post Natal Depression. I've read this book, and it fits what you're describing."

"No way. That's just a cop out! I can't have that. I'm just not capable. I can't do this," I repeated.

I'd never been completely honest about how difficult I was finding three children.

The shock on James's face said everything. "It's okay, Beck. I had no idea you were feeling so overwhelmed. I can help. Honey, I'll help out as much as you need."

"But I don't want to wake up tomorrow and do this again, James," I sobbed. "I don't want to do this anymore. I'm sick of it. I can't handle it!" I pleaded, begging him to hear my cries.

"It's okay, Beck. A lot of women go through this. There's nothing to be ashamed of," Jean said.

But how could I not feel ashamed when I was ready to pack up my own beautiful little girl and send her away? What kind of mother does that? James smirked a little bit, wondering how it would have all have taken place without his knowledge.

James and Jean sat on either side of me and agreed to check in on me more, while Jean would visit more during the day while James was at work.

"Can you please come around tomorrow?" I begged her.

She agreed, comforting James more than anything.

When Jean left, James tucked me into bed, assuring me everything would be fine.

It wasn't. Darker, more terrifying thoughts lurked beyond giving my daughter away. How could I admit I was terrified to be alone with my children for fear some strong force I couldn't resist, would urge me to pick up a heavy object and bludgeon them with it. I didn't want to hurt them, but I wasn't sure I wouldn't if I was left on my own, pushed further and further towards breaking point.

The next morning, James got ready for work before sitting beside me, gently stroking my hair while I slept, like he always did before leaving for the day. When I realised he was going, I burst into tears.

"What's wrong?" he asked.

"Please don't leave me, James," I begged, gripping his hand.

"It's okay, Jean will be here in a couple of hours."

"No, please, I can't do a couple of hours on my own. Please don't leave me. I'm terrified to be alone with the kids."

James brushed his hand over my head and assured me he'd stay.

When he left the room, I sobbed uncontrollably, realising I was in serious trouble.

Chapter 26

I had gone for as long as I could go both mentally and physically. The cracks created a chasm I collapsed into. James and Jean, my two biggest allies—the only ones who knew how unwell I was—supported me when the doctor formerly diagnosed me with Post Natal Depression (PND).

The doctor prescribed a low-dose anti-depressant. A decision that left me feeling like I'd been defeated by The Beast after all these years, after everything else I had gone through. But I knew, for my children's safety and my own, I had to accept I needed help. At least now, medication would help settle my anxiety and ease the non-stop chatter in my mind. A break I desperately needed in order to function and focus on being a mother. It wasn't just the exhaustion of a new routine; it was the exhaustion of constantly battling The Beast in my head.

I'd never taken anti-depressants before, despite doctors offering them to me over the years. What made this situation so different from all my other crises that I couldn't manage and sort my shit out like before? How was it that in this crisis I crumbled worse than ever? The battle became too strong to defend and overcome, and now I had to rely on this tiny round pill to carry the burdens, or at least take them away for a while. Surely this meant The Beast had won once and for all.

Taking medication would only be temporary and not a long-term solution, I insisted James knew that as much as I reminded myself. If this pill could work wonders to silence The Beast, so I could then figure out how to juggle everything—my family, the house, the errands, and manage my mind—then it was worth it. The shambles my mental state was in had compounded, and eventually I'd need to sift through a mountain of thoughts and pick out the culprits that tormented me, hold them up to the light, and challenge my beliefs around them. But now was not the time.

Once I'd been diagnosed with Post Natal Depression (PND), a whole team of people and mental health services were made available to keep an eye on my unstable mind: Psychologist appointments, access to a twenty-four-hour phone counselling line, as well as weekly home help by a local volunteer organisation of women. Initially, I took everything offered, especially the volunteer home visits, more so to ease James and Jean's minds that someone could be with me when they couldn't.

But after only a couple of visits, I cancelled the home help. Having strangers in my home, making me tea, helping with my children, felt weird and unnecessary, like the service should be for people who really desperately needed it. Besides, I was coping when they were there, far from feeling crazy or overwhelmed. Having home help me made feel like a lousy mum who couldn't do this on my own. I didn't need that kind of judgment.

PANDA, the Post Natal Depression helpline, became my go-to because the women on the other end of the phone had been through the same thing. They understood my fears and didn't judge me for the terrifying thoughts I'd never repeat to James or Jean. I didn't have to apologise for hating the same monotonous activities. And I could openly vent my truest thoughts. At any moment when thoughts or tasks overwhelmed me, I'd call PANDA and avoid bothering James while he was at work.

With medication and fortnightly visits to a psychologist, life began to settle down again. James rang me more often while he was at work, and on the weekends he took care of the kids while I had a break away from the house for a couple hours between feeds. Even if it was just a cup of coffee at a cafe. Sometimes it still felt selfish, like I was abandoning my children and piling more work onto James. But I was learning that I was an important person in the family too. Having time out did not make me a bad mum.

Frequent sessions with the psychologist helped me to develop more realistic expectations of myself, as well as challenge my perfectionist model of how mothers 'should' be. She worked with me to adopt healthier coping strategies when the day's plans went awry—as they often do with young children—as well as reframing my mountain of rigid beliefs around how life was 'supposed' to be with kids. Instead of trying to be Wonder Woman, like I thought I had to be, she coached me to prioritise daily tasks as important or not so important. Giving myself permission to let go of the unrealistic standards I thought I had to live up to.

Managing my moods became easier as the medication kicked in, so I didn't lash out at my children as much. Sometimes I'd notice my usual reaction ahead of time and stop myself from doing it altogether. I had more space in my head to manage the day-to-day tasks, without feeling as overwhelmed. I wasn't experiencing the lowest of lows anymore either, because the medication had more or less numbed the dark thoughts that caused a lot of my anxiety and panic. Obsessing over my health, my life, and lack of purpose moved to the back of my mind instead of the forefront. Little pains and aches still bothered me, but it didn't weigh me down with fears of a terminal diagnosis as much as it used to.

I was beginning to feel like my normal self again, something I hadn't felt in a very long time. James noticed it too as I relaxed more and more, enjoying motherhood again, laughing and having fun with my children, or enjoying a day out as a family. Sometimes, I'd notice myself smiling for no reason or even notice the absence of resentment or dread I'd usually feel doing the same daily tasks and wonder if it was the pills or the old me resurfacing again. Whatever it was, this normality felt refreshing. I could almost feel my body and mind untethered.

Putting on weight was the biggest downside to taking medication. It didn't seem like a fair trade: weight for sanity. I hated seeing my frumpy figure in the mirror and being unable to fit into my favourite jeans. But what could I do? My sanity was far more important than the added kilograms. Still, it bothered me. At the next psychologist appointment, I asked about swapping to another pill that didn't add the kilos. There were no guarantees other pills wouldn't have the same effect, but I was keen to try.

When you switch medications, you have to ween off one anti-depressant before you can start another. *Should be easy enough* since life had stabilised, and I was in a good place. I wasn't concerned this transition would affect me. Reducing my medication to every second day didn't make any difference. But as unmedicated days increased, my mood began shifting back to where I'd been. Resentment crept back in at waking to the same old routine.

Once again, I lost interest in doing anything or going anywhere with the kids. Even pulling out of a planned child free weekend away with my mum's group. Every chore became a drag. Every day became a more miserable prediction of the last as I felt myself sinking into a deep, dark hole with no way to pull myself out.

Old habits of mind resurfaced and tried to control and solve obstacles light years ahead. Thoughts centred around my traumatic upbringing. My non-existent family relationships surfaced and swirled around an already burdened mind.

I thought about my mother a lot.

She was back in my life again. After three years and the birth of my two sons, she turned up on my doorstep unannounced, ready to talk about her father, the abuse, and our relationship. I hoped her visit would be our chance to clear the air and begin again, hoping to switch our roles back to where they should have always been. Nothing would change overnight; I knew that much. But every time I uttered the words 'abuse' or 'paedophile' with her father's name in the same sentence, she'd turn away. Tears would spill down her face. Even after all this time, she still cowered like a child, not wanting to believe the truth about her dear Daddy. She apologised for not believing me, but it was insincere. Still, it felt obligatory, a way to come back into my life again. Despite my best efforts to have an honest discussion, deep in my heart, I knew I would not get a heartfelt, honest apology or recognition of the damage her disbelief and abandonment caused me.

There were certain things that had to change going forward in my attempt at a new start. She was no longer allowed to refer to her parents as 'my grandparents' or bring them up in conversation like we were talking about mutual friends or family I cared about. Her parents would never visit my children and play happy families. She had to know I would not join in her game of denial and pretence. And from here on in, the abuse was no longer a topic that could be swept under the rug.

There was still too much denial in Mum's heart to allow us to discuss anything deep, much less my mental health or struggles as a parent. Anything too real, too raw, and she'd revert to her usual tactic of smiling and pretending everything was fine and swiftly changing the topic, just like she'd always done. Rather than fight and demand for anything beyond that, I accepted we were not going to have the relationship I wanted. I'd go to Jean instead.

Weekly catch ups with my mum's group only magnified the absence of a deep connection between my mother and I, that other mums enjoyed. In comparison, mine felt more like an adopted daughter meets biological mother situation. They retold stories their mums told of their own childhood, while relating back to their grandchildren and similar traits they laughed about. I couldn't help feeling as though I was missing out on something really special. I sunk further into depression, realising everything I'd strived to correct with myself, with my mother, had actually done nothing. *Do I really want to raise my children without my ideal picture of what a family should look like? Like everyone else around me had?*

On my youngest son's fifth birthday, I treated us to one of our last dates together before he'd start school the following year. We went to my favourite café and ordered his favourite treat—a milkshake and cookie. Watching him with an adoring smile sucking down his chocolate milkshake and munch on his cookie, dark thoughts surfaced like a heavy rain cloud weighing on top of me.

I would not fall apart on my son's birthday. Not today. So, I zoomed in on every little thing my son was doing to ignore The Beast trying to bring me down. His little giggle at slurping as he sucked through his straw. His excited expression at finding a big chunk of chocolate in his cookie. Even mirroring his gasps of excitement. *You are just so beautiful. I just adore you, my baby boy.* Despite my best efforts, despair surged within, overpowering any will left to stay positive and hold The Beast back. *Come on, Beck, keep it together. Please, please, just breathe, just focus. We're nearly there.*

"Come on, let's go to day-care and play." I hustled my son into the car as a tsunami of tears burst their way out. I turned the radio up loud enough to drown out my long deep breaths so he wouldn't ask me if I was okay.

At home, I filled my mind with a list of jobs just to keep myself busy and resist any desire to fall apart. Eventually, it was no use. Sadness became too heavy to hold back as though my mind subconsciously knew there were no obstacles, or reasons to pretend.

The medication had well and truly worn off.

Slumped on the couch, alone with my heavy thoughts, tears welled as I stared out the window. I don't want to do this anymore. I don't want to be a mum who cannot give their children what I wanted for myself. A normal loving family, with normal loving parents and grandparents. My children do not deserve this. How could I bring life into this world and expect it to be different, when it wasn't and never would be? I adored my babies, but I just couldn't give them what I didn't have. Beyond the window was freedom, autonomy, life. If I stepped out that door, I'd be free, releasing the guilt and hopelessness that consumed me.

My children deserve better.

James deserves better.

I am not the right mother for these children.

The path to freedom was just ten feet away. *Open the door, Beck, walk away from the house and never look back. You are doing your family a huge favour. You'll be happy. They'll be happy. Get up and walk out the door.*

My eldest son was at kinder. My youngest son and daughter were in day-care. James was working about an hour away. Should I tell him, or just go? Who would collect the kids? Should I leave a note? I wanted to escape, but I had to tidy the loose ends up first. My kids were safe for now, but who would be here for them if I just walk out?

James didn't answer his phone, so I tried Jean; but she didn't answer either. I became increasingly impatient and anxious, wanting to run, but my conscience wouldn't allow me to until someone could collect the kids.

By now I was begging for James or Jean to answer. I texted Jean that I was leaving and I wasn't sure when I'd be back, asking if she could please get my children.

I got off the couch and crouched in the corner of the room, holding myself together in a tight ball. The weight of my sorrow, my failures, my inability to care for my kids, spilled out as I buried my head and sobbed.

My need for a steady, stable, and supportive mother was nowhere to be found. Hell, she had no fucking clue what I'd gone through these last couple of years. She was wilfully oblivious to my sorrow, the effects of the abuse, the absence of her love and care. I just wanted to ask her advice, have some extra help now and then. Someone I could turn to no matter what.

It all just felt hopeless. I thought I had recovered, but my reality was that it might never happen. My mum would never be the maternal figurehead I desperately wanted. She would never be the doting Nana to my own kids. She couldn't be trusted to protect me, there was no way I could trust her to protect what was mine.

For whatever reason, it mattered more to me now than it ever had before. I couldn't get past how sad it made me feel, and I couldn't let it go.

I didn't have any traditions from my own upbringing, nor any sage advice to pass on because I simply wasn't given any. Everything my kids would inherit started and ended with me, and the burden seemed impossible.

My family was a fucked up, dysfunctional system with no good stories to share, no positive relationships to be revered by my children. They had living great-grandparents they'd never know.

Guilt gnawed at me for having children at all when I couldn't give them a normal family with a strong legacy rich with traditions, and family members we loved and aspired to be like. My children would miss out and it was my fault for believing I could erase the history of abuse and dysfunction and start afresh.

Rocking back and forth, I thought about the life I was really giving my children. I wanted my story to be different. To be more than it was. But it wasn't. I had nothing good to offer them. How could I think that by creating my own family, I was giving them something better? How could I be so stupid to believe my children would benefit from my fresh start when I was still so screwed up? I couldn't share happy childhood stories. Instead, I'd have to hand-pick, edit, and delete information to stop their curious minds from asking why. Why weren't you allowed to celebrate a birthday from seven to nine? Why haven't we met your father or your grandparents? Where is your father? How come we don't have big family gatherings?

Jean rang, breaking my train of thought. "Beck, what's wrong?" she asked.

"Nothing, Jean. I just need you to get the kids. Will you be able to do that?"

"Why? Where will you be?"

"I'm just heading out, and I'm not sure when I'll be back."

"Beck, are you okay?"

"Yes, Jean," I lied, fighting back tears. "I just want to go, okay? Can you please just collect the kids, so James doesn't have to? That's all I'm asking."

"Hang on, Beck, I'll be there in a minute."

"No!" I screamed down the phone. "Please don't come. Please, just tell me you can pick up the kids. I don't need you now."

But Jean knew better. She hung up as I screamed out again, "Please! Just pick up my babies, please! Why can't you just do that?" I sobbed.

Ten minutes later, Jean knocked and let herself in as she called out to me. When she spotted me, I must have looked like a lost and confused little girl, my hair dishevelled, face all puffy and blotchy from crying.

Kneeling, Jean gently placed her hand on my knee.

"Beck?" She spoke softly. "What's wrong?"

"I'm fine. I just need you to pick the kids up, please?"

"Where are you going?"

"Nowhere, I'm just not going to be here."

"Beck, I think I need to take you to the doctor," she said, clearly worried.

"What for? They can't do anything."

"Let me just take you to the doctor and we'll have a chat."

"There's nothing to chat about, Jean. I just want to go."

"Come on, Beck, just come with me and see what the doctor has to say."

As she gently pulled me to my feet and half-carried me to the car, my body felt so lightweight, almost soulless, like I was reduced to a shell of myself. As Jean drove, I stared out the window, not recognising anything, completely detached from reality. Everything seemed so surreal. What's happened to me? Where have I gone? Who was I now? Would anything ever make sense again? Somewhere in the back of my mind, I had a husband. I had children. But was it real? I didn't know.

"Jean, do I have a family?" I quizzed.

"Yes, Beck, you do. You have a husband and three children."

"Oh, okay."

"You'll be okay, Beck. We'll get you some help," Jean assured me.

I glanced at Jean. I wanted to believe her. I hoped things made sense soon.

Chapter 27

After my latest episode, I was immediately placed back on medication. This was non-negotiable. For everyone's sake, I had to stay medicated for an indeterminate amount of time.

James relayed my phone call to him that day. When I couldn't reach him, I left a distressing message, saying I was leaving and could no longer handle the life of a mother and he'd be better off without me. Immediately, he dropped his tools, hopped in the car, and sped furiously down the highway. A parked police car happened to be detecting speedsters when James's car was clocked going 130km. When he was pulled over, James burst into tears as he explained my mental breakdown and his urgency to get home. The officer empathised, let him off with a warning, and offered to escort him.

I had no recollection of the events of that day. But hearing about it spoke volumes of how much I'd scared him.

No one outside James, Jean, and my doctor knew what happened that day. How could I explain the gap between finding motherhood difficult and wanting to quit and walk out on my family? I'd made small talk of my difficulties in mothers' group and with family, but no one knew how deep my troubles ran.

I continued seeing my psychologist, not only to expose unhealthy beliefs I knew were a factor in my illness, but also to learn to create a more realistic picture of life. A picture that wouldn't cripple me every time a curve ball was thrown my way. But as life settled down, James and I in a routine that supported my needs as well as his own - including weekly scheduled me-time locked in - and a reliable support network, a strong feeling I'd out-grown Rushton emerged. The urge to uproot my family and start a fresh became something I couldn't stop thinking about. Naturally, I scoffed at how absurd it was to even think, given how unstable I was. Besides that, we'd just completed an extension on the house to more comfortably accommodate our growing family and further cement our lives here. My friends, my biggest support, Jean, were here. My eldest son attended a school he and I both loved.

When I broached the idea to James, surprisingly, he wasn't completely against it. He too felt he'd outgrown his job and the city.

My mothers' group openly scoffed at the idea. *Why would you do that?* they argued. *Why would you want to move and start again? Haven't you got enough on your plate? Who would support you? Think of the money you'd be spending to leave?* I agreed. The idea seemed completely crazy. Could I be bothered starting from scratch? Having to find a new doctor and psychologist I felt comfortable with did dampen the idea, knowing those supports were an absolute priority if we did move.

More than logistics, I had to consider if this wasn't just me pulling out my old bag of tricks. Was I just trying to escape again? Believing my problems wouldn't follow me? Am I really in the right frame of mind to do this? My medication had barely kicked in, and I knew I couldn't afford to have another incident, especially without support. But despite all the obvious reasons not to, and friends convincing me it was stupid, everything in my mind and body knew. It just felt right. It was time for a new beginning.

James and I began making the necessary steps to plan our move, remov-ing both our sons from the following year's school enrolment. Packing. Selling furniture we wouldn't be taking. James applied for a relocation within his company to a position up north. Everything worked seamlessly: no obstacles, no fear, no difficulties arose. Despite some decisions feeling harder, like leaving Jean, my biggest ally and my truest confidante outside of James, my resolve to move got stronger with each day. Despite knowing how much the kids and I would miss her dearly, my family needed this change. I needed a fresh start.

We focused on the positives of what this new life and new experiences in a different environment would give our children—even it was temporary, even if we tried it and decided we didn't like it. I accepted there'd be challenges and a period of adjustment, yet I still felt a strange sense of ease and calm I couldn't explain.

On the 7 January 2013, just four months after making our momentous decision, we moved to Queensland, settling in a peaceful suburb with everything we needed: school, medical facilities, and a local shopping cen-tre. The town's landscape was reminiscent of the one we left behind: long stretches of suburban roads with cow grazing paddocks on one side and lush green ovals and public walking tracks on the other. Tree-lined streets and large acreages were visible from the fringes of the built-up residential areas and bustling housing estates. The effects of a sub-tropical area, which recorded massive amounts of rain Rushton wouldn't see in a year, made a picturesque view of gorgeous verdant land for as far as the eye could see.

Within a week of moving, James left to begin his fly-in, fly-out (FIFO) job, working in a remote town five hours away on a two and one roster. Two weeks away and one week home. James's absence would be the biggest and most difficult adjustment to our move.

We'd discussed the potential challenges his new role would have on our family, and my ability to cope becoming a single mum to three kids under six while he was away. We both agreed staying on medication was essential, knowing he couldn't reach me quickly like before if something did hap-pen. James needed assurance I was well enough to manage everything.

Pretty soon, the challenges of the move and James's absence became clear. No longer could I count down the hours before he came home to share the load. Now I had to multi-task cooking, homework, cleaning, and the kid's bedtime routine alone. Properly alone. Most days my legs ached from the constant demands of running the house and taking care of the kids.

Once the kids were asleep, the one part of the day I most looked forward to—curling up alongside James with a cup of tea and relaying Herculean tales, thwarting public tantrums, ticking off to-do lists, and the remarkable feat of getting three little people in bed at once, causing a collective sigh, knowing we'd made it—was replaced with the sound of ticking clocks and a humming fridge.

With James's new role, his days were long and exhausting too. Early starts and late finishes meant my usual time to offload my day seemed to burden his overloaded mind. Half the time our conversations were brief, checking in to make sure I was okay before he retired for the evening.

A couple of months flew by, and despite missing James and the daily challenges I still faced, I still believed moving was the right decision. Though I missed catching up with friends back home. I missed seeing Jean and watching her spoil my children. Sometimes I missed teaching. I purposely hadn't applied to teach in Queensland when we moved, deciding instead to use the one day a week my two-year-old daughter was in day care and the boys in school full time, to have much needed time to myself.

Generally, I was coping quite well. A part of me was super proud that I'd stuck to my decision to move and not run back to the comfort of my old home, as I imagined was a possibility in the early days after moving.

Most of my illness was an open book now. I committed to communicating with James when days were hard, when I felt low, or too exhausted and struggling to feel positive.

Sometimes I even revealed darker thoughts that in the past I would never have admitted to him, just so he could help me challenge how realistic they were. Even then James would talk me through more healthy, realistic thoughts by offering new perspectives, before they escaped to dangerous levels. I'd learned many times what happened when I dismissed the signs.

The more I spoke honestly about my illness, the more James learned what triggered my anxiety and tuned more into the thoughts I shared that would alert him I was in potential danger of sinking down the rabbit hole of doom. More and more, James became vocal, taking the reins of my mind, pulling me back from heading down the path of madness.

He would hear my fears and respond gently, "It's okay, Beck. Just take a breath. Do what you can today. The kids are okay. You're doing a good job." I relied on James and his comforting words to keep me grounded.

Sometimes I did miss the warning signs—the little moments of anxiety; worrying repetitive thoughts that sometimes lingered in my mind, activating subtle waves of panic. Thankfully, the medication took the edge off succumbing to a full-blown panic attack. It slowed my racing mind, helping me become aware of all the responses my body went through: nerves burning, a tight chest, rapid breathing, dizziness. As I became more aware, I always told James, no matter what. No matter how small, trivial or ridiculous it seemed.

Chapter 28

Six months after we moved, I started waking in the middle of the night in a pool of sweat.

Normally something like this started an avalanche of self-diagnosed terminal illnesses, rocket-launching my body into panic before I'd even managed to strap myself in for the ride. I'll admit, I entertained this briefly. It was a habit my mind and body performed automatically. But in my quest to stop panicking and self-diagnose, I rang James, knowing he would offer a saner, more logical reason than I ever would. James thought it might have been the sub-tropical weather. My GP suggested it was the new medication I'd swapped to back in Rushton. So I decided to go back to the original medication I started on.

While I began weening off my medication, I wondered if this was my golden opportunity to get off medication entirely. After all, I was coping so well, managing the children and everything else on my own for six months better than I thought I would. Even though my body often bubbled with nerves, my head still dizzy most days, I didn't fret about it as much. I just carried on and adjusted to the physiological symptoms like they were part of the deal. Surely that meant I was acing it? Medication was only meant to be temporary, and I'd already been on them for two years now. Eventually I'd have to learn how to cope without it, and maybe now was the time to try.

I presented my case to James, who of course was not sharing my confidence at all, especially knowing what happened last time. This time neither he nor Jean could be there if I did fall apart again. But I assured him I'd go back on them immediately if I wasn't coping.

He knew I was too headstrong and trying to change my determined mind was pointless. Reluctantly, he agreed.

Coming off this particular medication was more difficult than the last time. As I decreased the dosage, my brain zapped repeatedly throughout the day, like an electrical wire short circuiting. This did nothing to ease my anxiety and panic I was determined to be rid of. Every zap awakened an underlying fear that something more sinister was at play. A brain tumour perhaps? Just the thought sent a ripple of terror through my body. *What other explanation could there be?* Well, maybe this time there is another explanation, I told myself sternly. *We're not going down this path again, Beck! I promised James I would try not to entertain worst case scenarios.*

At the very least, I could have shared my concerns with my GP, but that's not how Health Anxiety aka Hypochondria works. No, you feel something, an ache, or striking jab, and immediately link it to the worst possible disease from an already prepared list of diseases, waiting to be hand picked.

The more you feel it, the more you convince yourself it must be stage four cancer. Then begins the obsessive thought looping around your mind. Once you've allowed one symptom to escalate to a terminal disease, it consumes you. That's when the panic comes in. The small wave becomes a tsunami, and before you know it, you're on the ground in a full-blown panic attack, wondering if this is the moment you'll meet your untimely death.

Googling your 'disease' can be your best friend or worst enemy, depending on what symptoms you type into the search bar. The answer will either confirm your worst fears or allay them, or worse yet, find a new disease to worry over, continuing the never-ending cycle of torture.

I realised some time ago that googling symptoms only made my anxiety worse, so I stopped doing it. Besides, I already had a list of the top diseases I could pinpoint on any ache or pain I had. But this brain zapping was something completely new. Hard evidence, something must be wrong. I had to know, without really wanting to know. Ignore it and you let it slowly kill you. Have your diagnosis confirmed and you live every terrifying moment knowing you'll die. That's the torture of anxiety and panic holding you hostage.

When the brain zaps eventually subsided, fear of a terminal brain tumour resolved itself for now. With an anxiety disorder though, if you drop one worry, you have to pick up another. An anxious mind doesn't like rest. No space to be still. That is a fear worse than any disease I could imagine.

Just like when I was pregnant with my daughter, the same fears and anxieties resurfaced. I felt incapable of handling life again. How would I get stuff done without James's help, despite the fact I'd been doing fine? The smallest tasks snowballed and became too difficult to handle. Added on top was the stress of difficult tenants in our Victorian house we were renting out while we lived away.

My body now shook constantly, my nerves-endings burned in every limb. I was constantly lightheaded and dizzy. My chest tightened, choking me at the mere thought of everything I was dealing with. Every physical sensation combined to a more dangerous thought: I must be dying. The mounting pressures of life and endless non-stop shit got to me again, but this time I actually had to deal with it, without Jean to run to, without James rescuing me, without medication to block my fears.

Was life meant to be this way? Why do I never seem to get a break? I cannot deal with this! I am exhausted. Why is there never an endpoint? My thoughts demanded. *Is there ever a time when I won't have to run multiple errands, organise the children's schooling, appointments, homework, or clean the damn house?* The to-do list seemed insurmountable. Everything I had to manage was like trying to juggle a dozen glass balls with one hand and the consequences would be disastrous if I dropped one. My worries projected far into a future I couldn't control. Life felt like one giant obstacle I needed to figure out instantly or be squashed under the boulder size weight.

The hardest part was ignoring the chatter in my head that urged me to collapse in panic. To give up and give into the truth. *You can't handle life, Beck. It's too much. It's too hard.*

As much as I tried to focus on my children and their needs, The Beast swooped in, repeatedly whispering defeat and hopelessness, reminding me of the sky-high list of things to do. I lashed out at my kids, screaming to a simple request for help, or to play, in an attempt to silence The Beast. The sting of my words added guilt to the list things I couldn't get right.

I now knew I was well and truly off my medication.

The most obvious thing to do was to go back on medication, knowing my struggle to cope was invading my life yet again. But was rushing straight back to medication just to bathe in the sweet sanity I craved the answer? I insisted to James, medication was only ever temporary. Wasn't two years enough? When would I call "time" on this inner battle that was five years running now? Medication clearly was the perfect antidote to my anxiety and overthinking. But would I ever learn to truly deal with life if I kept relying on medication to get me through? Maybe it was time to try and defeat this on my own, without any help at all.

Armed with determination, advice from my psychologist three years ago to breathe, and a quick go-to mantra of, "I'm okay", I gathered my bag of defences to destroy The Beast and prove to myself and to James that I could do this. I placed the medication I was meant to go back on high up on the kitchen cupboard, out of plain sight, but still within arm's reach, just in case.

Every second my mind wandered to anywhere beyond the here and now, I chanted my mantra, *I'm okay, I'm okay*. Every moment my body burned up and threatened to bring me down—which almost happened with every tick of the clock—I forced myself to breathe and repeat, *I'm okay*. I repeated this hundreds of times a day, as I cleaned the house, walked through the shopping centre, caught up with people, made dinner, even while my children played loudly. Despite my mind feeling heavy and exhausted at the end of each day—trying to ward off thoughts, like swatting an infestation of flies—incessantly repeating my mantra got me through. But not before another curve ball, which seemed more like an elephant-sized boulder, threatened to prove life really was too difficult to handle.

My youngest son, now six-years-old, fell severely ill with Salmonella after eating dodgy chicken for dinner. He spent three nights in hospital hooked up to a drip, trying to keep fluids down and regain the three kilos he'd already lost through constant vomiting. Struggling to manage, I begged James to come home early, just so someone could sit with our son at the hospital while I nursed my eldest son and my daughter with mild Salmonella back at home, before succumbing to food poisoning myself.

Burdening an already worried mind, life's obstacles were just too much. How would I ever cope long-term if things like this kept happening? How do I juggle everything and do it well?

Pushing through the long days, dragging my ever-constant burning body around, fighting The Beast screaming at me, *you're not coping, life really is too difficult. You can't do this! Give up! Surrender!*

"No," I fought back, screaming out loud. "No, I'm fine! I'm okay. Yes, I am!" Each time louder and more determined.

Just when I'd got through one health crisis, another one appeared. My left eye began throbbing to the point where a glimpse of light sent stabbing pains through to my head. I went to the optometrist and had my eyes re-tested to check if my prescription glasses were the source of my pain. But when the optometrist mentioned that if it wasn't my glasses creating the intense pain, which had me taking 'round the clock painkillers, then they'd need to send me to a specialist for further investigation. My entire body froze with terror as the words 'eye cancer' flashed across my mind.

Could it be that The Beast was right all along? The evidence against me was certainly mounting, and I wasn't even sure I had the strength to fight back anymore. I had nothing to prove I was doing okay, despite telling myself I was.

I rang James more frequently, for help, support, to cry, trying to juggle health stuff, tantrums, and daily fights for cooperation from a strong-willed middle child.

"Just ground me and tell me I'm okay," I'd plead to James. "Don't tell me to go back on medication. Please, just tell me I'm okay," I begged.

Constantly trying to talk over The Beast, who was now controlling more and more of my mind, was taking its toll. My tactics weren't working, and I knew it, no matter how many times I repeated *I'm okay* in my head, or out loud. No matter how many times I tried to brush off my burning body, my heavy legs, my dizzy mind, as nothing, trying to pretend I was fine, it wasn't relieving my symptoms, nor was it banishing the constant torment in my head. Instead, it gained momentum. Getting stronger and stronger.

James rightly worried that my determination to stay off medication, despite everything I was managing without him, on top of dealing with my ailing mental health, was not realistic. I took his words to heart, and I believed he didn't think I was strong enough. Now more than ever, I was more resolute.

I sought out my next best ally in a book—my private therapist I could take anywhere. Finding a second-hand book called *Instant Calm* by Paul Wilson, I fished through the '100 stressful techniques for relaxing the mind and body' and found a page I could read over and over reminding myself I really was okay. Even if I didn't believe it yet.

The ongoing struggle to keep off the meds was now at a critical point. James had one last two-week work rotation before his annual four-week Christmas break. Secretly, I wished he could stay at home, but I couldn't bring myself to beg him like I wanted to. It would prove I wasn't coping. *Just two more weeks*, I reminded myself.

My routine had to be as predictable as possible. Praying no more curve balls, no more issues would be thrown at me.

I committed to focusing on each day as it came, slowly breathing through every tantrum, every shouted demand from my children, every thought trying to bring me down. Even looking forward to a special evening James and I had arranged for ourselves when he came home. We rarely went out without the kids.

James was just days away from coming home. Knowing he would be there to rescue me so I could stop working overtime to keep myself from falling apart, I unconsciously relaxed the stronghold on all the strategies I'd stringently held in place to keep me from losing it.

The day he was due home, I dragged my heavy body around, struggling to get through every single moment, like the clock had stopped ticking. Pressure to hold on became too much, and I felt myself being sucked into a black hole that would sweep me away. Frantically I grabbed my phone, crouched in my bedroom closet, and phoned James, praying he would answer.

"James," I whispered. "I'm having a panic attack. Please come home now," I begged.

"Oh, honey, hang on. I'll be home in just a few hours," he assured me.

"But, James, I'm losing it. I can't hold on until you get home. I'm terrified. Please, James, help me."

"Okay, honey, just breathe. You're okay. Can you see if you can get to the doctors now?" he asked.

When I arrived at the doctors, I relayed my panicked state and urgency just to sit and regain ground somewhere safe before she quickly interrupted to ask if I was taking the medication she'd suggested I swap to five months earlier.

"No, I'm trying to get through without it," I insisted.

She immediately raised her eyebrows in surprise, before urging me to go back on medication to stabilise my mental health.

"No," I snapped back, while wiping away tears of defeat. "I know it's hard and I'm struggling, but I know I can do this. James will be home tonight, and he will help me through it. I want to learn how to manage without medication. I need to do this."

I stared at my doctor through blotchy, swollen eyes, desperately seeking her support.

She gazed at me with a reassuring smile. Knowing it was pointless to state the evidence was stacked against me, I could see she wanted this for me as much as I wanted it for myself.

While James and I prepared for our date, I still worried I wouldn't get through the night, as my nerves constantly burned, and my mind was still full of thoughts that something would swallow me up. I repeatedly told myself *I will be fine,* and I knew James would be right by my side. We'd both looked forward to this evening, and I was determined not to spoil it.

By midnight, we returned home, both exhausted, pleasantly full of good food and fine wine. We went to bed and fell asleep immediately. Success.

During the night I stirred, trying to find a comfortable position. Thoughts of impending doom flooded my half-woken mind at incredible speed. With no time to adjust, my mind went into complete meltdown, unable to control a tsunami of panic surging through me.

I screamed out to James, "Please, help me!"

"What, Beck?" he murmured, too groggy to recognise my terrified state.

"James, I don't know where I am! James, please help me," I begged, while clinging on to him, certain that if I didn't hold on, the world would swallow me up.

Clutching his arm tight, I whispered, "Please help me. Please help me. Please help me," over and over until I too fell back asleep.

The next morning, as soon as I opened my eyes, my body felt weightless, like I was floating in space and being sucked into a pitch-black atmosphere. I let out a blood curdling scream. "James! James!"

"What's wrong"?" he shouted, alarmed as he rushed to my side.

Nothing looked familiar. Nothing made sense. Closing my eyes or keeping them open sent me free-falling into a sinkhole that went nowhere.

"Please don't leave me," I begged, as I squeezed his hand tight to keep me from slipping away.

"Just keep breathing, honey. You're okay," he repeatedly reassured me.

My entire body now trembled continuously, without a break. There was nothing I could do but fixate on breathing through every moment, as I clutched tightly on to James's hands, trying desperately to ground myself.

For three long days I lay stiff as a board on the couch, terrified for my life, purposely staring at furniture and objects around the room, repeatedly labelling them, reminding myself I was still in a place that would make sense, eventually. "That is my table. I'm still here. That is my kitchen. I'm still here. That is my son. I'm still here." Too terrified to close my eyes and sleep unless James sat with me and held my hand, I summoned whatever energy remained just to keep breathing, slowly and deeply, through my constantly trembling body. I couldn't eat or drink, except for the times James insisted at I least sip water.

No matter how hard I tried, or how much James reassured me I was here and safe, nothing pulled me from the fear of impending doom.

James insisted on taking me to the doctor for an urgent appointment. As soon as we arrived, I was immediately whisked in, ahead of waiting patients.

While I sat in a zombie state, vacantly staring into space, James and the doctor's muffled voices explained the events of the last couple of days. I couldn't distinguish their words other than, "Beck, this," and "Beck, that." My ears only pricked up when I heard the word Valium, as a quick fix to relax my panicked state.

"No," I blurted out, still staring into space. "Not Valium. It's too addictive."

While James held my hand, the doctor spoke loudly, slowly enunciating every word, making sure I understood. "Beck. You need to go back on medication. I know you don't want to. But for now, it is the best thing. Okay?"

I hung my head in defeat. I'd tried so hard not to go back to medication. With tears in my eyes, I looked at both her and James and nodded.

The moment we got home, James handed me a tablet and a glass of water.

James had planned a pre-Christmas camping trip with the kids, while I was meant to go back to Victoria to catch up with friends. The medication had not kicked in yet, so it wasn't safe for me to go, much less be alone. I joined him and the kids instead.

While we settled into our camping spot, the kids excitedly unloaded their bikes and shuffled through their bags to grab their bathing suits. I anchored myself on a camping chair without any visual obstructions, keeping James in view at all times as a constant reminder I was still here. Even though my body burned and bubbled like a perpetual boiling pot, seeing James told my dubious mind I really was okay.

The next day, as the sun scorched the earth, the kids wanted to play in the caravan park's waterpark. Knowing I was doing everything to keep it together, James suggested we all go. I stared at him, trying to swallow the lump of guilt and shame wedged in my throat. The burden I'd placed on James to not only look after our children practically by himself, but to watch his wife with an eagle eye—so concerned was he that I might lose the plot in front of the children if he wasn't there.

"No," I insisted as my voice quavered. "You have some time to yourself. We'll be fine."

I gathered the children, along with my *'Instant Calm'* book, and headed to the waterpark. As soon as the children splashed into the water, I slouched into the beach chair, clutching my book, ready to use it if needed. I convinced myself I'd be fine if I glued my eyes on the children splashing their arms and legs in the water, fixating on their laughs, anything out there, whilst ignoring anything going on in my mind and body.

Despite my best efforts, the trembling and shaking began, overheating an already boiling body. A wave of panic rippled through. Despite repeating, *I'm okay, I'm okay, I'm okay*, I was not able to convince myself, much less hold back the surge of terror flooding my entire body. I struggled to hold on. *James,* I cried inside. *I need help. What am I going to do?*

I decided not to call him. *He does not need to rescue me.* I ripped my book open to a bookmarked page, scrambling to find one line to instantly reassure me, in place of James's steady hands. The words 'In Case of Emergency' headlined the page. Underneath it read, 'mentally reassure yourself that good breathing is the most effective way ever conceived to control feelings of stress and anxiety.'

Breathe, Beck, breathe, I commanded my body.

So I began breathing slow. So slow as to control every single particle of air moving through my body, trying to extinguish the burning sensation in every limb. Focusing on nothing but the sound of air wheezing through my nose and amplifying its sound in my ears, drowning out every other noise or voice, to focus solely on the sound of my breath and nothing more. The Beast's power felt stronger than ever. My breath shuddered with every inhale, trying to control the surge of power rushing through my body. I needed something else to latch onto. I flicked through the book and came to a page where I'd highlighted the words, 'Repeat, repeat, repeat. Affirmation is an enormously powerful technique for long-term change.' Immediately, I began chanting over and over without pausing. *I'm okay, I'm okay. Beck, you're okay.* My voice whimpered under the increasing pressure to survive this panic attack, scratching at the pores on my skin's surface.

After what felt like an hour, the panic passed, taking every ounce of energy with it, leaving me completely exhausted. The kids and I would have to leave soon and return for dinner. I wasn't even sure I had the energy to walk on my own, much less dry off their wet bodies and carry their water-soaked towels. The moment I rose, my feet felt like blocks of concrete. My head was dizzy, blurring my vision. While I concentrated on putting one foot in front of the other, taking care not to fall, I kept the kids walking ahead of me before letting them run wildly back to the campsite as soon as they saw James. As I dragged myself closer to James, I could feel the tears welling in my eyes, knowing the battle I'd just overcome without him. I threw my arms around him, seeking his comfort and protection, before he guided me to bed.

James was due to go back to work in just over a week and I could tell the medication was beginning to take effect. I was regaining my sense of self without always needing James in sight, nor needing his constant hand to keep me grounded. Feelings of panic and overwhelm were subsiding, the burning sensations were easing. Though not completely gone, the fog that shrouded my existence was clearing, giving me some head space to think and see things more clearly.

I began to reflect on what was my worst mental breakdown to date. I hadn't been back to the doctor nor a psychologist since that day to label and dissect my latest event, because I didn't need a formal diagnosis to tell me what I already knew. I was seriously unwell, and it was obvious I needed to be medicated to stabilise my mind and life.

I hated relying on a tablet. It was a daily reminder I couldn't do this on my own. It felt as though The Beast had toppled me for good. I had actually failed not once, but twice now. Sitting with this bothered me because that wasn't who I was. I never gave up. I'd been through so much in my life so far and I'd consciously fought hard not just to survive but to work through my problems. Even when it was tough, I worked through it. I couldn't accept that this time the problems I had couldn't be resolved.

It was only three weeks ago that I'd collapsed and was incapable of even closing my eyes, and yet now I was pretty much back to normality. What was that telling me? The only difference was the medication. A tiny tablet that acted as a shield to prevent my fears and worries from resurfacing, suppressing the very fears I needed to confront and deal with for good. That was the only way. It wouldn't be the easiest choice, but then again, I never took the easy road.

I wasn't sure if I was mentally or physically capable, but knowing I'd recently worked through a panic attack at the waterpark without James, I had a strong point of reference. Proof that I could do it. I'd survived my toughest challenge on my own, without running away, without needing James's hand to hold, without collapsing. It could be done. I could do this. And I was determined to do it again and again until it *was* done!

Three weeks after starting my medication again, I announced to James, with determination that surpassed any doubt in my mind, that I was quitting them for good! It was time to face my fears head on and deal with it.

Chapter 29

Following my decision to stop taking medication indefinitely in January 2014, I hid the almost full packet away and out of sight. My aim was complete recovery. No more panic attacks. No more dreaded, fearful thoughts to bring me to my knees. I wanted a normal life. To see the world differently and enjoy it with my family. To give my children a mother they deserved. To handle it all without fear gripping me at every turn.

If I was to take on this ambitious plan, James's only condition was to see a psychologist who could support me during recovery.

Once a week, I unloaded my anxiety, laying it bare in the hope the psychologist would unravel my tangled mind like a knotted ball of wool and pinpoint where the problems lay. I aired my most common worries and the physical symptoms that accompanied it all: I can't cope. Life's too hard. There's so much to juggle. And of course, the big one that peppered every thought: I'm a big fat failure as a mother.

As she sat back and listened, her advice was always the same: just take it one day at a time. Leaving each session, I found myself more irritated and just as anxious as when I'd arrived. She didn't understand anxiety like I did. If I could get through a day, I wouldn't be wasting my time seeing a psychologist.

Anxiety disorders grip on and strangle you every waking second, and even during sleeping time too. Every dark minute ahead becomes a mountain to climb. Just when you think you've overcome one, another Everest is there waiting. Until eventually you get through a whole twenty-four hours feeling like you've used up enough energy for an entire week. Most days I'd beg for a deal with The Beast just to let me get through the next five minutes before it took me hostage again.

Even though I had reached that familiar point where my body vibrated like a malfunctioned switch and the weight of The Beast's words in my head pressed down heavier and heavier, I abandoned any further appointments with the psychologist, knowing I needed more than she was giving me. I needed a deeper approach beyond the single layer cognitive therapy that was offered. Besides, dumping my problems onto a psychologist somehow felt like I was depending on her for results, for quick fixes, believing only she had the answers, and I didn't. What power did that give me? Where was I in all this?

Maybe it was time to ask myself the hard questions. Face the fears I was running away from and be my own coach, my own help, and stop placing my life in the hands of a professional and take the reins myself.

Part of my recovery was taking full responsibility for my current condition. Not from a place of judgement, but objectively, like a friend observing how I'd arrived at this point in my life. Full ownership gives me back the power to choose what I do with what I created. It didn't matter if I created it out of fear or self-preservation. How I arrived here was not so much the focus, but what could I do now that I knew for certain I wanted something completely different for my life? That's what was important.

What did I want my life to look like?

If I dedicated myself to the answer to that question, I believed I could achieve long-term recovery. More than anything, I wanted to stop being afraid and to face it all with courage, with faith, so that I could live as others lived. I adored my three children and so desperately wanted to be their happy, healthy mum again. To embrace their lives with laughter and enjoy the moments that were passing me by at rapid speed. To be the mum they looked to for strength and support and actually be able to give that to them instead of trying to survive every moment, trying to keep my anxious body and mind from flipping out. I was sick of dividing my life between surviving two weeks on my own and waiting for James to come home and rescue me.

One thing I knew for certain, I was not always like this. Despite every obstacle, every tortured moment, for all the times I ran to the shower seeking refuge, my anxiety had never escalated to the point it was at now. Each new breakdown became worse than the last, barely needing the smallest thing to set me off, triggering an uncontrollable series of panic, anxiety, and overwhelm.

My thoughts worsened, becoming more terrifying as I gave them more power and authority, scaring me into believing them as truths, which in turn set off alarm bells as quick as a switch with the all too familiar cocktail of symptoms that quickly flooded my mind and body.

To achieve my goal of recovery and the normality I craved, I needed a calm body and a free mind. So I pragmatically broke my illness into two separate parts: mind and body. Both needed equal work, but not together. I was not superwoman. Nor would I try to be.

Tackling one thing at a time was far more realistic and sensible. Far more pressing was bringing my body back to calm rather than a constant state of fight or flight, falsely believing it was always under attack, hypervigilant to every threat, perceived, imaginary, or otherwise. I would deal with The Beast and my untamed mind later.

Trying to raise three children under seven with a body that constantly burned up like a furnace while my legs either felt so lightweight I struggled to stay upright, or like concrete boulders I dragged around, had become a near impossible task that I could no longer manage, nor did I want to anymore.

The trick was to become aware of the automatic pattern my mind and body were running on. Recognising that my thoughts, consciously or otherwise, sent a terrifying message to my body to panic, and that response showing up in my body was now my signal that a fear-inducing thought was behind it. Now I had to retrain myself that regardless of what my mind was trying to convince me of, there was no actual threat. I was not in danger and I really was okay.

It was a bold plan, but I needed to remind myself that I had run this pattern for so long now and each time after the perceived threat was over, no matter how real or terrifying it felt in the moment, my body always returned to calm and everything was okay.

That was my proof that I was running a faulty system with a faulty alarm.

Waking up to a new day, it wasn't long before my body burned up again as it usually did, right about the moment I started to think about the twenty things I needed to do in the ninety minutes before school drop off as well as the rest of the day's demands. No medication, no James, no psychologist. Only me to take charge.

"Okay, I'm worrying about something," I said out loud. "Yep, okay, body, you burn up and do all the things you want, but this time I'm not believing you. You want me to be afraid. You want me to believe I'm in danger, that I'm sick. Go ahead. Do what you will. Harden my legs, I will still drag them around. Blur my vision, tighten my chest, shake my body. I am NOT in danger. I am ok. So if you want to hang around trying to frighten me, you're wasting your time."

Still, like clockwork, my body did as I'd trained it to do. But this time, I chose not to be pulled into the game I no longer wished to play. Every day, scores of times a day, I stood up to myself, choosing only to observe the alarm bells going off. *Ting!* We have shaking legs. *Ting!* Now a racing heart. And of course, my favourite: itchy, crawling, burning skin. *Ting!* It was like welcoming circus performers on stage, letting them belt out their best show yet, while I went about my day, no matter how uncomfortable it got. Leaving them all to tag along whenever I went out with the kids, while doing the housework or running errands. I did not give in.

Every day James was away I checked in with him, keeping him informed of my progress. He still worried I was taking on too much and all my efforts would crumble without professional support or medication. I understood his fears. But I also knew going in, this would not be easy. There would be times I would fall. There would be times I would give in and allow fear to grip on and take me down that familiar path. I was under no illusion this would go away overnight. It would take constant intentional effort every single day until my body no longer automatically went into panic mode.

My biggest test would come when I'd have to calmly sit my way through a panic attack without being sucked into the black sink hole. And it wouldn't be long before that would eventuate.

After a couple of weeks of allowing all the anxiety-related symptoms to hitch on and follow me everywhere, repeatedly telling my body I was okay and there was no danger, the weight of it all became too heavy to carry, too exhausting to keep taking the hits.

One afternoon, I picked up my sons from school with my daughter strapped in her car seat. The loud noise coming from my boys eagerly sharing their school stories was enough to break through my exhausted self-talk. Instantly my body burned up like a boiled pot, and I gasped for air, trying to take a deep breath but not being able to. As soon as I got home, I shuffled the kids inside and ran to my bedroom, slammed the door, and fell to my hands and knees.

This was the first panic attack since the waterpark. As a wave of panic and fear surged viciously through my body, doing its best to seize control and surrender to the terror I'd succumbed to every time before, I quickly moved to a meditative position. Crossing my legs, I closed my eyes, wrapped my hands tight over my knees and began breathing through the thickest and heaviest surge of fear I'd ever felt. My breath shuddered and trembled as the emotional tsunami rushed through my body, scorching every single cell.

Channelling every bit of strength I could muster, I calmly instructed myself with fierce determination to stand up to my body. *It's okay, Rebekah. You're okay. We are not in danger. There is no threat. You are stronger than this. Your body doesn't have to do this anymore. It doesn't need to be afraid. We don't have to play this game anymore. This force is strong. But you are stronger. Hold on, Beck, hold on. It will pass. This is the hardest part. And once we get through this, it will get easier. Just hold on.*

I don't know how much time passed, but eventually the powerful surge subsided. As I opened my eyes, I immediately felt the heaviness of my exhausted body, as though it were filled with wet sand. Leaning forward, I dropped my face into my hands and cried out of sheer exhaustion and pride that I survived my first panic attack without medication, without ringing James. I'd done this on my own.

If this was my hardest battle to face, then I had triumphed. Now I knew I could do this as many times as I needed to. And if this was the worst, then nothing I would face again would ever be so hard.

Every day forward, I focused on bringing my body back to calm. Slow, purposeful breathing and using self-talk to remind my body over and over that the danger was gone, and I was okay. Though circumstances, life, children, and ongoing to-do lists still piled up and overwhelmed me at times, my body was learning to gauge situations so that panic was not the first response. Creating stillness and space between a thought and my body's reaction to it.

Over the next couple of months, sensations in my body changed. Chains that had bound and tightened my chest for years were loosening, so much so that I could breathe a full breath of air without gasping. Even my heart that often raced like a jackhammer had begun to slow down to an even, rhythmic pace. The fog and blur that often left me lightheaded and my vision blurred was also clearing. For years my body felt like it was trapped in a heat wrap, numbing my arms or legs to a cool breeze or my children's hands while clasped in mine. Now the cold air smacking my face and the warm touch of my children's hands felt amazing.

Now that my body was calmer, and it didn't panic nearly as much as it used to, it was time to tackle the culprit that set it all off in the first place.

My thoughts. To face off with The Beast that had enthroned itself in the corner of my mind, hurling out lies upon lies like confetti.

I was under no illusion this war would be easy, either. After all, this was at least six years of torment and repeatedly cementing lies as truth. I'd long employed the tactic to repeat a phrase, like "I'm okay" until I'd convinced my mind and body the threat was over. But it only worked until the next thought crept in shortly after. Trying to block out the yammering in my head never worked either. Eventually, the weight of my thoughts always took over.

For true long-term recovery, I would need to intentionally and bravely face my thoughts head on. Allow them to rise to the surface and expose them under the light for the bullshit lies they were. The more I stood up to these untruths and fought back with evidence, gumption, and courage, the more these false narratives would disappear into thin air, draining each one of its meaning and power over me.

But I would need more than one strategy.

I peppered my world with a whole bunch of tricks up my sleeve to outwit and outsmart The Beast for good.

Armed with a fierce determination to see it through, no matter how hard it would be, this time I would stick at it. I realised the reason I had failed before was in some part due to giving up before I got the results I wanted.

I remembered my psychologist's words three years earlier, "*Breathe, relax.*" At the time, his advice grated on me and I deemed it too simple and nonsensical.

But now, with renewed commitment, I stuck a note on my kitchen cupboard above that read, *BREATHE. This is not forever, it's just TODAY!* Reminding me not to let my thoughts get away from me.

Any second my mind wandered to anything beyond the here and now, I brought it back to this mantra: *BREATHE. This is not forever. It is just today.* I repeated this statement hundreds of times a day, as I cleaned the house, walked through the shopping centre, caught up with people, and prepared dinner while the children played loudly. Despite my mind feeling heavy and exhausted by the end of each day, trying to ward off an influx of thoughts coming at me like a swarm of bees, it got me through. Pulling me out of the vicious cycle that would have usually set off waves of panic.

Now, instead of reacting in fear and letting these untamed thoughts set off an automatic chain reaction, I magnified every single word. Stretched it right across my mind, amplifying The Beast's words in my ears, ready to face the thoughts masked as truths that tormented me for years, and expose them all for the lies they were.

Waking up to the same routine, with a long list of chores and errands to run, as well as getting the kids ready for the day, The Beast began throwing out the same intrusive thoughts as though they were hand grenades.

There's too much to do today. Beck, you can't do this!

But it seemed The Beast had not received the memo that I was not taking his crap anymore. His words were lies, and I was ready to take them on.

I began my rant as I got dressed, firing back answers with a vengeance for everything the Beast tried to hurl at me. *Oh, really? Says who? I've done it before, why can't I do it now?*

The Beast, unwilling to give up so easily, fought back harder, digging up all the instances and images he could to try to prove I couldn't handle life. *What about all the times you've crumbled? All the times you've broken down?* It hissed as it continued. *You couldn't do it last month when you escaped your children and hyperventilated in your room.*

So what? I shouted back. *I've failed many times. But I'm still here and I can do it; and I will do it. Because despite every fucking time you tell me I can't, I'm still here.*

Everywhere I went, The Beast followed, insisting on taking me down like it had so many times before. Out with my children at a busy shopping centre, he'd whisper all the ways I was disappointing my children, failing as a mother, like my mother had failed me.

How could you take them to a busy shopping centre and drag them around? What sort of a mother would do that?

The belittling mother tactics hurt the most and were the taunts that might have succeeded in bringing me down. But I knew better than to listen, despite my body joining forces with the merciless Beast, adding what felt like twenty-kilogram weights to my ankles.

Still, I refused to crumble and dragged my heavy body around, anyway. Retaliating with equal force. *You are not the bearer of truth anymore. I am a good mum. I love my children. Taking them out to a shopping centre just to shop does not make me a bad mum.*

When it got too much and I needed support, I'd ring James, ticking off every strategy like a checklist and facing every scary thought that appeared. James grounded me. He praised my efforts and assured me he was there any time I needed to call and feel safe again.

Six months had passed since I'd taken any medication. I'd managed to bring my body back to an almost peaceful and calm state. No longer ravaged daily by bubbling sensations, a racing heart, and a tightened chest. Sometimes they came to visit, but now my mental state was stronger. The same pesky thoughts still at times tried to come to the surface and scare me, but they no longer had power over me like they once did. Like watching a twig ride a river's current, I had learned to observe the train of thoughts in my head and not to react.

Though, if I was to banish The Beast permanently, I'd need to go to the source. Where it all stemmed from. My beliefs. Seeds planted long ago in my unstable childhood, from years of insecurity to three years of religious brainwashing, instilling rigid, airtight rules and weaving perfectionist ideologies into my being. Repeatedly watching my own mother avoid dealing with life and pretending problems weren't there, despite a mountain of evidence to the contrary. All these experiences I could now see formed incredibly strong beliefs that programmed my thinking, setting up a false narrative of how the world was supposed to be.

Right around this time when epiphanies started exploding in my mind that if mere mortals in my childhood had shaped my views and beliefs of the world, I could rewrite them, a friend introduced me to quantum physics. A concept that completely obliterated the notion of a Zeus-like God, throning himself above the evil sinners below, watching like eagles for us to screw up and banish us to hell for all eternity.

Instead, we lived in a field of potentiality, an energy source, free of criticism, condemnation, of rules, and free of the construct of a vengeful God, ready to punish. An energetic field that gives us all the ability to shape and design our lives by the thoughts we construct ourselves.

So fascinated was I by this new idea that could free me not just from my own rigid beliefs that cornered my every move, but it could once and for all get the monkey off my back that paraded as a 'loving God' while reminding me of my sinful ways. I could fully be in charge and do away with ridiculous ideologies that held me hostage.

Now when a dark or bad thought came up, not only did I challenge the absurdity of it, I dug deeper to the belief behind it to ask, what's really behind that? My long list of well-used thoughts like, *you can't handle life and there's too much to do, I have to be a perfect mother,* were flicked off like a scab to reveal deeper beliefs that were the source of all my thoughts. Life shouldn't be this hard. Life is meant to be long stints of smooth sailing. No issues, obstacles, or opposition. Mothers must be perfect.

Working through the pile of beliefs programmed into me and delivered by The Beast himself, learning all I could to let go of religion masked as 'control and love', I only had to ask myself one question.

Do I have to believe any of this crap anymore?

Like a scene from Buffy the Vampire Slayer, The Beast was vanquished. The God in the sky that had kept a watchful and judgemental eye, like an ever-present dark cloud since I was six years old, had also disappeared.

I was my own person, and I could choose to believe whatever the hell I wanted without fear or condemnation. I was human, with flaws. Someone who makes mistakes and won't always get it right with my children. And that was actually okay. I would do *my* best.

Choosing now to see the world as fluid, with ups and downs, curveballs, boulders, and yeah, even avalanches. That not every little thing that happens is a *big deal*. Perhaps it's just a tiny bump in the road? Life can be challenging with three young kids, and it's even more difficult when my husband works away. It is natural to be overwhelmed at times with my busy life. But it didn't have to mean I wasn't capable, or that I wasn't coping.

I was no longer looking ahead to try and predict problems way into the future. I finally understood that today was all I had, was all I could see, and all I could control. That was it. The cliché that inked itself in every book I'd ever read finally made sense! I would learn to tackle everything as it came and know that I can only do my best in that moment.

No one person or eye in the sky was asking anything more of me. Even if I did stuff up, it didn't spell doom. The sun would still shine. The earth would still spin. Life would continue regardless. Learning to accept things that came my way and deal with them accordingly, brought me more peace than the five years of panic, fear, and chronic anxiety I created trying to control everything ever did.

Chapter 30

2014 was a year of powerful personal transformation. I'd spent every moment of every day exhaustingly retraining my mind and body, so that calm was my new normal instead of panic and fear. Chronic anxiety and daily panic attacks had all but vanished. Thoughts came and went like the wind. Standing upright without any dizziness was an achievement in itself and boy did that feel good.

Recovery was one of the most challenging yet rewarding periods of my life. My children had their mother back. James, my unfailing husband, was enjoying a much happier, relaxed partner again. Most importantly, I had myself back. I was the happiest and the most at peace I'd been in years. For the first time in my life, I felt more me than I ever had.

These days, life is well-balanced. Mentally, I'm in a great place. I still have moments where I feel anxious and begin to walk down that well-trodden path of panic when some new ache in my forty-something body arises, or the humdrum of life feels a bit much and has the potential to topple me—more so now as my children are growing up and life feels so much busier than ever. I may even entertain the ghost of The Beast at times, but I notice what I'm doing pretty quickly now and make sure to never let it escalate to where it was.

James catches it earlier than me sometimes when hears me chatter around the chaotic moments that sound like anxiety is rearing its ugly head again, and he'll quickly pull me up. "Beck," he'll say. "Remember where this leads. It's okay." The temptation to allow The Beast into my life is dealt with swiftly, using solid strategies well programmed into me. So now when the first signs of anxiety or overwhelm signal, I grab any one of my ready-to-use tools and resources: focused breathing, staying only in the present moment, prioritising what's most important, going for a walk, or just taking a break. All the while reminding myself, *it's all good, I've got this.*

Because I've gone through so much—I've walked the most difficult paths and weathered many storms—I now know in the grand scheme of life, despite how hard some days feels, despite how burdened I feel by expectations either from what society expects or those that I place on myself, the sun will still shine, the earth will spin regardless. So I get through it as best I can without ridiculous expectations and an inner critic trying to badger me with perfection that simply does not exist. I know there will always be challenges in life, but there are also rewards. An abundance of them if we choose to see them. And I do. Now I do.

On the 28th of June 2017, I turned forty. It was one of the happiest days of my life. I don't say that flippantly, or to throw a cliché to the milestone that turning forty often creates. I say it with a heart of sheer, unbridled joy, realising I made it to forty the way I had imagined fifteen years earlier.

Standing at the warm heater one evening talking to Jo, my mentor, I shared my dreams for my future self. "I think I'll write a book in my forties," I said, a little sheepish of my own admission.

"Really, what about?" Jo asked.

"Probably a story of my life and how I overcame my trauma."

"Beck, I believe you will achieve that," she said, beaming with pride, like she could already see my vision as a reality.

Now, looking back, it was a bold goal for someone who was still in throes of personal turmoil, not knowing just how much more tumultuous life would become. Though something in my twenty-five-year-old self knew I was destined to deal with my trauma at a relatively young age. A deep existential knowing I couldn't shake. A universal reason why every time I hit the proverbial rock bottom, some new wisdom appeared that would help me keep going and not give up.

I reflected on my twenty-five-year-old self and smiled with pride. Grateful for her belief in herself for a better future, and as I recollected how far she'd come, I cried tears of happiness.

James asked me if I wanted anything special for my milestone birthday.

"No, I truly have everything I ever wanted," I replied, beaming brighter than the sun.

There were no big celebrations, no elaborate gifts because I had my gift—a gift I'd earned. A gift I'd fought for. A gift no one could give to me but myself.

I had given myself the gift of a life I deserved to live.

Even more so, I had my husband James—a man who gallantly stood by me and never ran from the scores of painful and difficult times, and my three amazing children. Nothing in this world could have prepared me for the delight they bring to my life.

Nothing could wipe away my smile or the tears of joy from my face as I realised all that I wanted to become, all I had imagined for my future self, had come to fruition. To not only be happy and enjoying life and have a family, but more than anything, I wanted to live each day without the weight of trauma dragging me down.

I dreamed of living a normal life, like I imagined everyone else around me seemed to be living. From my earliest turning point, I believed so ardently that if others were living as I imagined, then it was possible for me too. Trauma wasn't the hero in this story, nor would I let it be. I never saw myself as someone who was fixed, as though trauma was some permanent tattoo I couldn't remove. At the very least, I wanted to experiment with what I could and couldn't change. I had nothing to lose that I hadn't already lost. Sink or swim were the only options I saw. And I'd be damned if I'd sink without giving myself a chance.

Even if it meant stripping back every part of me to rebuild, repair, and re-parent myself. Surrounding myself with people who were willing to guide me, to love me, to teach me, and help me see my own worth. To read books on anything that would help me learn about life, love, and relationships.

Memories will always be there. I can't erase those. Flashbacks, life events that once tried to destroy me, still come up at times. More so when I'm with my children and teachable moments immediately throw me back to all I wasn't taught or given. I notice how diametrically opposed my parenting is to what was parented to me; especially with my daughter, who is now at the age I was when I was abused.

Sometimes I can't help but look at my daughter and wonder what my life would have been like without trauma. How different my life could have been, had I not gone through all that I did. But it's quickly overshadowed by immense gratitude that she gets to live a happy childhood. She gets to be that little girl I didn't get to be. She gets to know nothing other than safety and protection and feel so secure in her parents' love that she can grow into her own self with confidence, as can my sons.

By refusing to pass on a deeply embedded tapestry of pain, trauma, and abandonment woven through my family's generations, I have strived to heal and repair myself, snipping away all the damage that should never have been mine to bear, therefore sewing unblemished threads into a new and beautiful tapestry for my children.

That is my gift to them.

Resources

Lifeline - lifeline.org.au

PANDA - panda.org.au

Mindspot - mindspot.org.au

Headspace - headspace.org.au

Beyond Blue - beyondblue.org.au

Reach Out - au.reachout.com

Sane Australia - sane.org

About Beck

Beck Thompson doesn't much like the terms 'survivor' or 'thriver' but instead made it her personal mission to change the way trauma had tainted her view of the world and the way she behaved. Her approach was determined and unabashedly honest, getting real with the girl within to repair and renew her sense of worth and value despite an Everest of obstacles that continuously stood in her way. Giving up simply wasn't an option.

If you ask Beck what she's achieved in her forty plus years, in a worldly sense, she is a devoted mother and holds a Bachelor of Education but Beck's most prized achievement is her sense of normalcy and peace. Something she worked tirelessly behind the scenes for. Beck is tenacious, determined and has an unwitting ability to cut through the rubbish and get to the heart of problems. She lives in Queensland with her husband and three children.

For public speaking bookings or events, please go to www.beckthompson.com.au